BBC

DOCTOR WHO

PRISONERS OF TIME

VOLUME 3

BBC

DOCTOR WHO

PRISONERS OF TIME

VOLUME 3

Cover by
FRANCESCO FRANCAVILLA
Collection Edits by
JUSTIN EISINGER and **ALONZO SIMON**
Collection Design by
TOM B. LONG

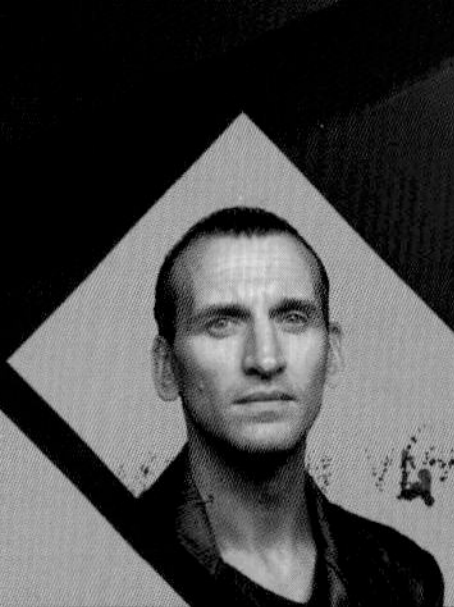

9TH DOCTOR
2005

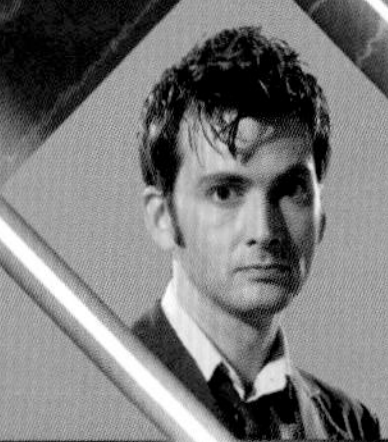

10TH DOCTO
2005 - 2

ISBN: 978-1-61377-822-7 16 15 14 13 1 2 3 4

IDW founded by Ted Adams, Alex Garner, Kris Oprisko, and Robbie Robbins

IDW®

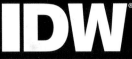

Ted Adams, CEO & Publisher
Greg Goldstein, President & COO
Robbie Robbins, EVP/Sr. Graphic Artist
Chris Ryall, Chief Creative Officer/Editor-in-Chief
Matthew Ruzicka, CPA, Chief Financial Officer
Alan Payne, VP of Sales
Dirk Wood, VP of Marketing
Lorelei Bunjes, VP of Digital Services

Special thanks to Kate Bush, Georgie Britton, Brian Minchin, Richard Cookson, Matt Nichols, and Ed Casey at BBC Worldwide for their invaluable assistance.

Originally published as DOCTOR WHO: PRISONERS OF TIME issues #9–12.

Written by
SCOTT & DAVID TIPTON

Art by
DAVID MESSINA
with **GIORGIA SPOSITO, ELENA CASAGRANDE, MATTHEW DOW SMITH,** and **KELLY YATES**

Colors by
SCARLETGOTHICA, ARIANNA FLOREAN
with **AZZURRA M. FLOREAN,** and **CHARLIE KIRCHOFF**

Letters by
TOM B. LONG

Series Edits by
DENTON J. TIPTON

11TH **DOCTOR**
2010 - 2013

NOV 04 2014

PTER 9
ERY DATE'"
by Francesco Francavilla

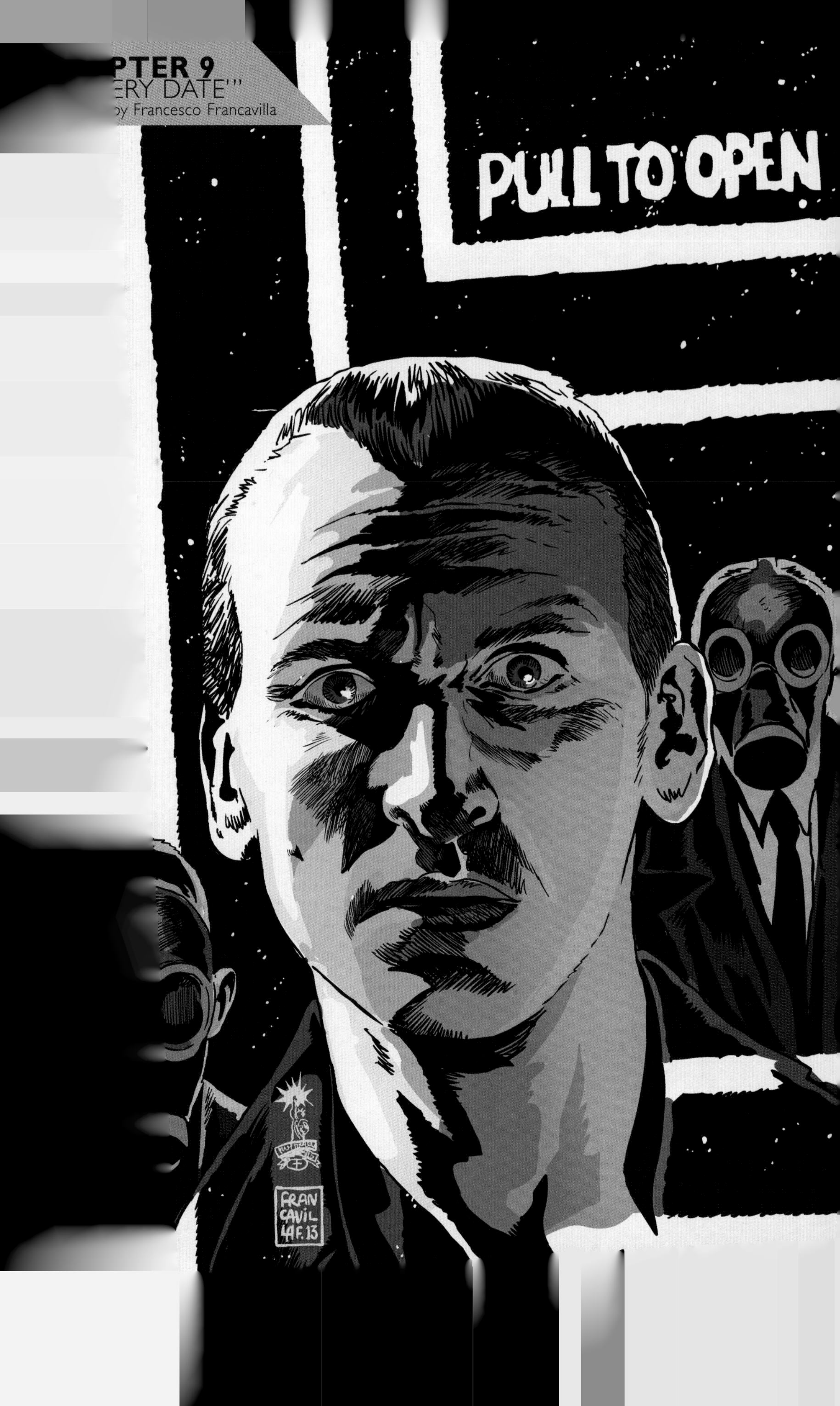
PULL TO OPEN
FRAN
CAVIL
LA F. 13

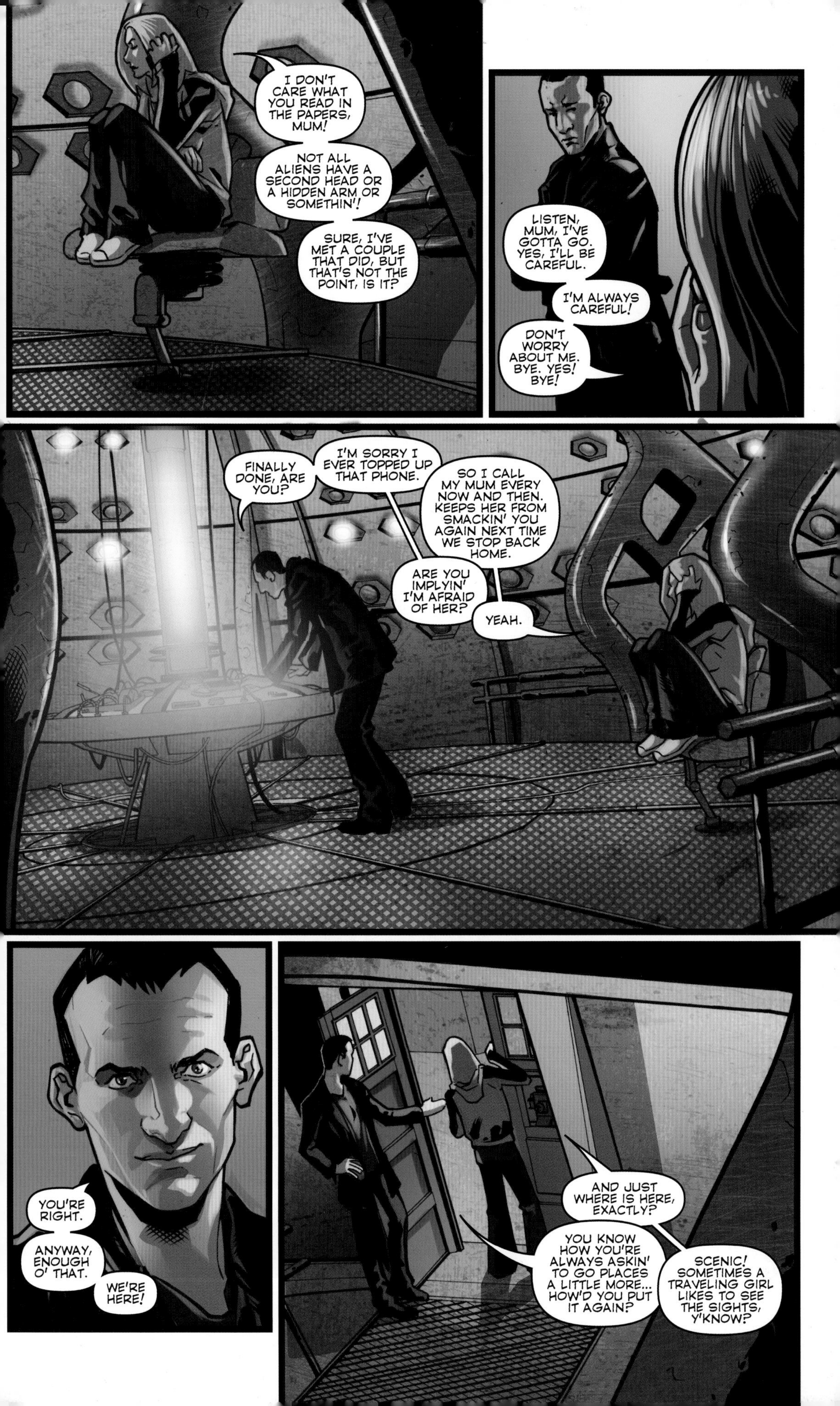
I DON'T CARE WHAT YOU READ IN THE PAPERS, MUM!
NOT ALL ALIENS HAVE A SECOND HEAD OR A HIDDEN ARM OR SOMETHIN'!
SURE, I'VE MET A COUPLE THAT DID, BUT THAT'S NOT THE POINT, IS IT?
LISTEN, MUM, I'VE GOTTA GO. YES, I'LL BE CAREFUL.
I'M ALWAYS CAREFUL!
DON'T WORRY ABOUT ME. BYE. YES! BYE!
FINALLY DONE, ARE YOU?
I'M SORRY I EVER TOPPED UP THAT PHONE.
SO I CALL MY MUM EVERY NOW AND THEN. KEEPS HER FROM SMACKIN' YOU AGAIN NEXT TIME WE STOP BACK HOME.
ARE YOU IMPLYIN' I'M AFRAID OF HER?
YEAH.
YOU'RE RIGHT.
ANYWAY, ENOUGH O' THAT.
WE'RE HERE!
AND JUST WHERE IS HERE, EXACTLY?
YOU KNOW HOW YOU'RE ALWAYS ASKIN' TO GO PLACES A LITTLE MORE... HOW'D YOU PUT IT AGAIN?
SCENIC! SOMETIMES A TRAVELING GIRL LIKES TO SEE THE SIGHTS, Y'KNOW?

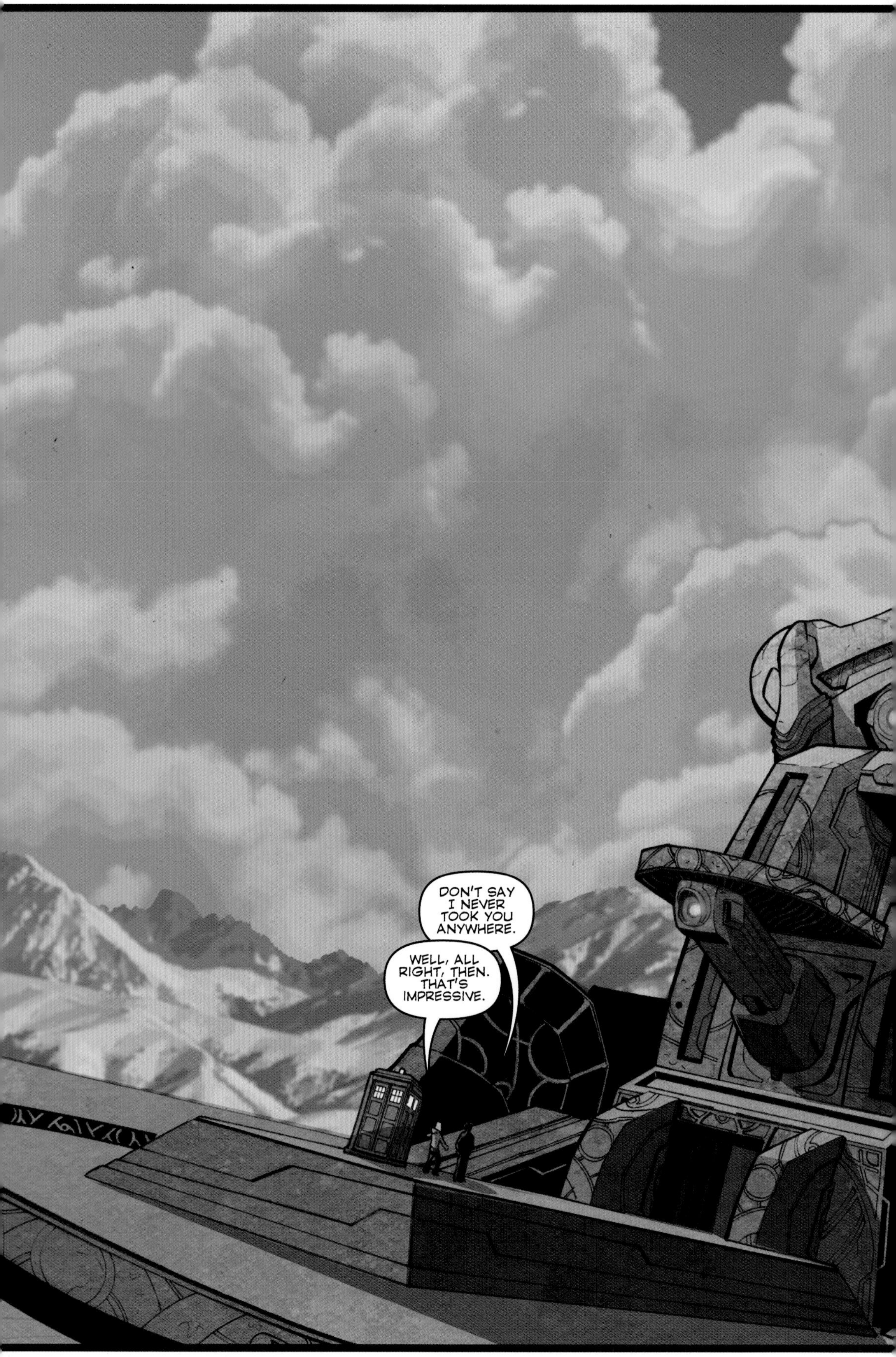
DON'T SAY I NEVER TOOK YOU ANYWHERE.
WELL, ALL RIGHT, THEN. THAT'S IMPRESSIVE.

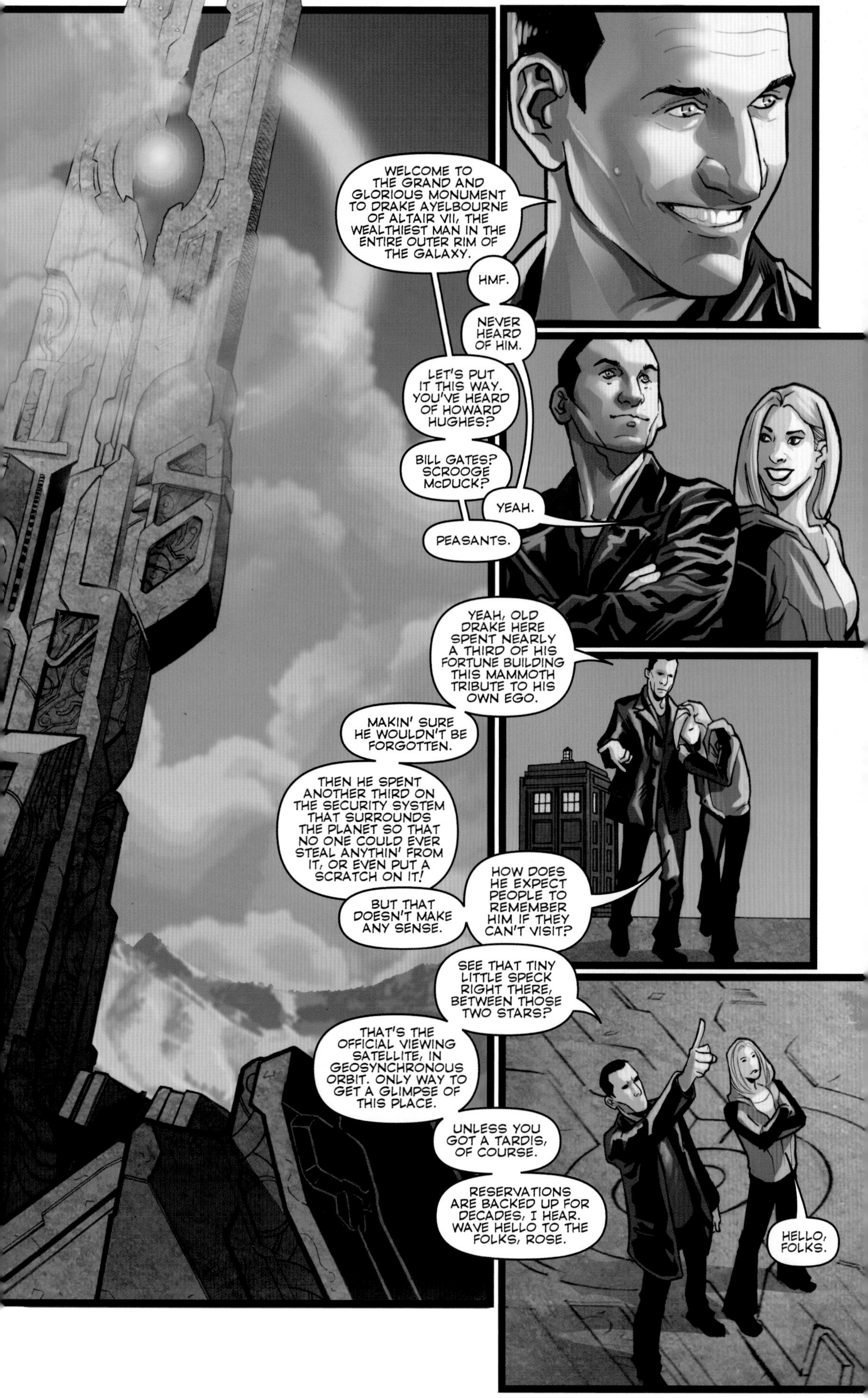
WELCOME TO THE GRAND AND GLORIOUS MONUMENT TO DRAKE AYELBOURNE OF ALTAIR VII, THE WEALTHIEST MAN IN THE ENTIRE OUTER RIM OF THE GALAXY.
HMF.
NEVER HEARD OF HIM.
LET'S PUT IT THIS WAY. YOU'VE HEARD OF HOWARD HUGHES?
BILL GATES? SCROOGE McDUCK?
YEAH.
PEASANTS.
YEAH, OLD DRAKE HERE SPENT NEARLY A THIRD OF HIS FORTUNE BUILDING THIS MAMMOTH TRIBUTE TO HIS OWN EGO.
MAKIN' SURE HE WOULDN'T BE FORGOTTEN.
THEN HE SPENT ANOTHER THIRD ON THE SECURITY SYSTEM THAT SURROUNDS THE PLANET SO THAT NO ONE COULD EVER STEAL ANYTHIN' FROM IT, OR EVEN PUT A SCRATCH ON IT!
BUT THAT DOESN'T MAKE ANY SENSE.
HOW DOES HE EXPECT PEOPLE TO REMEMBER HIM IF THEY CAN'T VISIT?
SEE THAT TINY LITTLE SPECK RIGHT THERE, BETWEEN THOSE TWO STARS?
THAT'S THE OFFICIAL VIEWING SATELLITE, IN GEOSYNCHRONOUS ORBIT. ONLY WAY TO GET A GLIMPSE OF THIS PLACE.
UNLESS YOU GOT A TARDIS, OF COURSE.
RESERVATIONS ARE BACKED UP FOR DECADES, I HEAR. WAVE HELLO TO THE FOLKS, ROSE.
HELLO, FOLKS.

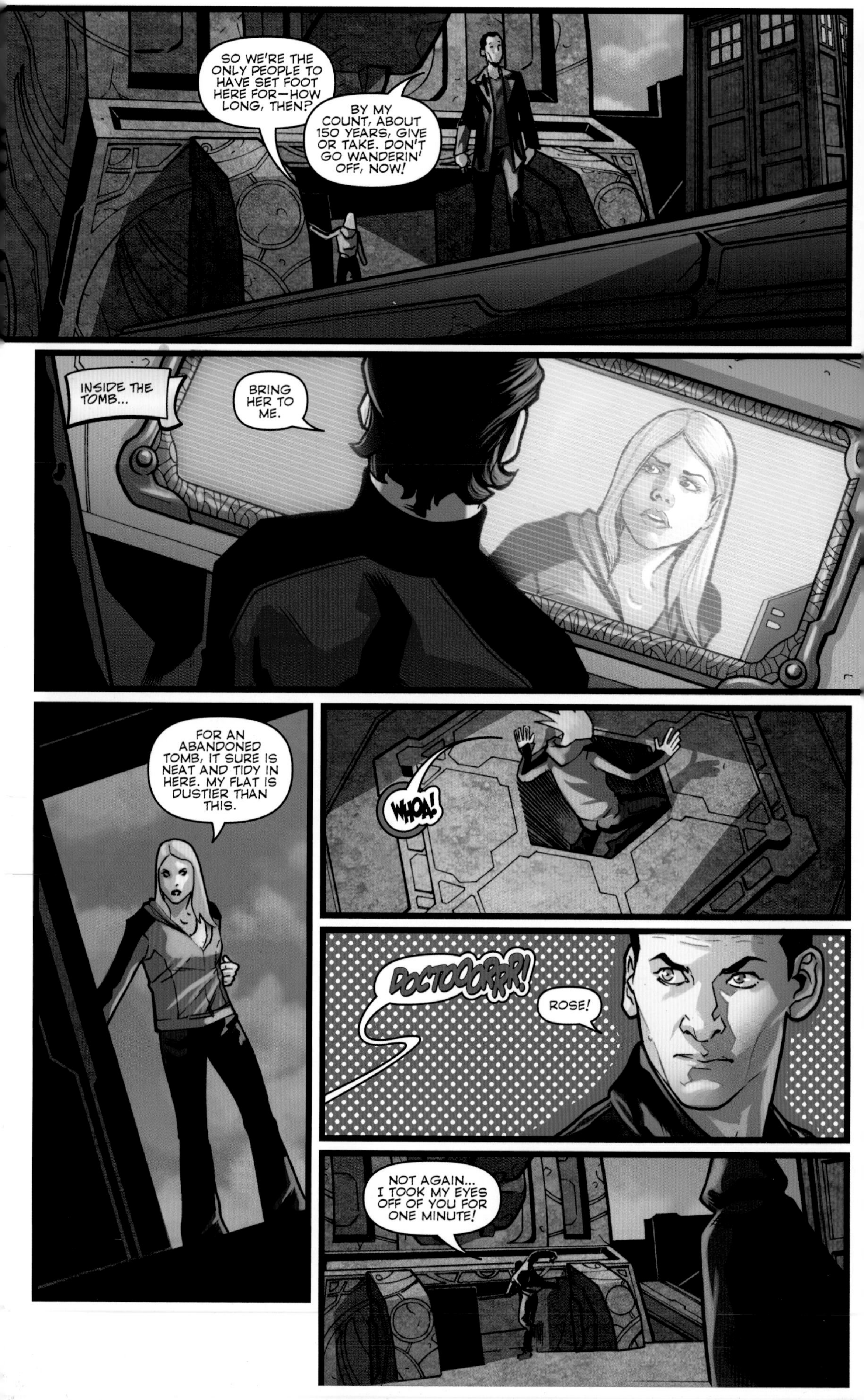
SO WE'RE THE ONLY PEOPLE TO HAVE SET FOOT HERE FOR—HOW LONG, THEN?
BY MY COUNT, ABOUT 150 YEARS, GIVE OR TAKE. DON'T GO WANDERIN' OFF, NOW!
INSIDE THE TOMB...
BRING HER TO ME.
FOR AN ABANDONED TOMB, IT SURE IS NEAT AND TIDY IN HERE. MY FLAT IS DUSTIER THAN THIS.
WHOA!
DOCTOOORRR!
ROSE!
NOT AGAIN... I TOOK MY EYES OFF OF YOU FOR ONE MINUTE!

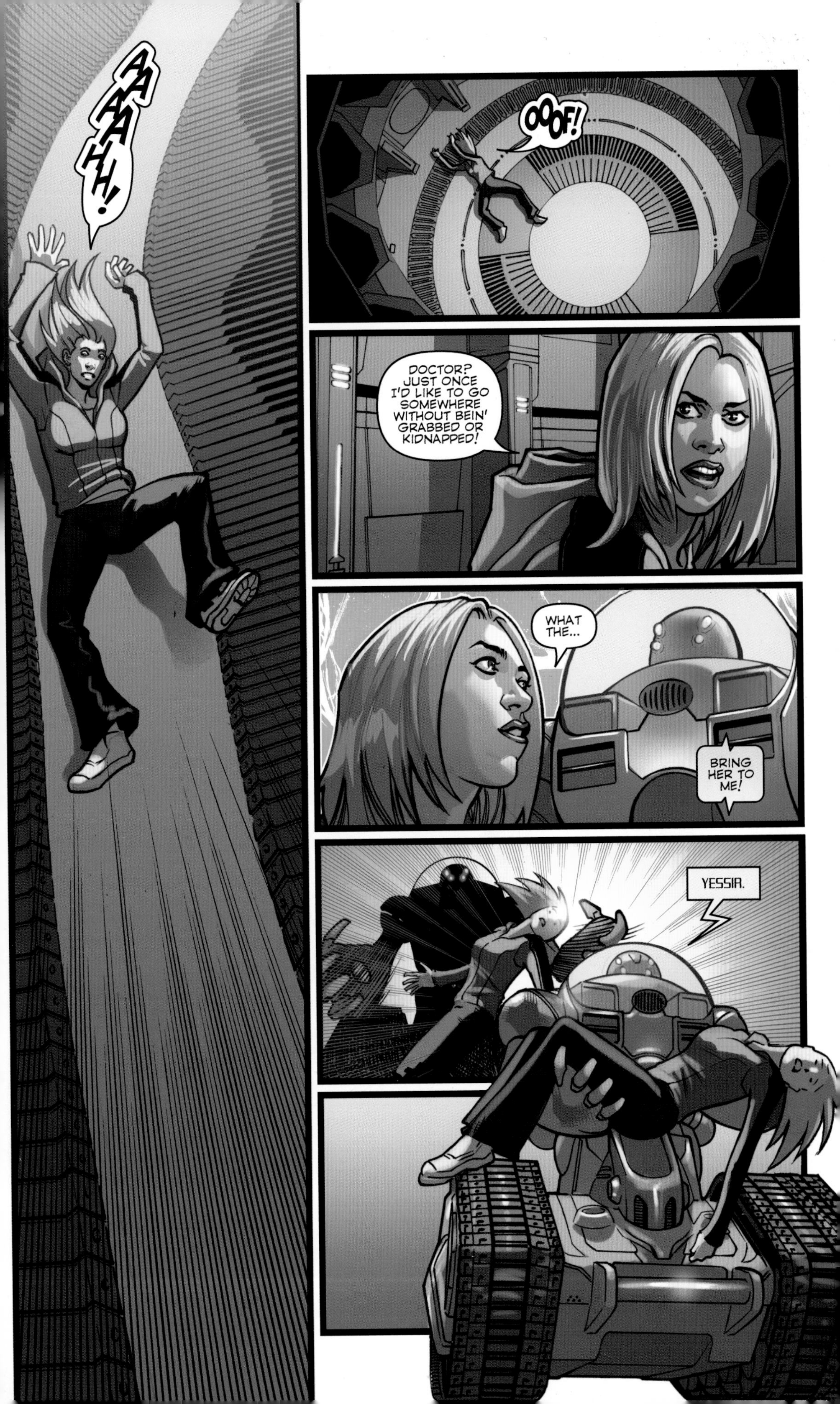
AAAAHH!
OOOF!
DOCTOR? JUST ONCE I'D LIKE TO GO SOMEWHERE WITHOUT BEIN' GRABBED OR KIDNAPPED!
WHAT THE...
BRING HER TO ME!
YESSIR.

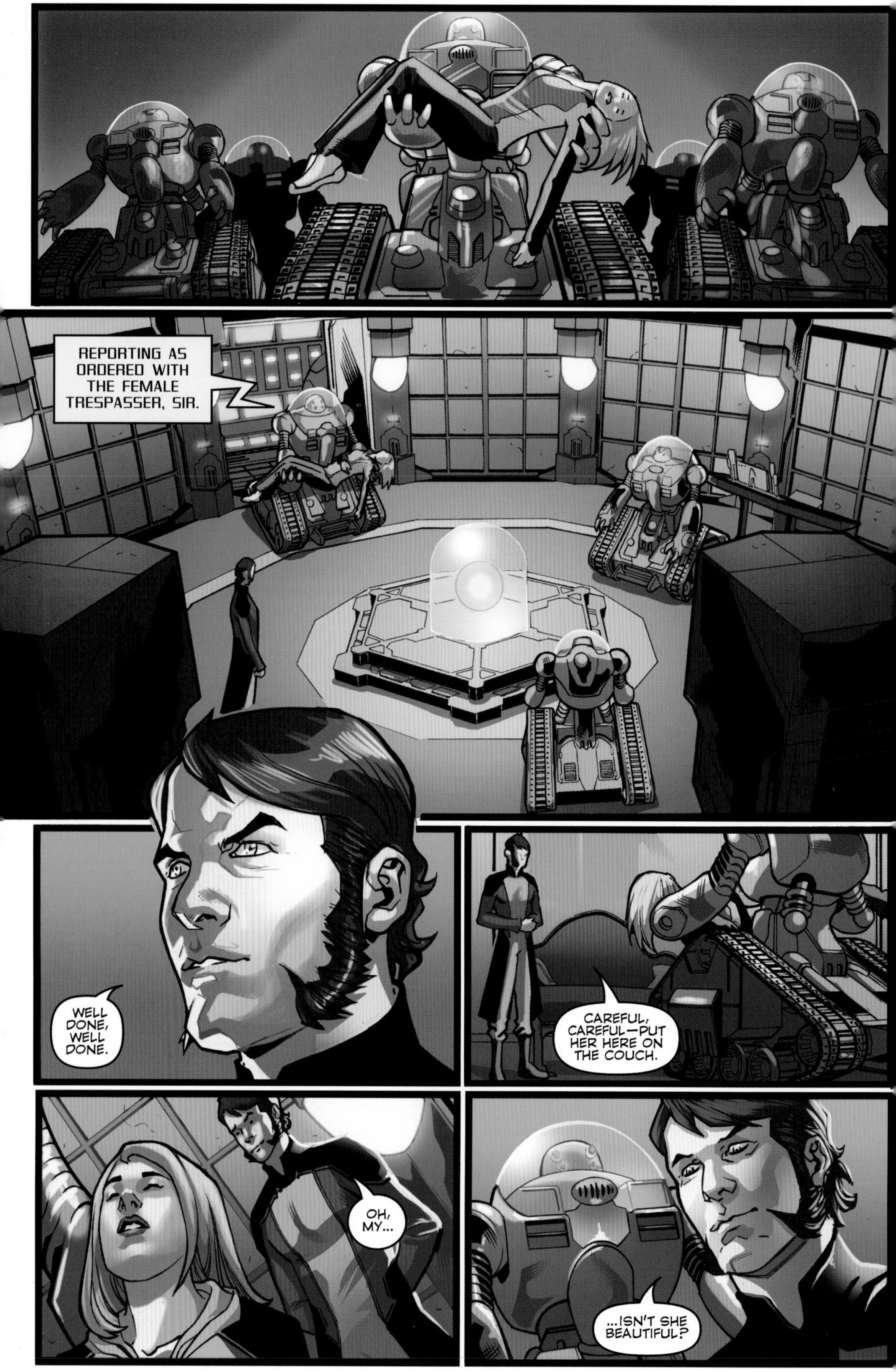
REPORTING AS ORDERED WITH THE FEMALE TRESPASSER, SIR.
WELL DONE, WELL DONE.
CAREFUL, CAREFUL—PUT HER HERE ON THE COUCH.
OH, MY...
...ISN'T SHE BEAUTIFUL?

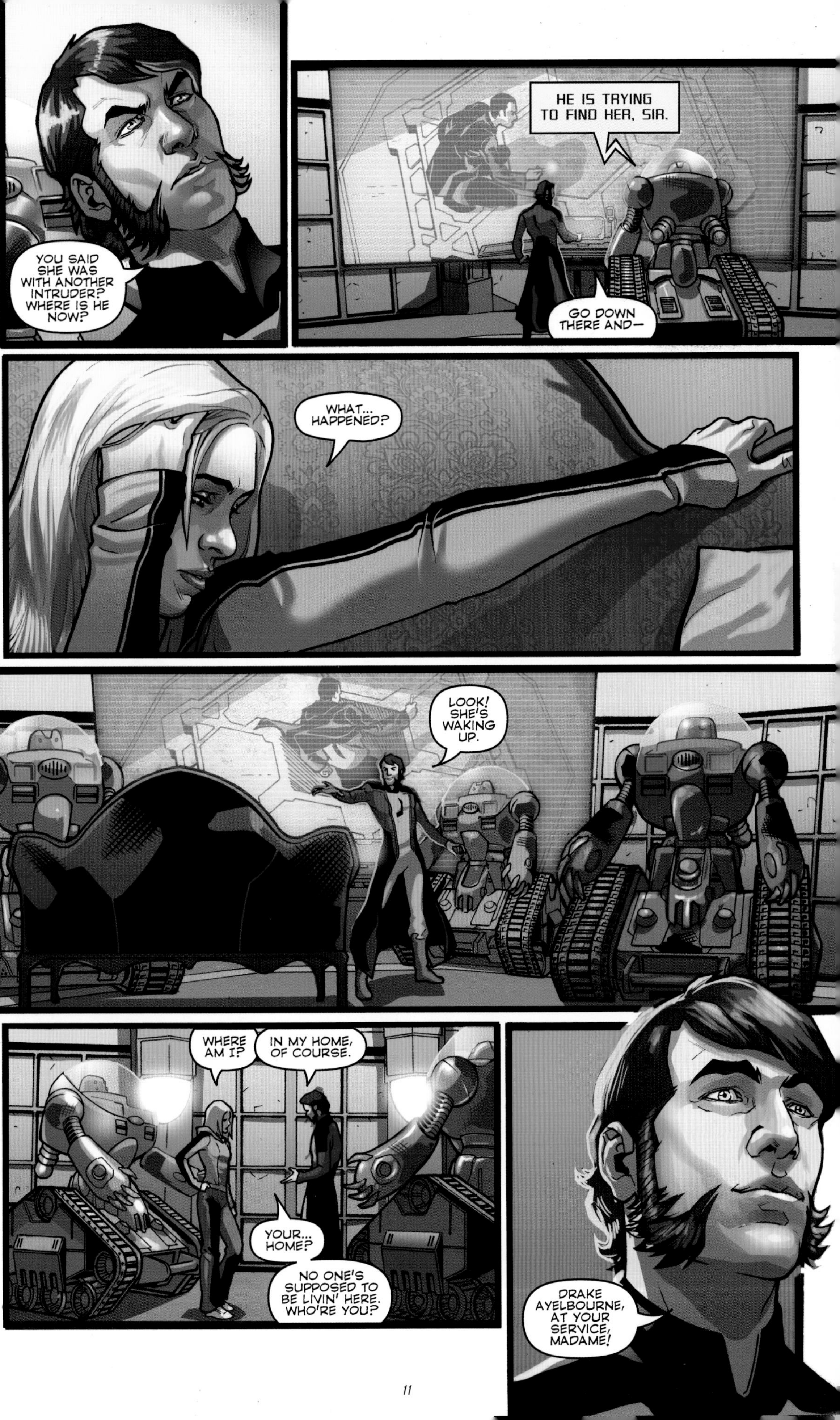
YOU SAID SHE WAS WITH ANOTHER INTRUDER? WHERE IS HE NOW?
HE IS TRYING TO FIND HER, SIR.
GO DOWN THERE AND—
WHAT... HAPPENED?
LOOK! SHE'S WAKING UP.
WHERE AM I?
IN MY HOME, OF COURSE.
YOUR... HOME?
NO ONE'S SUPPOSED TO BE LIVIN' HERE. WHO'RE YOU?
DRAKE AYELBOURNE, AT YOUR SERVICE, MADAME!

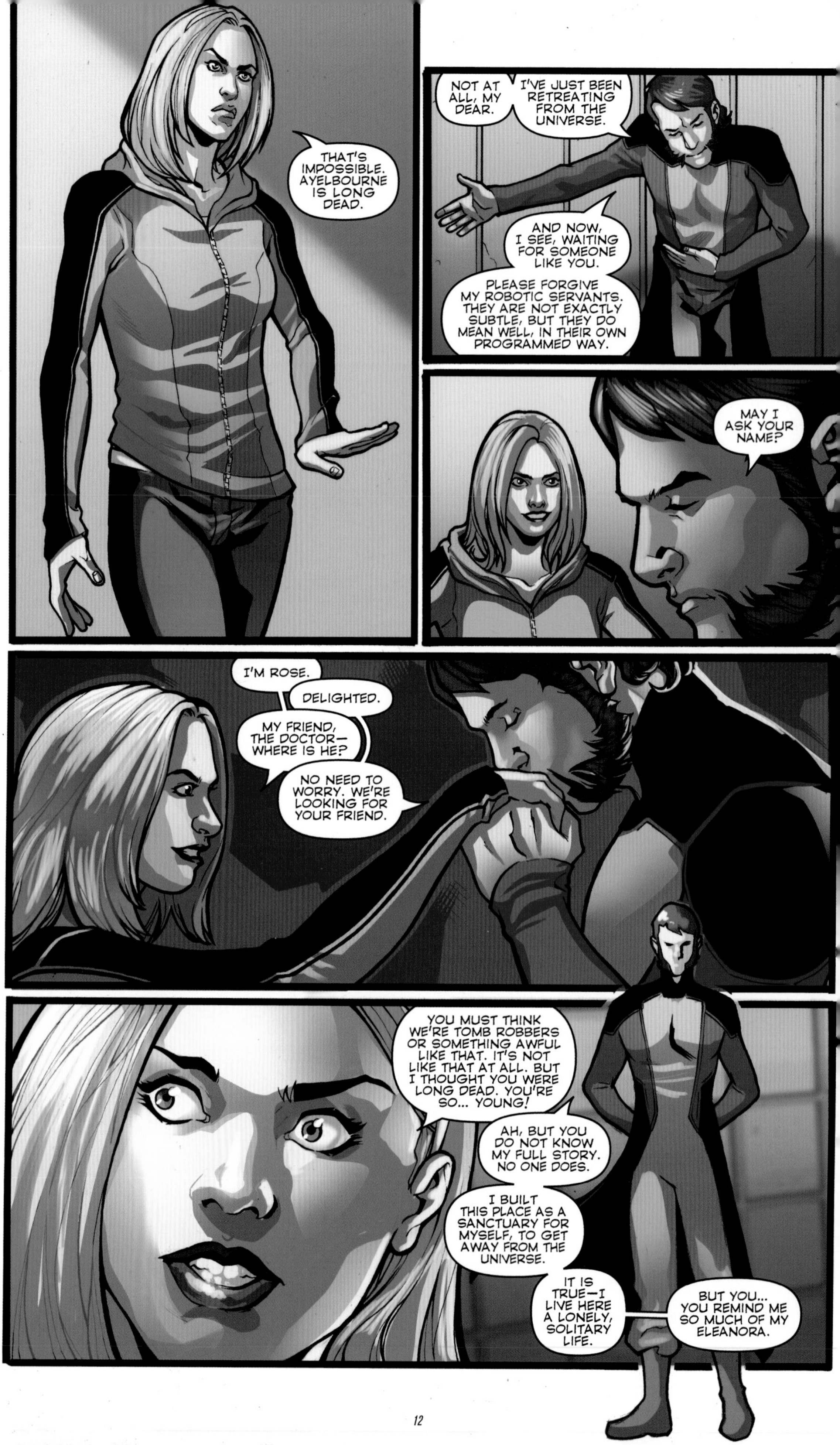
THAT'S IMPOSSIBLE. AYELBOURNE IS LONG DEAD.
NOT AT ALL, MY DEAR.
I'VE JUST BEEN RETREATING FROM THE UNIVERSE.
AND NOW, I SEE, WAITING FOR SOMEONE LIKE YOU.
PLEASE FORGIVE MY ROBOTIC SERVANTS. THEY ARE NOT EXACTLY SUBTLE, BUT THEY DO MEAN WELL, IN THEIR OWN PROGRAMMED WAY.
MAY I ASK YOUR NAME?
I'M ROSE.
DELIGHTED.
MY FRIEND, THE DOCTOR— WHERE IS HE?
NO NEED TO WORRY. WE'RE LOOKING FOR YOUR FRIEND.
YOU MUST THINK WE'RE TOMB ROBBERS OR SOMETHING AWFUL LIKE THAT. IT'S NOT LIKE THAT AT ALL. BUT I THOUGHT YOU WERE LONG DEAD. YOU'RE SO... YOUNG!
AH, BUT YOU DO NOT KNOW MY FULL STORY. NO ONE DOES.
I BUILT THIS PLACE AS A SANCTUARY FOR MYSELF, TO GET AWAY FROM THE UNIVERSE.
IT IS TRUE—I LIVE HERE A LONELY, SOLITARY LIFE.
BUT YOU... YOU REMIND ME SO MUCH OF MY ELEANORA.

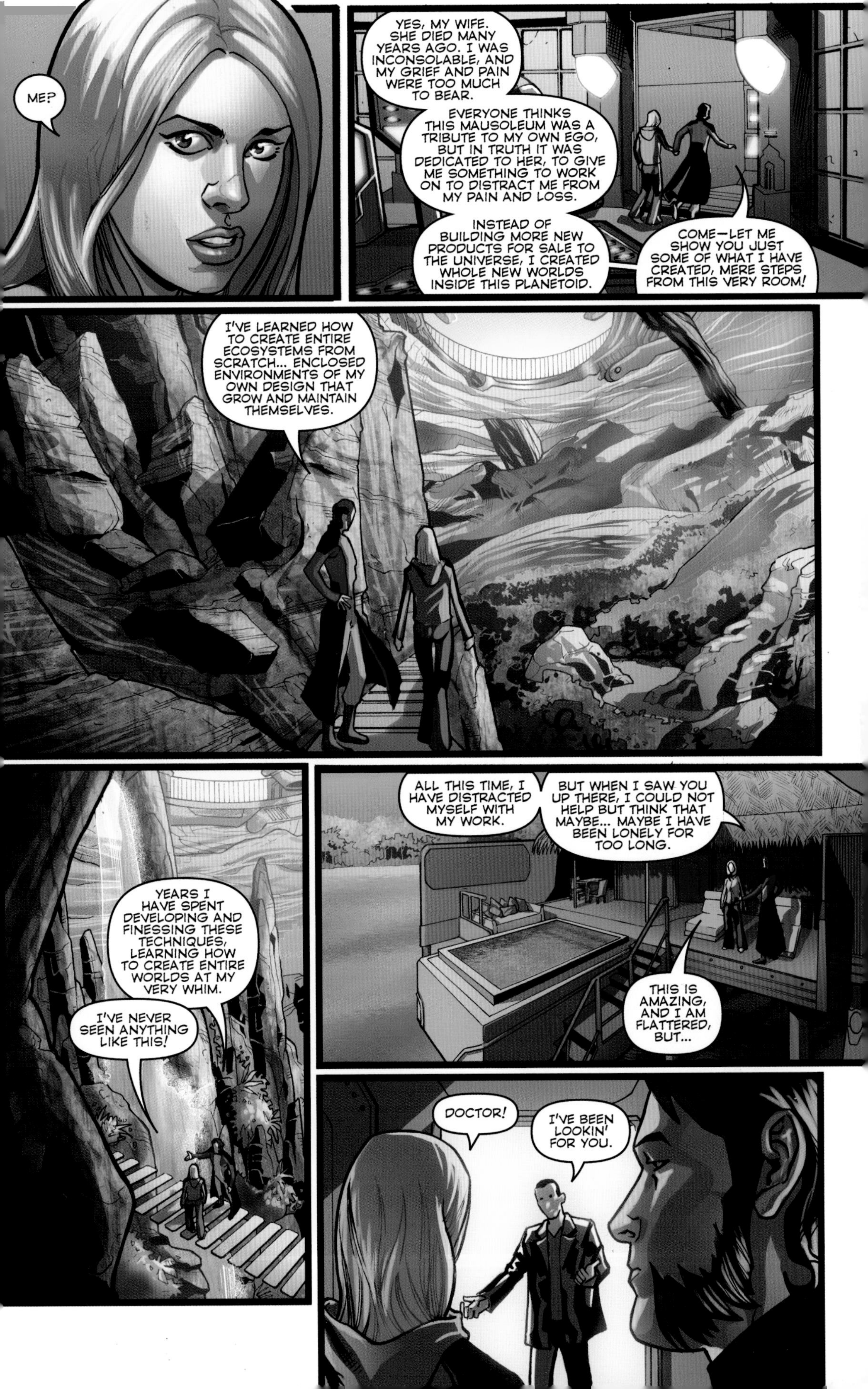
ME?
YES, MY WIFE. SHE DIED MANY YEARS AGO. I WAS INCONSOLABLE, AND MY GRIEF AND PAIN WERE TOO MUCH TO BEAR.
EVERYONE THINKS THIS MAUSOLEUM WAS A TRIBUTE TO MY OWN EGO, BUT IN TRUTH IT WAS DEDICATED TO HER, TO GIVE ME SOMETHING TO WORK ON TO DISTRACT ME FROM MY PAIN AND LOSS.
INSTEAD OF BUILDING MORE NEW PRODUCTS FOR SALE TO THE UNIVERSE, I CREATED WHOLE NEW WORLDS INSIDE THIS PLANETOID.
COME—LET ME SHOW YOU JUST SOME OF WHAT I HAVE CREATED, MERE STEPS FROM THIS VERY ROOM!
I'VE LEARNED HOW TO CREATE ENTIRE ECOSYSTEMS FROM SCRATCH... ENCLOSED ENVIRONMENTS OF MY OWN DESIGN THAT GROW AND MAINTAIN THEMSELVES.
YEARS I HAVE SPENT DEVELOPING AND FINESSING THESE TECHNIQUES, LEARNING HOW TO CREATE ENTIRE WORLDS AT MY VERY WHIM.
I'VE NEVER SEEN ANYTHING LIKE THIS!
ALL THIS TIME, I HAVE DISTRACTED MYSELF WITH MY WORK.
BUT WHEN I SAW YOU UP THERE, I COULD NOT HELP BUT THINK THAT MAYBE... MAYBE I HAVE BEEN LONELY FOR TOO LONG.
THIS IS AMAZING, AND I AM FLATTERED, BUT...
DOCTOR!
I'VE BEEN LOOKIN' FOR YOU.

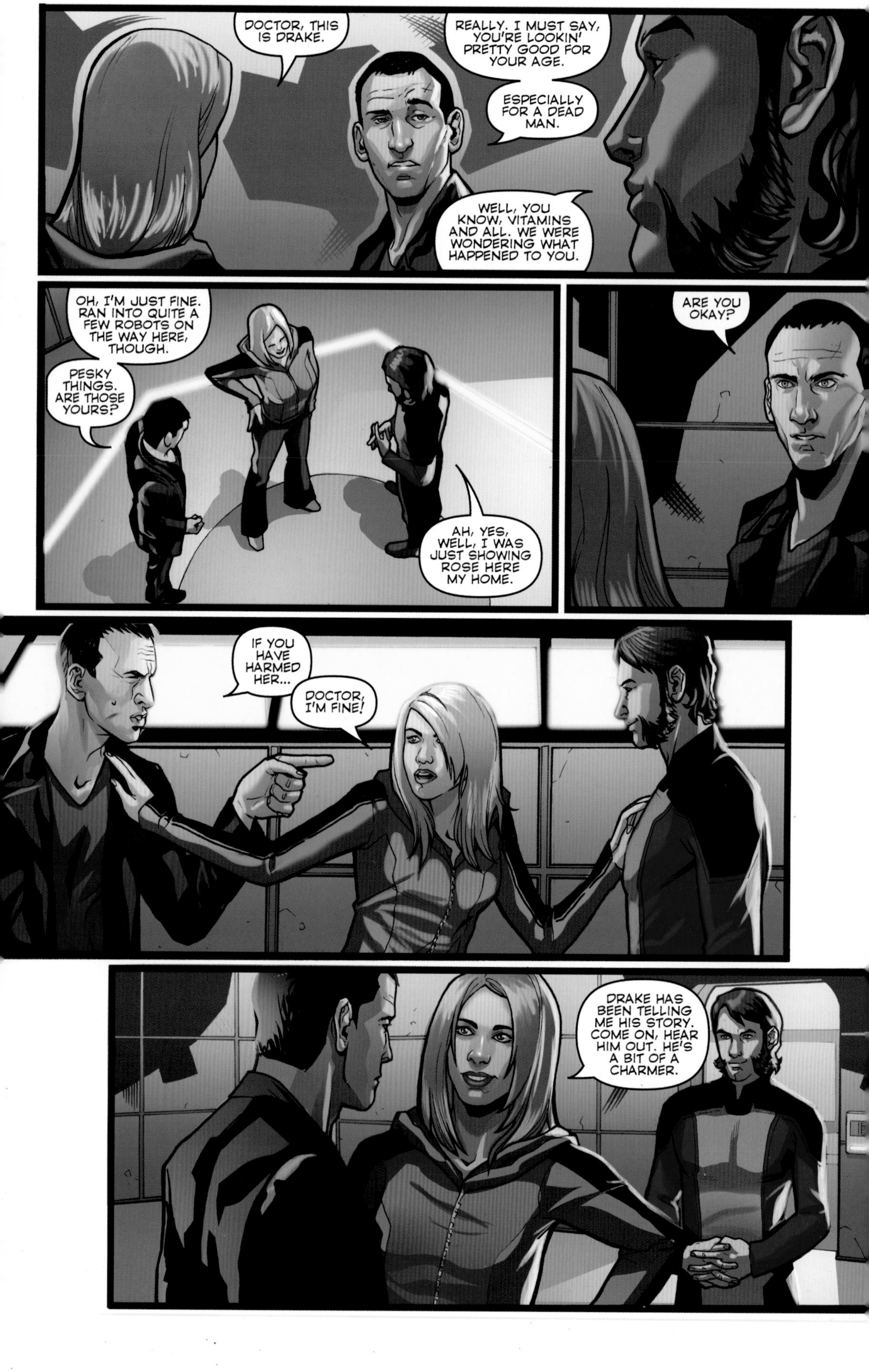
DOCTOR, THIS IS DRAKE.
REALLY. I MUST SAY, YOU'RE LOOKIN' PRETTY GOOD FOR YOUR AGE.
ESPECIALLY FOR A DEAD MAN.
WELL, YOU KNOW, VITAMINS AND ALL. WE WERE WONDERING WHAT HAPPENED TO YOU.
OH, I'M JUST FINE. RAN INTO QUITE A FEW ROBOTS ON THE WAY HERE, THOUGH.
PESKY THINGS. ARE THOSE YOURS?
AH, YES, WELL, I WAS JUST SHOWING ROSE HERE MY HOME.
ARE YOU OKAY?
IF YOU HAVE HARMED HER...
DOCTOR, I'M FINE!
DRAKE HAS BEEN TELLING ME HIS STORY. COME ON, HEAR HIM OUT. HE'S A BIT OF A CHARMER.

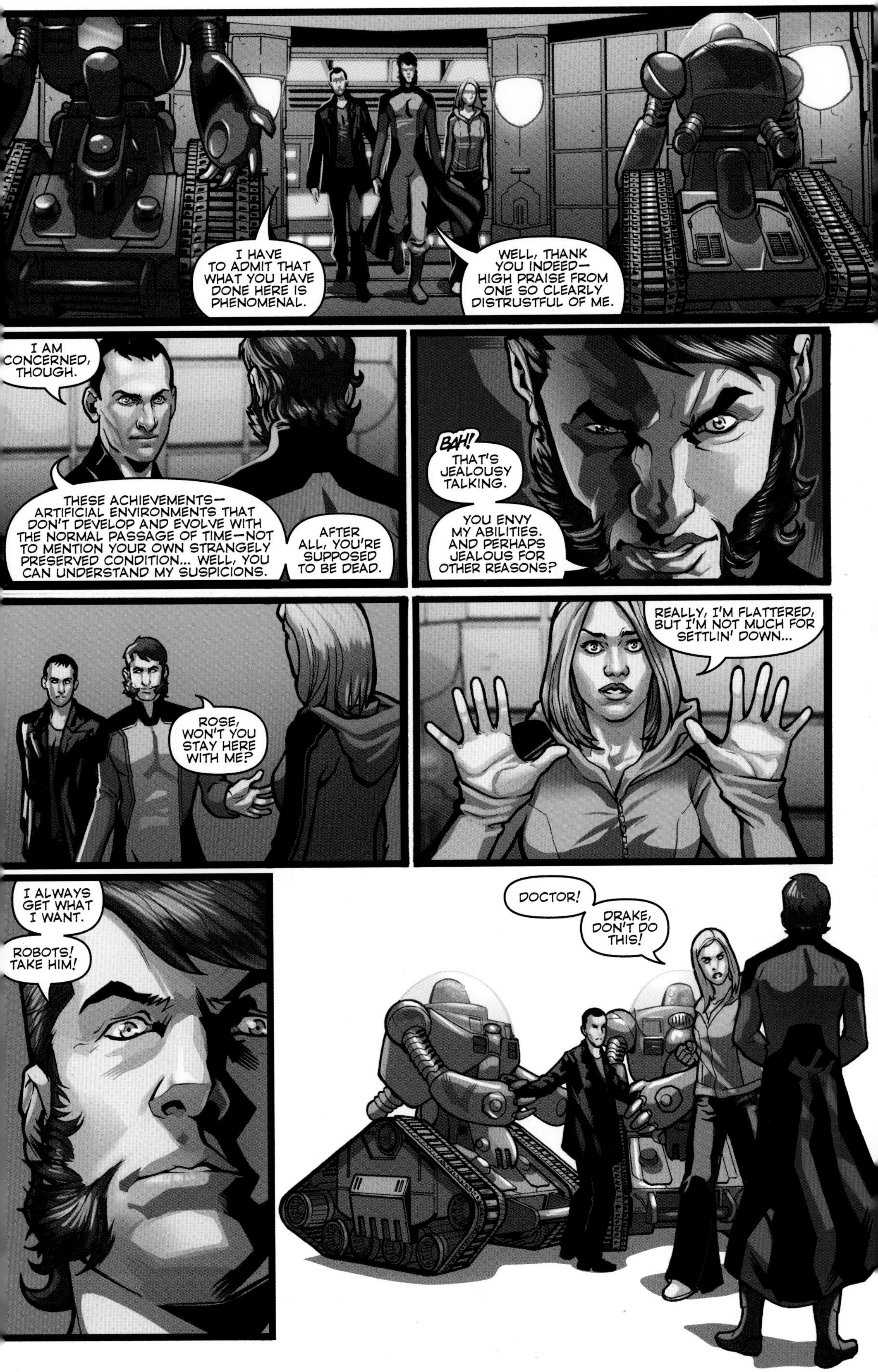
I HAVE TO ADMIT THAT WHAT YOU HAVE DONE HERE IS PHENOMENAL.
WELL, THANK YOU INDEED— HIGH PRAISE FROM ONE SO CLEARLY DISTRUSTFUL OF ME.
I AM CONCERNED, THOUGH.
THESE ACHIEVEMENTS— ARTIFICIAL ENVIRONMENTS THAT DON'T DEVELOP AND EVOLVE WITH THE NORMAL PASSAGE OF TIME—NOT TO MENTION YOUR OWN STRANGELY PRESERVED CONDITION... WELL, YOU CAN UNDERSTAND MY SUSPICIONS.
AFTER ALL, YOU'RE SUPPOSED TO BE DEAD.
BAH! THAT'S JEALOUSY TALKING.
YOU ENVY MY ABILITIES. AND PERHAPS JEALOUS FOR OTHER REASONS?
ROSE, WON'T YOU STAY HERE WITH ME?
REALLY, I'M FLATTERED, BUT I'M NOT MUCH FOR SETTLIN' DOWN...
I ALWAYS GET WHAT I WANT.
ROBOTS! TAKE HIM!
DOCTOR!
DRAKE, DON'T DO THIS!

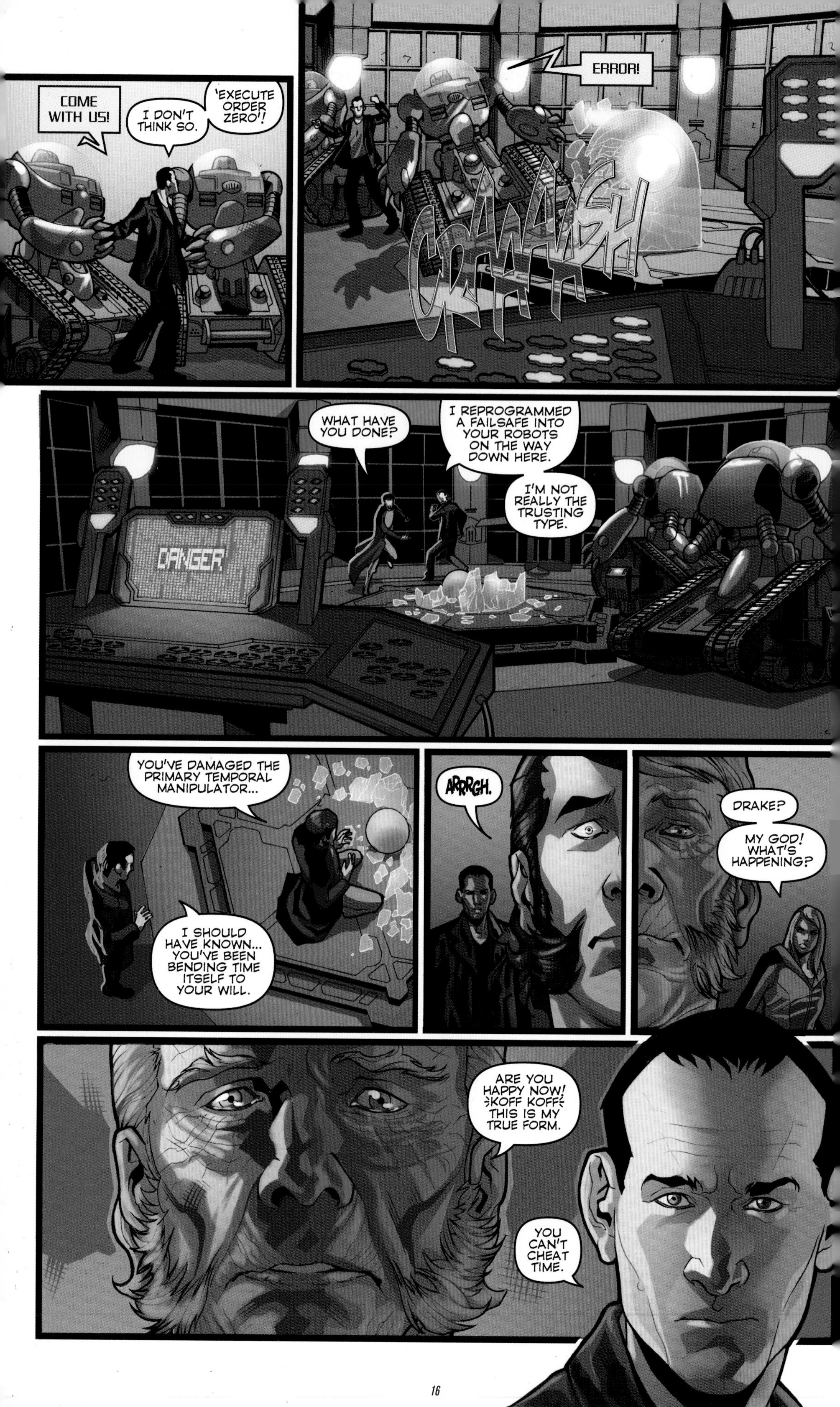
COME WITH US!
I DON'T THINK SO.
'EXECUTE ORDER ZERO'!
ERROR!
CRAAASH
DANGER
WHAT HAVE YOU DONE?
I REPROGRAMMED A FAILSAFE INTO YOUR ROBOTS ON THE WAY DOWN HERE.
I'M NOT REALLY THE TRUSTING TYPE.
YOU'VE DAMAGED THE PRIMARY TEMPORAL MANIPULATOR...
I SHOULD HAVE KNOWN... YOU'VE BEEN BENDING TIME ITSELF TO YOUR WILL.
ARRRGH.
DRAKE?
MY GOD! WHAT'S HAPPENING?
ARE YOU HAPPY NOW! *KOFF KOFF* THIS IS MY TRUE FORM.
YOU CAN'T CHEAT TIME.

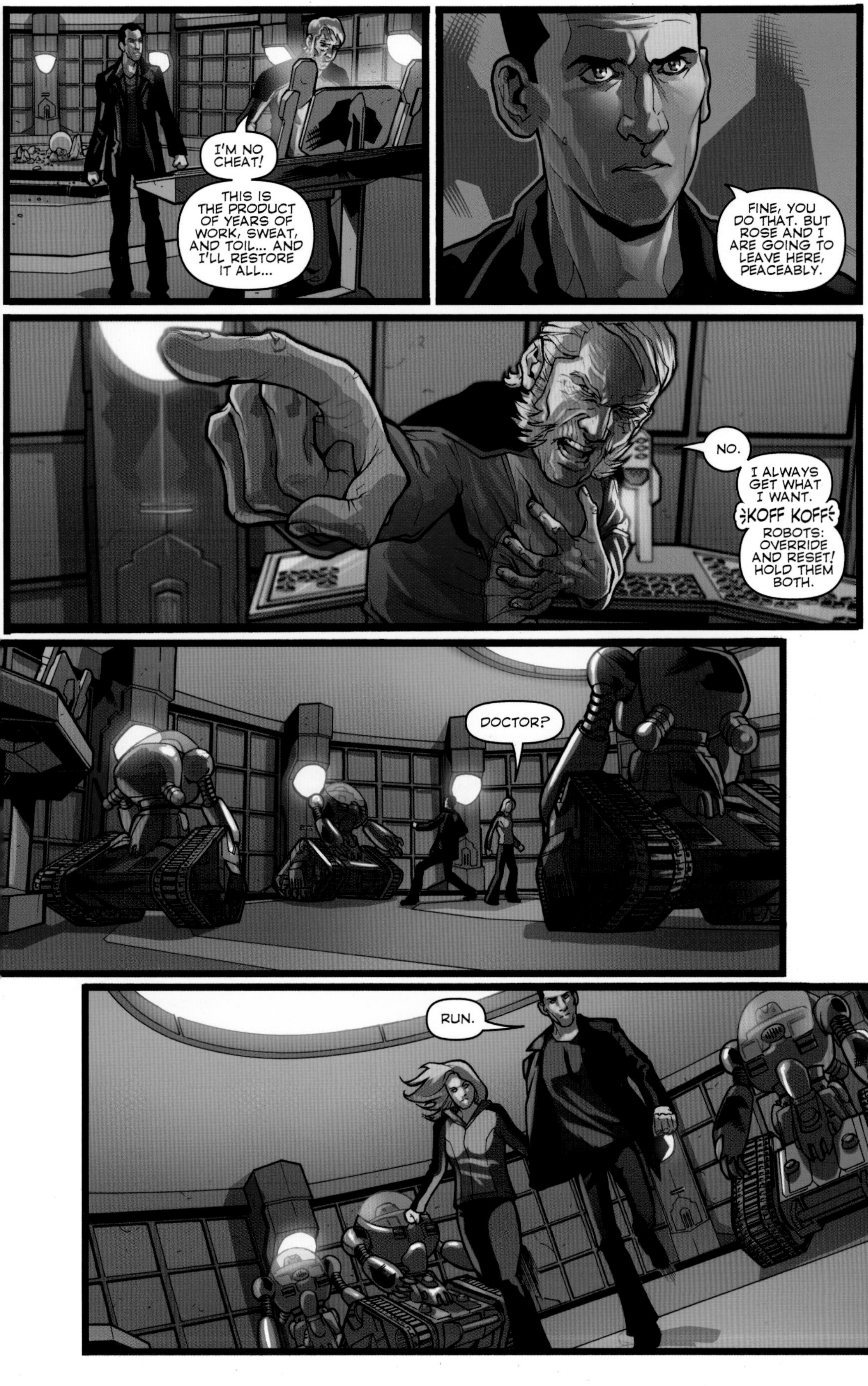
I'M NO CHEAT!
THIS IS THE PRODUCT OF YEARS OF WORK, SWEAT, AND TOIL... AND I'LL RESTORE IT ALL...
FINE, YOU DO THAT. BUT ROSE AND I ARE GOING TO LEAVE HERE, PEACEABLY.
NO.
I ALWAYS GET WHAT I WANT.
KOFF KOFF
ROBOTS: OVERRIDE AND RESET! HOLD THEM BOTH.
DOCTOR?
RUN.

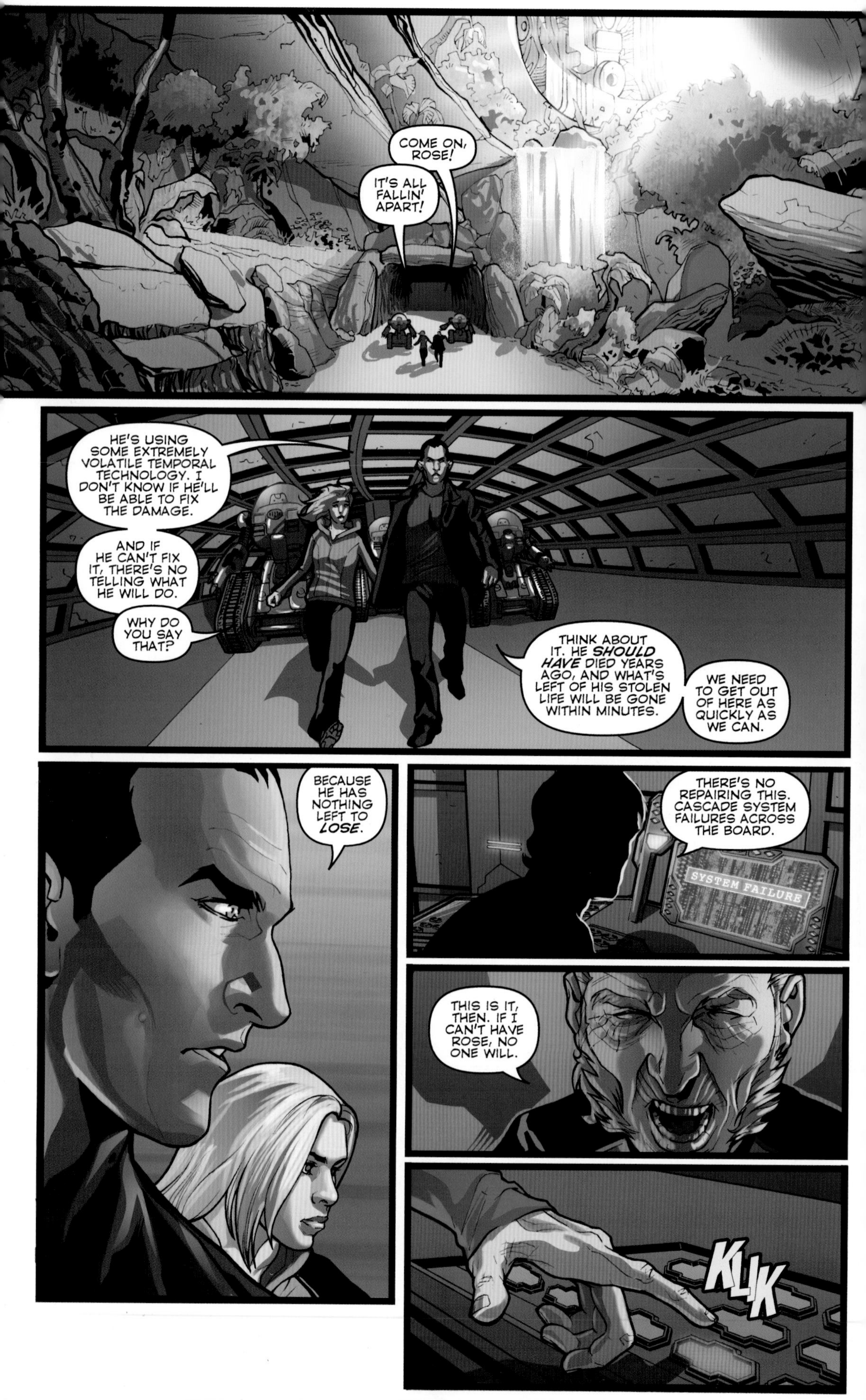
COME ON, ROSE!
IT'S ALL FALLIN' APART!
HE'S USING SOME EXTREMELY VOLATILE TEMPORAL TECHNOLOGY. I DON'T KNOW IF HE'LL BE ABLE TO FIX THE DAMAGE.
AND IF HE CAN'T FIX IT, THERE'S NO TELLING WHAT HE WILL DO.
WHY DO YOU SAY THAT?
THINK ABOUT IT. HE SHOULD HAVE DIED YEARS AGO, AND WHAT'S LEFT OF HIS STOLEN LIFE WILL BE GONE WITHIN MINUTES.
WE NEED TO GET OUT OF HERE AS QUICKLY AS WE CAN.
BECAUSE HE HAS NOTHING LEFT TO LOSE.
THERE'S NO REPAIRING THIS. CASCADE SYSTEM FAILURES ACROSS THE BOARD.
SYSTEM FAILURE
THIS IS IT, THEN. IF I CAN'T HAVE ROSE, NO ONE WILL.
KLIK

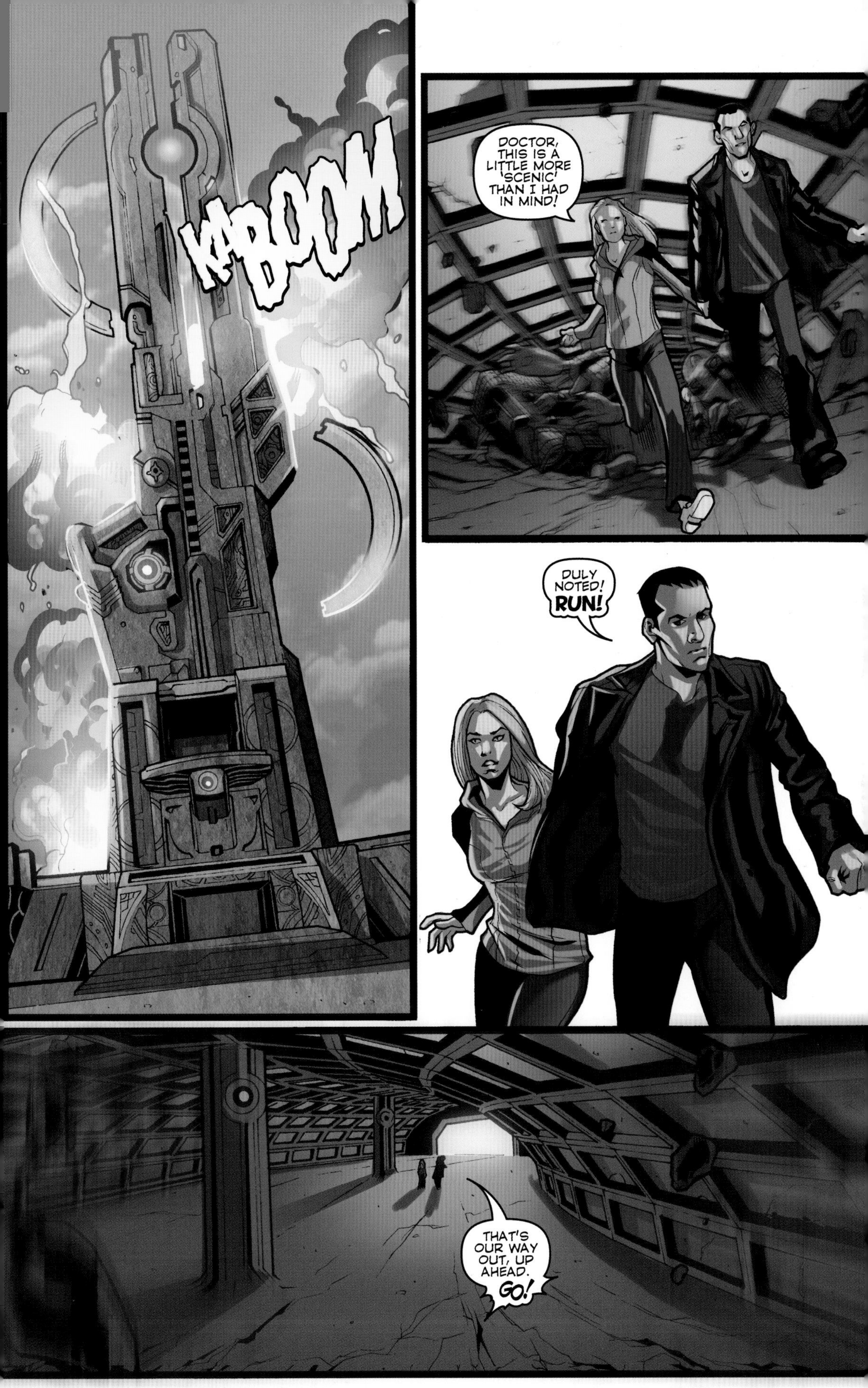
KABOOM
DOCTOR, THIS IS A LITTLE MORE 'SCENIC' THAN I HAD IN MIND!
DULY NOTED! RUN!
THAT'S OUR WAY OUT, UP AHEAD. GO!

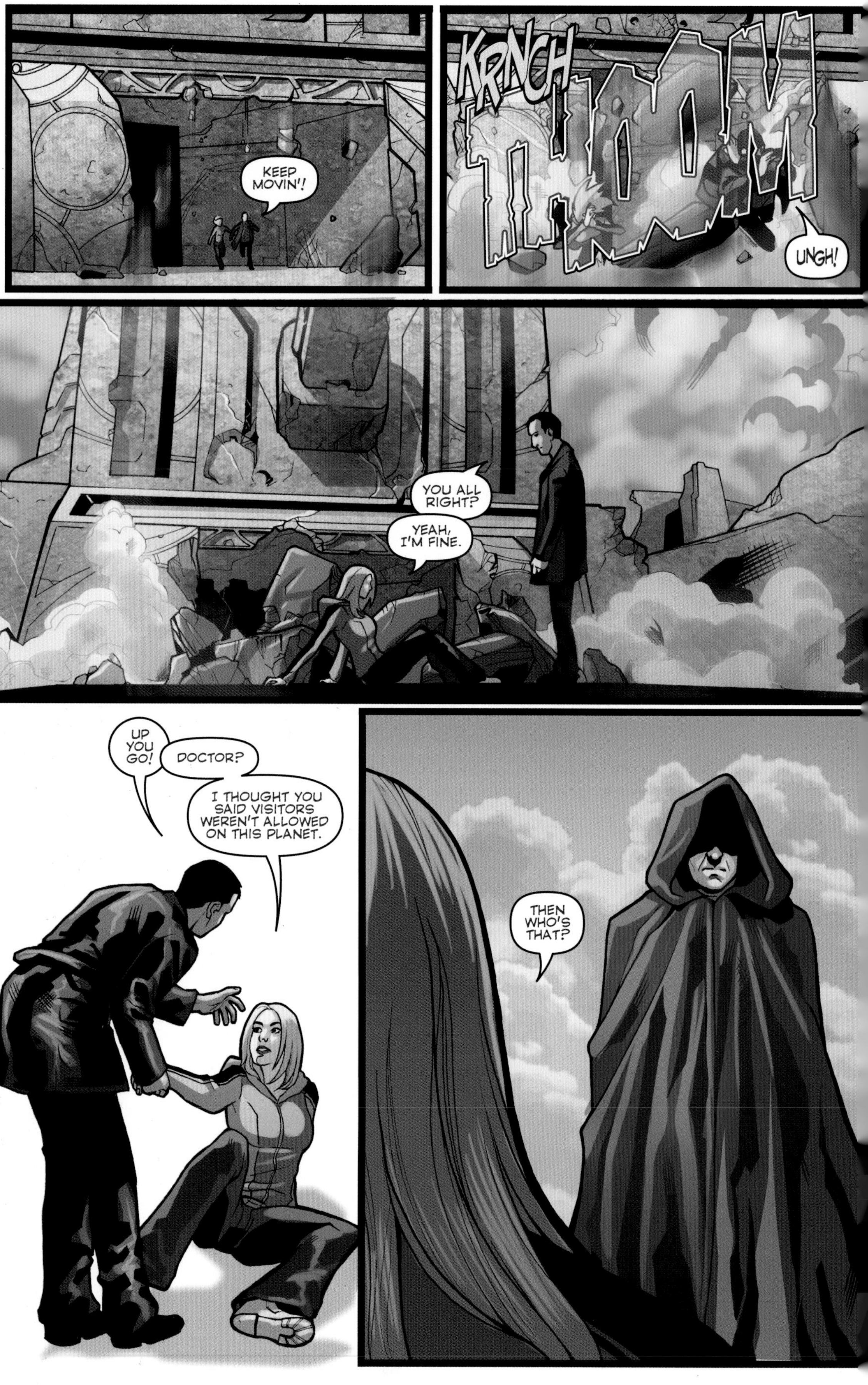
KEEP MOVIN'!
KRNCH
UNGH!
YOU ALL RIGHT?
YEAH, I'M FINE.
UP YOU GO!
DOCTOR?
I THOUGHT YOU SAID VISITORS WEREN'T ALLOWED ON THIS PLANET.
THEN WHO'S THAT?

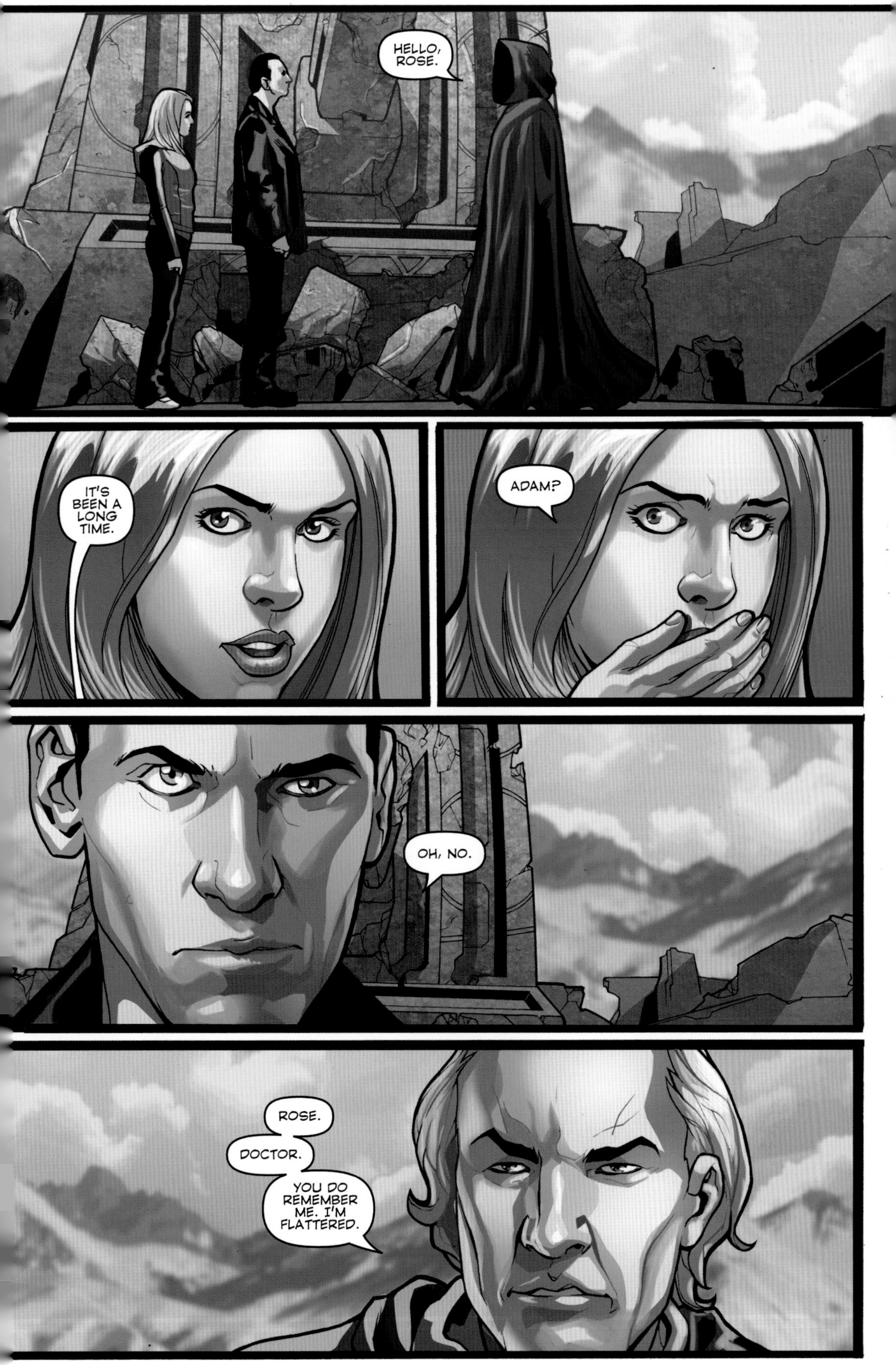

HELLO, ROSE.
IT'S BEEN A LONG TIME.
ADAM?
OH, NO.
ROSE.
DOCTOR.
YOU DO REMEMBER ME. I'M FLATTERED.

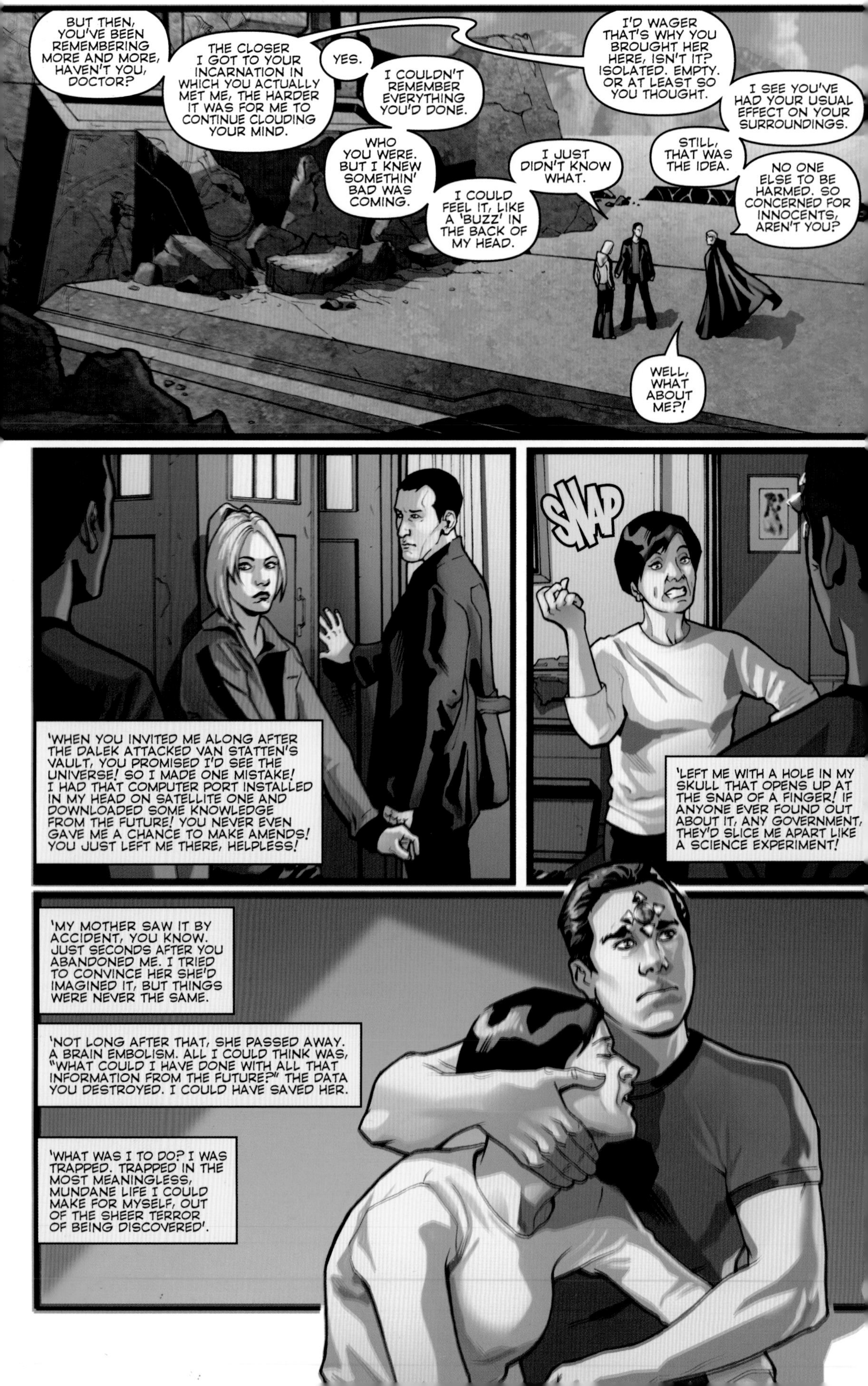

BUT THEN, YOU'VE BEEN REMEMBERING MORE AND MORE, HAVEN'T YOU, DOCTOR?
THE CLOSER I GOT TO YOUR INCARNATION IN WHICH YOU ACTUALLY MET ME, THE HARDER IT WAS FOR ME TO CONTINUE CLOUDING YOUR MIND.
YES.
I COULDN'T REMEMBER EVERYTHING YOU'D DONE.
WHO YOU WERE. BUT I KNEW SOMETHIN' BAD WAS COMING.
I COULD FEEL IT, LIKE A 'BUZZ' IN THE BACK OF MY HEAD.
I JUST DIDN'T KNOW WHAT.
I'D WAGER THAT'S WHY YOU BROUGHT HER HERE, ISN'T IT? ISOLATED. EMPTY. OR AT LEAST SO YOU THOUGHT.
STILL, THAT WAS THE IDEA.
I SEE YOU'VE HAD YOUR USUAL EFFECT ON YOUR SURROUNDINGS.
NO ONE ELSE TO BE HARMED. SO CONCERNED FOR INNOCENTS, AREN'T YOU?
WELL, WHAT ABOUT ME?!
'WHEN YOU INVITED ME ALONG AFTER THE DALEK ATTACKED VAN STATTEN'S VAULT, YOU PROMISED I'D SEE THE UNIVERSE! SO I MADE ONE MISTAKE! I HAD THAT COMPUTER PORT INSTALLED IN MY HEAD ON SATELLITE ONE AND DOWNLOADED SOME KNOWLEDGE FROM THE FUTURE! YOU NEVER EVEN GAVE ME A CHANCE TO MAKE AMENDS! YOU JUST LEFT ME THERE, HELPLESS!
SNAP
'LEFT ME WITH A HOLE IN MY SKULL THAT OPENS UP AT THE SNAP OF A FINGER! IF ANYONE EVER FOUND OUT ABOUT IT, ANY GOVERNMENT, THEY'D SLICE ME APART LIKE A SCIENCE EXPERIMENT!
'MY MOTHER SAW IT BY ACCIDENT, YOU KNOW. JUST SECONDS AFTER YOU ABANDONED ME. I TRIED TO CONVINCE HER SHE'D IMAGINED IT, BUT THINGS WERE NEVER THE SAME.
'NOT LONG AFTER THAT, SHE PASSED AWAY. A BRAIN EMBOLISM. ALL I COULD THINK WAS, "WHAT COULD I HAVE DONE WITH ALL THAT INFORMATION FROM THE FUTURE?" THE DATA YOU DESTROYED. I COULD HAVE SAVED HER.
'WHAT WAS I TO DO? I WAS TRAPPED. TRAPPED IN THE MOST MEANINGLESS, MUNDANE LIFE I COULD MAKE FOR MYSELF, OUT OF THE SHEER TERROR OF BEING DISCOVERED'.

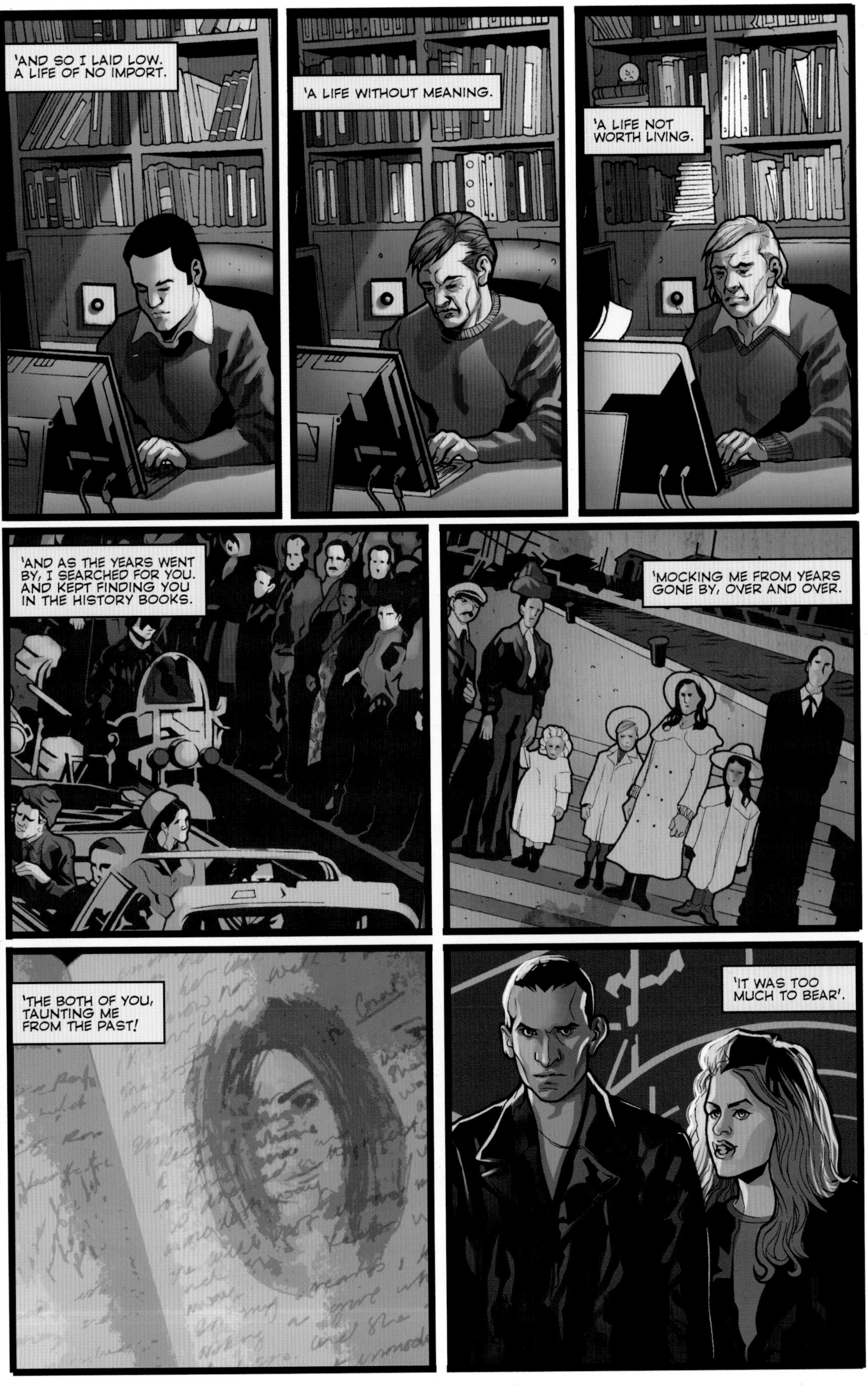
'AND SO I LAID LOW. A LIFE OF NO IMPORT.
'A LIFE WITHOUT MEANING.
'A LIFE NOT WORTH LIVING.
'AND AS THE YEARS WENT BY, I SEARCHED FOR YOU. AND KEPT FINDING YOU IN THE HISTORY BOOKS.
'MOCKING ME FROM YEARS GONE BY, OVER AND OVER.
'THE BOTH OF YOU, TAUNTING ME FROM THE PAST!
'IT WAS TOO MUCH TO BEAR'.

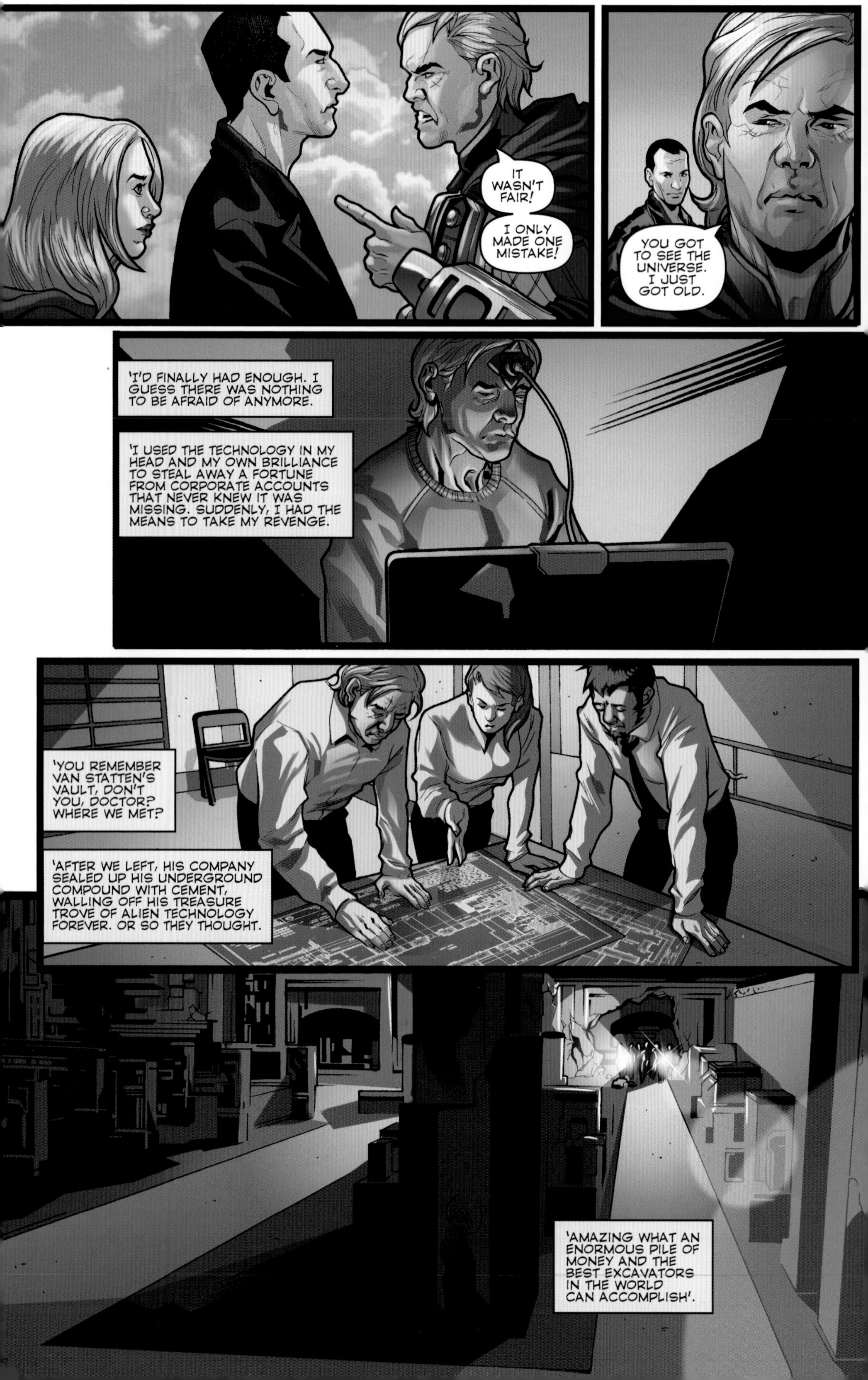
IT WASN'T FAIR!
I ONLY MADE ONE MISTAKE!
YOU GOT TO SEE THE UNIVERSE. I JUST GOT OLD.
'I'D FINALLY HAD ENOUGH. I GUESS THERE WAS NOTHING TO BE AFRAID OF ANYMORE.
'I USED THE TECHNOLOGY IN MY HEAD AND MY OWN BRILLIANCE TO STEAL AWAY A FORTUNE FROM CORPORATE ACCOUNTS THAT NEVER KNEW IT WAS MISSING. SUDDENLY, I HAD THE MEANS TO TAKE MY REVENGE.
'YOU REMEMBER VAN STATTEN'S VAULT, DON'T YOU, DOCTOR? WHERE WE MET?
'AFTER WE LEFT, HIS COMPANY SEALED UP HIS UNDERGROUND COMPOUND WITH CEMENT, WALLING OFF HIS TREASURE TROVE OF ALIEN TECHNOLOGY FOREVER. OR SO THEY THOUGHT.
'AMAZING WHAT AN ENORMOUS PILE OF MONEY AND THE BEST EXCAVATORS IN THE WORLD CAN ACCOMPLISH'.

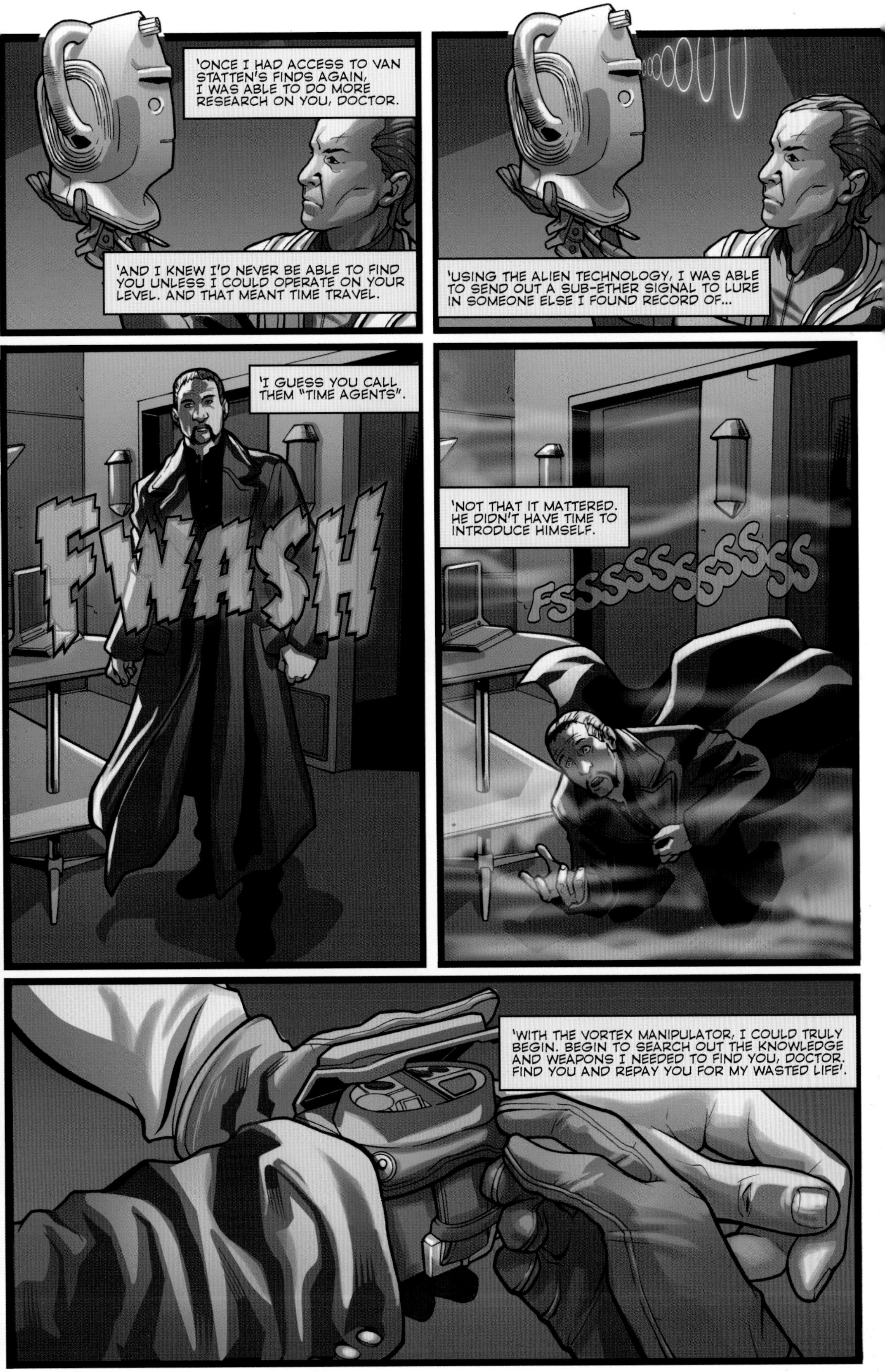
'ONCE I HAD ACCESS TO VAN STATTEN'S FINDS AGAIN, I WAS ABLE TO DO MORE RESEARCH ON YOU, DOCTOR.
'AND I KNEW I'D NEVER BE ABLE TO FIND YOU UNLESS I COULD OPERATE ON YOUR LEVEL. AND THAT MEANT TIME TRAVEL.
'USING THE ALIEN TECHNOLOGY, I WAS ABLE TO SEND OUT A SUB-ETHER SIGNAL TO LURE IN SOMEONE ELSE I FOUND RECORD OF...
'I GUESS YOU CALL THEM "TIME AGENTS".
FWASH
'NOT THAT IT MATTERED. HE DIDN'T HAVE TIME TO INTRODUCE HIMSELF.
FSSSSSSSSSSS
'WITH THE VORTEX MANIPULATOR, I COULD TRULY BEGIN. BEGIN TO SEARCH OUT THE KNOWLEDGE AND WEAPONS I NEEDED TO FIND YOU, DOCTOR. FIND YOU AND REPAY YOU FOR MY WASTED LIFE'.

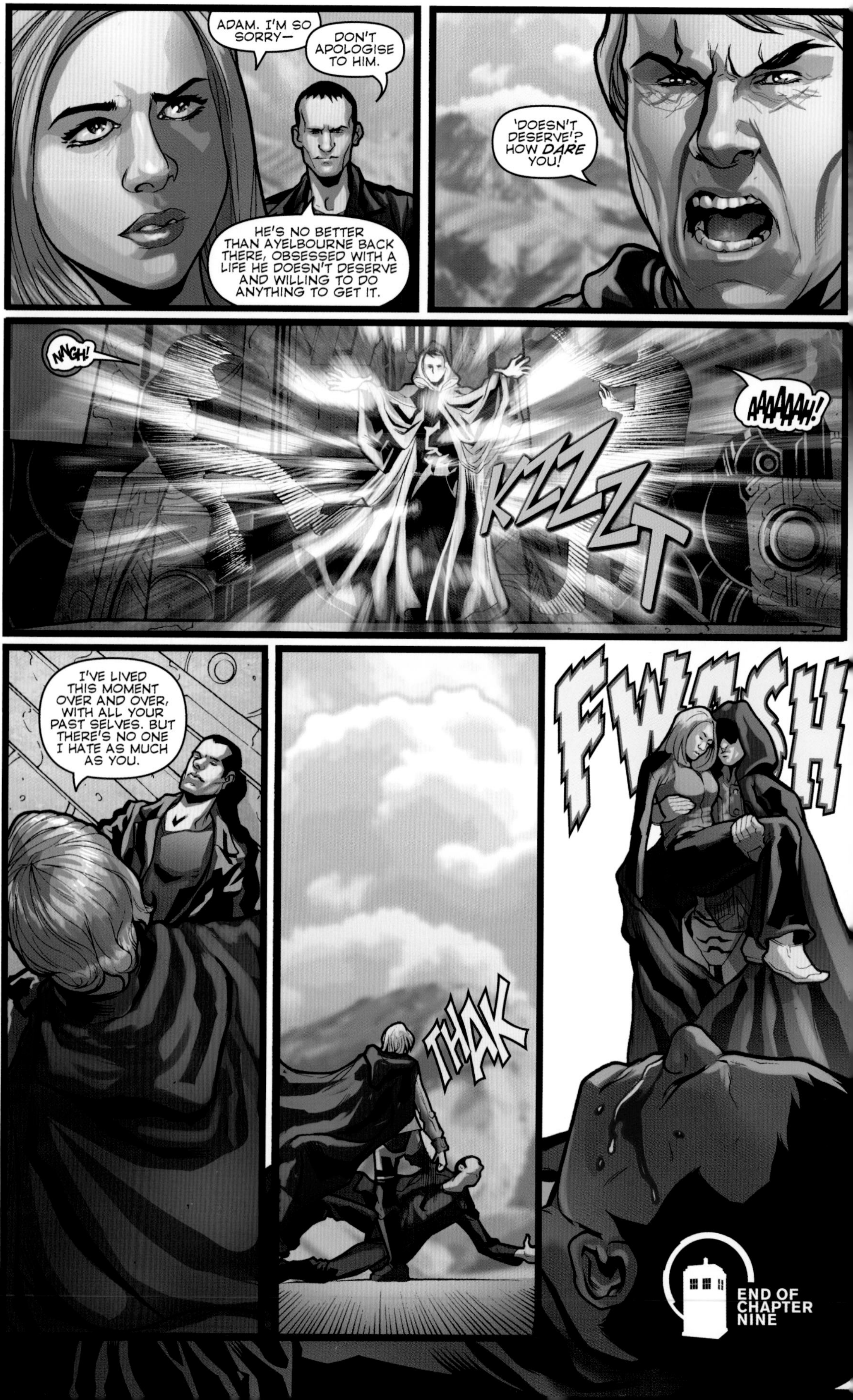

ADAM. I'M SO SORRY—
DON'T APOLOGISE TO HIM.
HE'S NO BETTER THAN AYELBOURNE BACK THERE, OBSESSED WITH A LIFE HE DOESN'T DESERVE AND WILLING TO DO ANYTHING TO GET IT.
'DOESN'T DESERVE'? HOW *DARE* YOU!
NNGH!
AAAAAAH!
KZZZZT
I'VE LIVED THIS MOMENT OVER AND OVER, WITH ALL YOUR PAST SELVES. BUT THERE'S NO ONE I HATE AS MUCH AS YOU.
THAK
FWOSH
END OF CHAPTER NINE

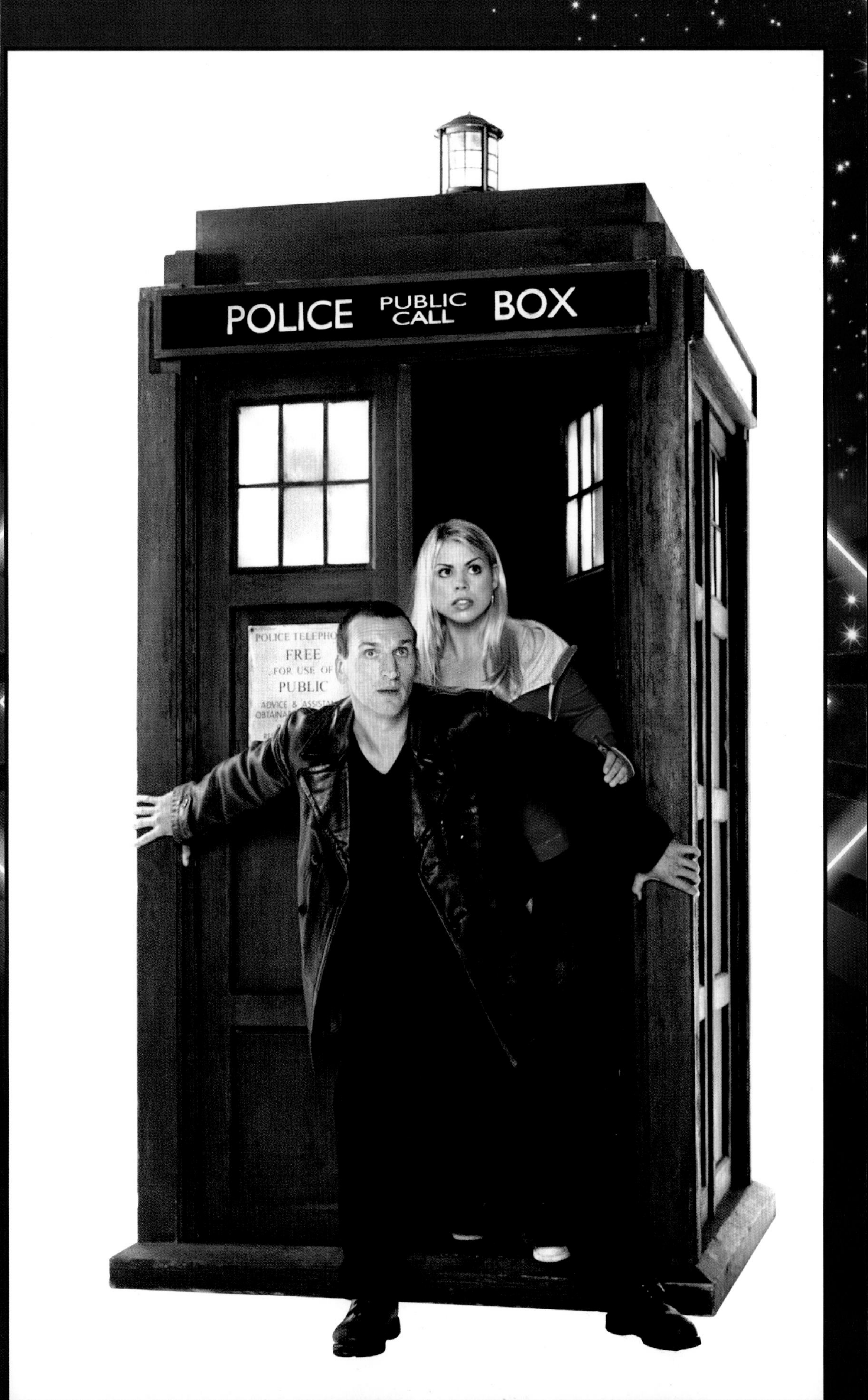
POLICE PUBLIC CALL BOX
POLICE TELEPHO
FREE
FOR USE OF
PUBLIC

CHAPTER 10
"QUIET ON THE SET"
Cover Art by Francesco Francavilla

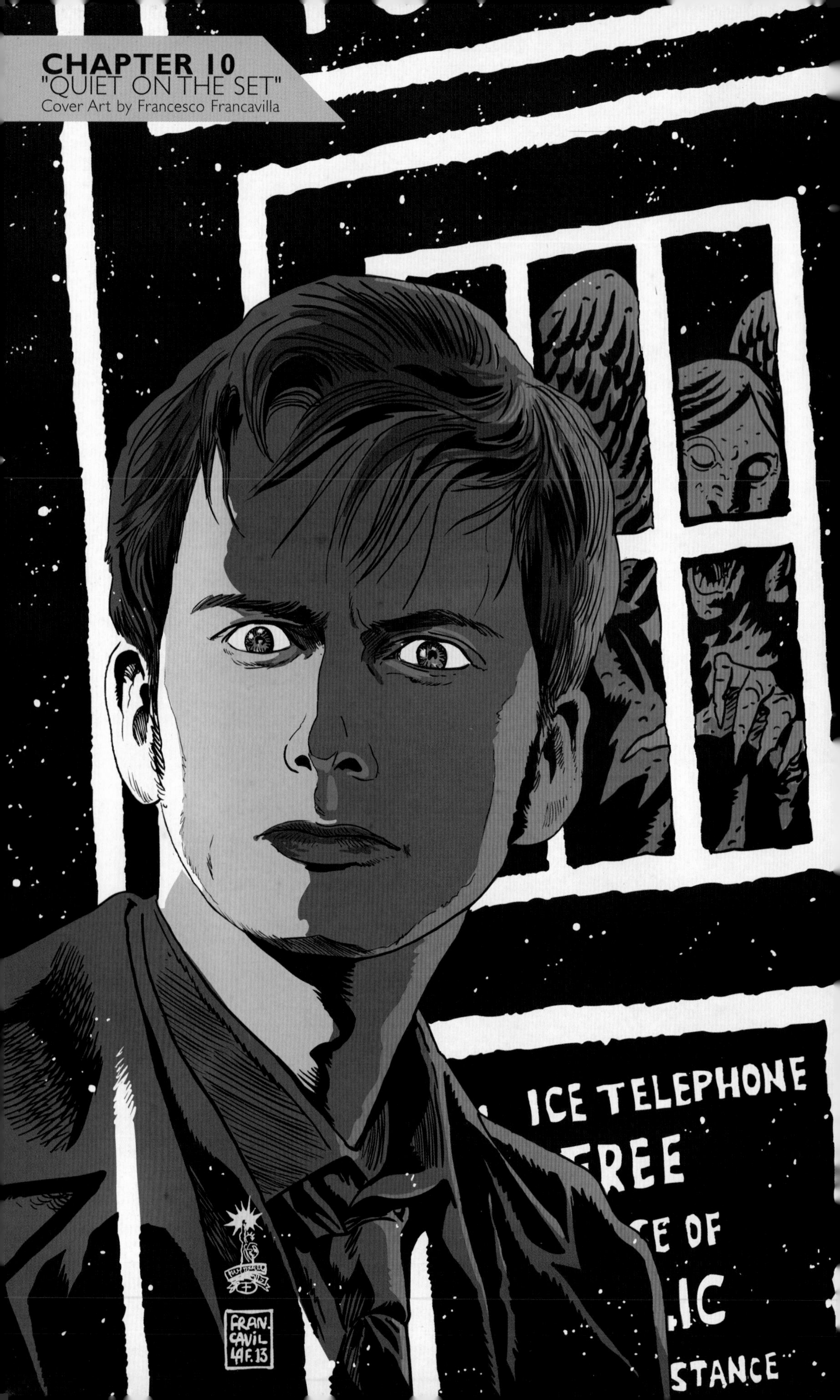
ICE TELEPHONE
FREE
CE OF
LIC
STANCE
FRAN. CAVIL LA F. 13

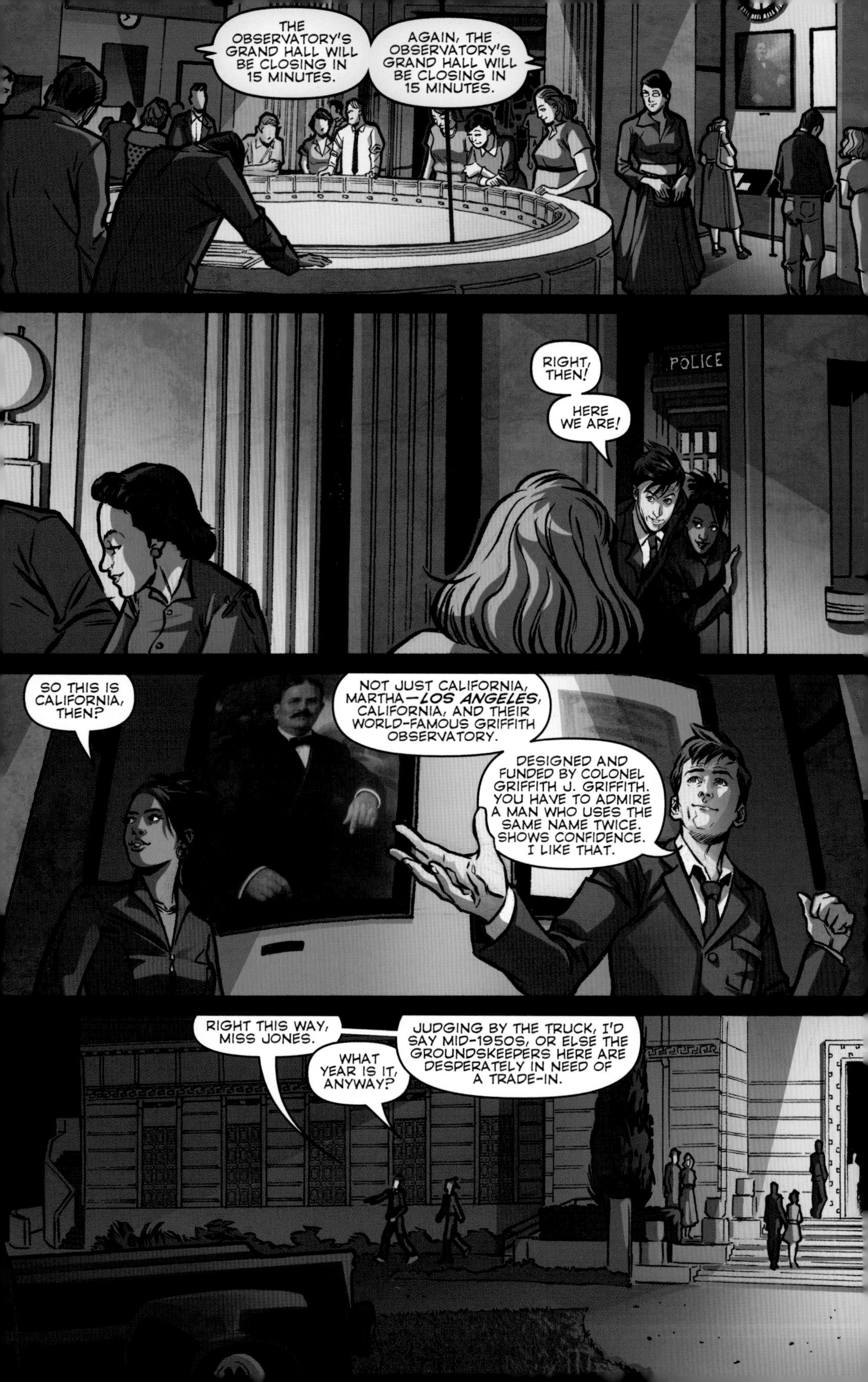
THE OBSERVATORY'S GRAND HALL WILL BE CLOSING IN 15 MINUTES.
AGAIN, THE OBSERVATORY'S GRAND HALL WILL BE CLOSING IN 15 MINUTES.
POLICE
RIGHT, THEN!
HERE WE ARE!
SO THIS IS CALIFORNIA, THEN?
NOT JUST CALIFORNIA, MARTHA—*LOS ANGELES*, CALIFORNIA, AND THEIR WORLD-FAMOUS GRIFFITH OBSERVATORY.
DESIGNED AND FUNDED BY COLONEL GRIFFITH J. GRIFFITH. YOU HAVE TO ADMIRE A MAN WHO USES THE SAME NAME TWICE. SHOWS CONFIDENCE. I LIKE THAT.
RIGHT THIS WAY, MISS JONES.
WHAT YEAR IS IT, ANYWAY?
JUDGING BY THE TRUCK, I'D SAY MID-1950S, OR ELSE THE GROUNDSKEEPERS HERE ARE DESPERATELY IN NEED OF A TRADE-IN.

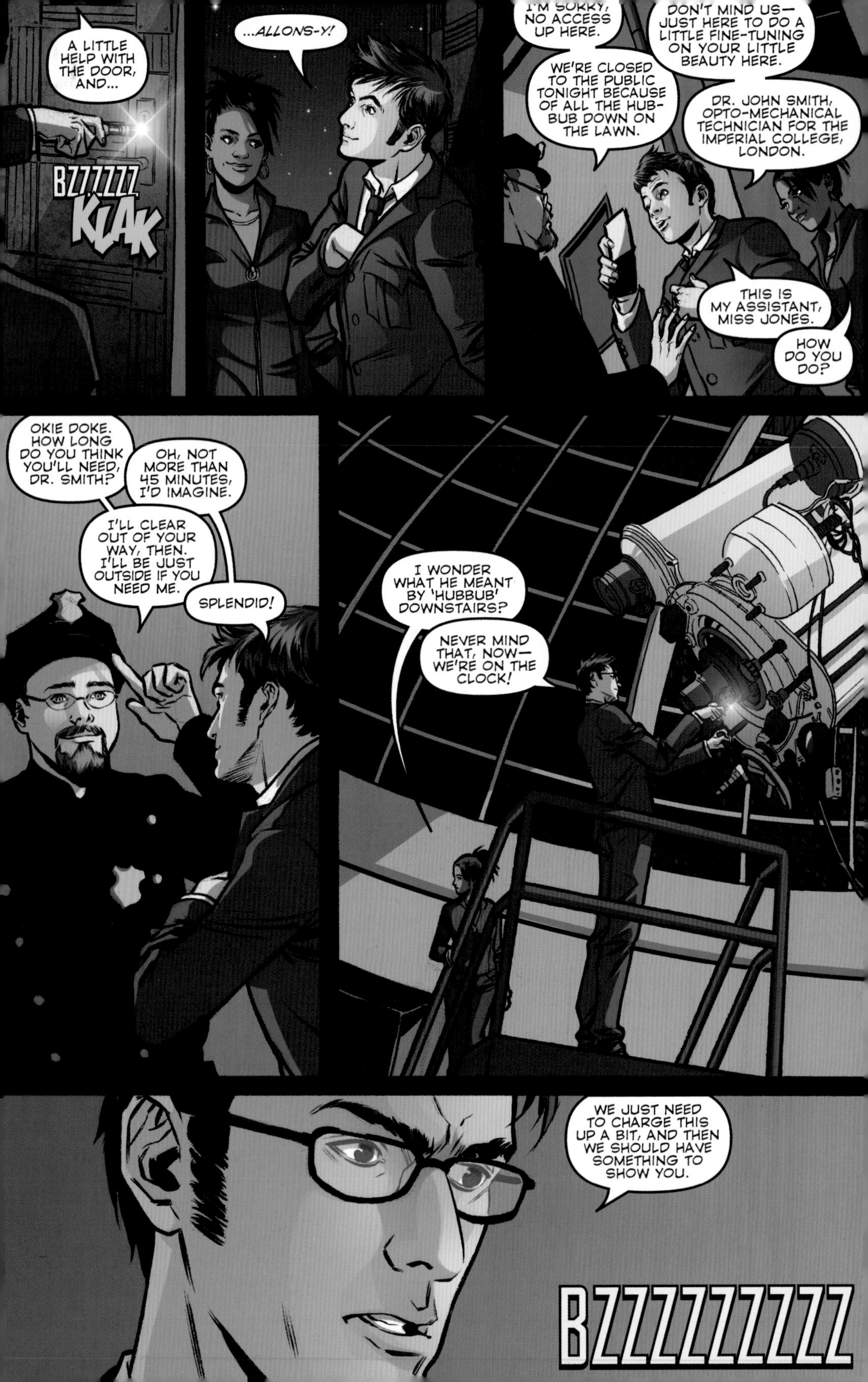
A LITTLE HELP WITH THE DOOR, AND...
BZZZZZZ
KLAK
...ALLONS-Y!
I'M SORRY, NO ACCESS UP HERE.
WE'RE CLOSED TO THE PUBLIC TONIGHT BECAUSE OF ALL THE HUB-BUB DOWN ON THE LAWN.
DON'T MIND US— JUST HERE TO DO A LITTLE FINE-TUNING ON YOUR LITTLE BEAUTY HERE.
DR. JOHN SMITH, OPTO-MECHANICAL TECHNICIAN FOR THE IMPERIAL COLLEGE, LONDON.
THIS IS MY ASSISTANT, MISS JONES.
HOW DO YOU DO?
OKIE DOKE. HOW LONG DO YOU THINK YOU'LL NEED, DR. SMITH?
OH, NOT MORE THAN 45 MINUTES, I'D IMAGINE.
I'LL CLEAR OUT OF YOUR WAY, THEN. I'LL BE JUST OUTSIDE IF YOU NEED ME.
SPLENDID!
I WONDER WHAT HE MEANT BY 'HUBBUB' DOWNSTAIRS?
NEVER MIND THAT, NOW— WE'RE ON THE CLOCK!
WE JUST NEED TO CHARGE THIS UP A BIT, AND THEN WE SHOULD HAVE SOMETHING TO SHOW YOU.
BZZZZZZZZZZ

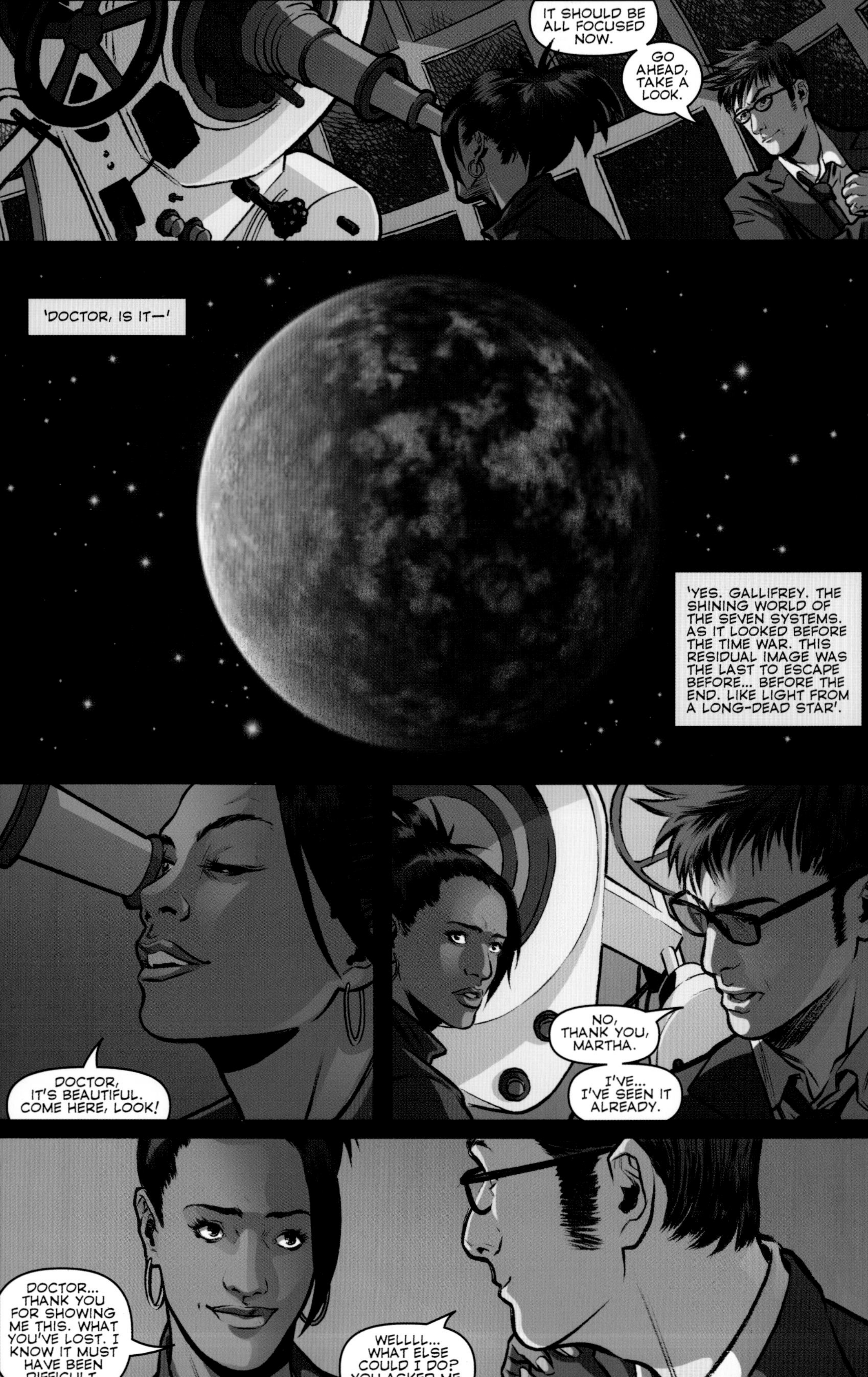
IT SHOULD BE ALL FOCUSED NOW.
GO AHEAD, TAKE A LOOK.
'DOCTOR, IS IT—'
'YES. GALLIFREY. THE SHINING WORLD OF THE SEVEN SYSTEMS. AS IT LOOKED BEFORE THE TIME WAR. THIS RESIDUAL IMAGE WAS THE LAST TO ESCAPE BEFORE... BEFORE THE END. LIKE LIGHT FROM A LONG-DEAD STAR'.
DOCTOR, IT'S BEAUTIFUL. COME HERE, LOOK!
NO, THANK YOU, MARTHA.
I'VE... I'VE SEEN IT ALREADY.
DOCTOR... THANK YOU FOR SHOWING ME THIS. WHAT YOU'VE LOST. I KNOW IT MUST HAVE BEEN DIFFICULT.
WELLLL... WHAT ELSE COULD I DO? YOU ASKED ME.

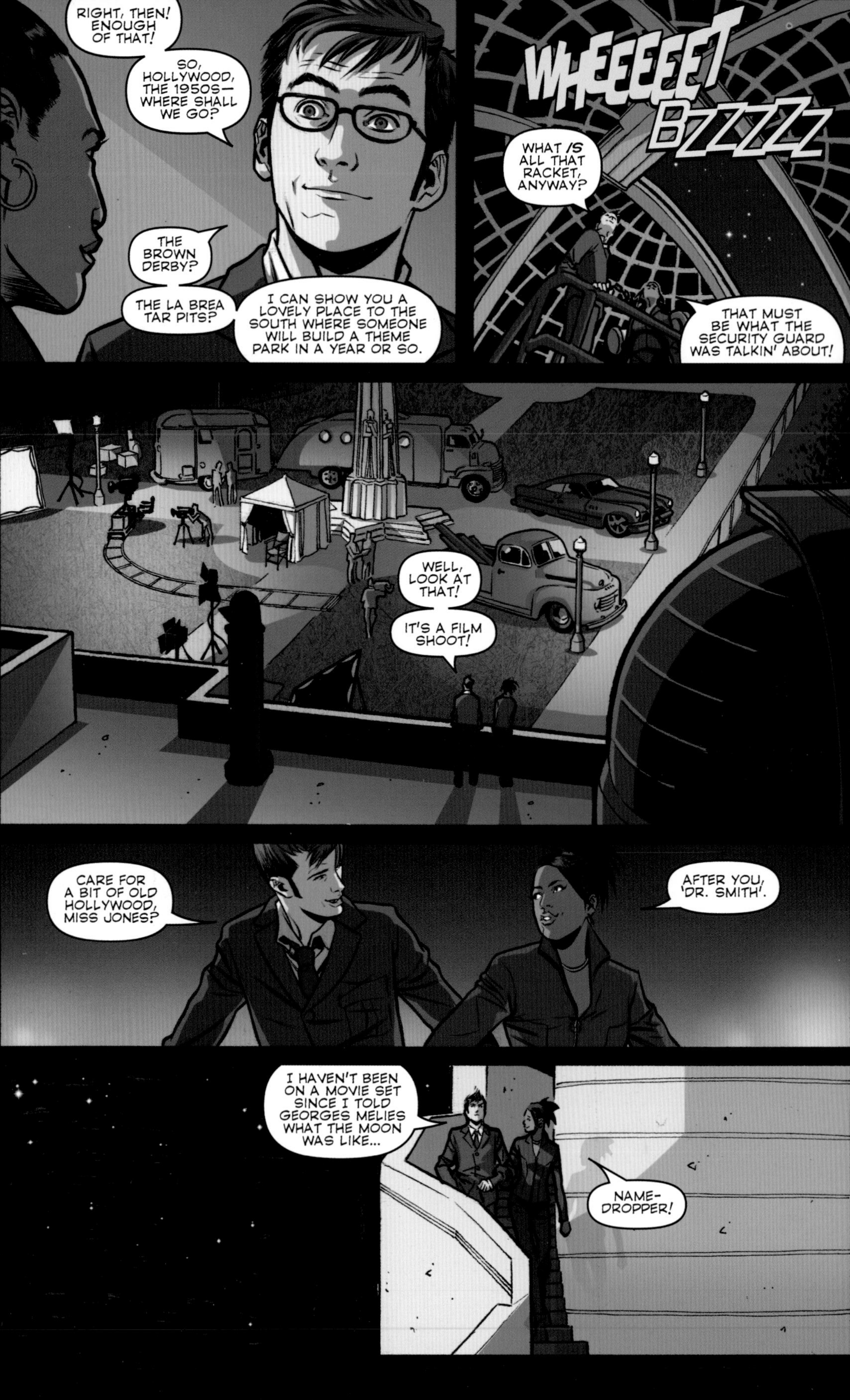
RIGHT, THEN! ENOUGH OF THAT!
SO, HOLLYWOOD, THE 1950S— WHERE SHALL WE GO?
THE BROWN DERBY?
THE LA BREA TAR PITS?
I CAN SHOW YOU A LOVELY PLACE TO THE SOUTH WHERE SOMEONE WILL BUILD A THEME PARK IN A YEAR OR SO.
WHEEEEET
BZZZZZ
WHAT IS ALL THAT RACKET, ANYWAY?
THAT MUST BE WHAT THE SECURITY GUARD WAS TALKIN' ABOUT!
WELL, LOOK AT THAT!
IT'S A FILM SHOOT!
CARE FOR A BIT OF OLD HOLLYWOOD, MISS JONES?
AFTER YOU, 'DR. SMITH'.
I HAVEN'T BEEN ON A MOVIE SET SINCE I TOLD GEORGES MELIES WHAT THE MOON WAS LIKE...
NAME-DROPPER!

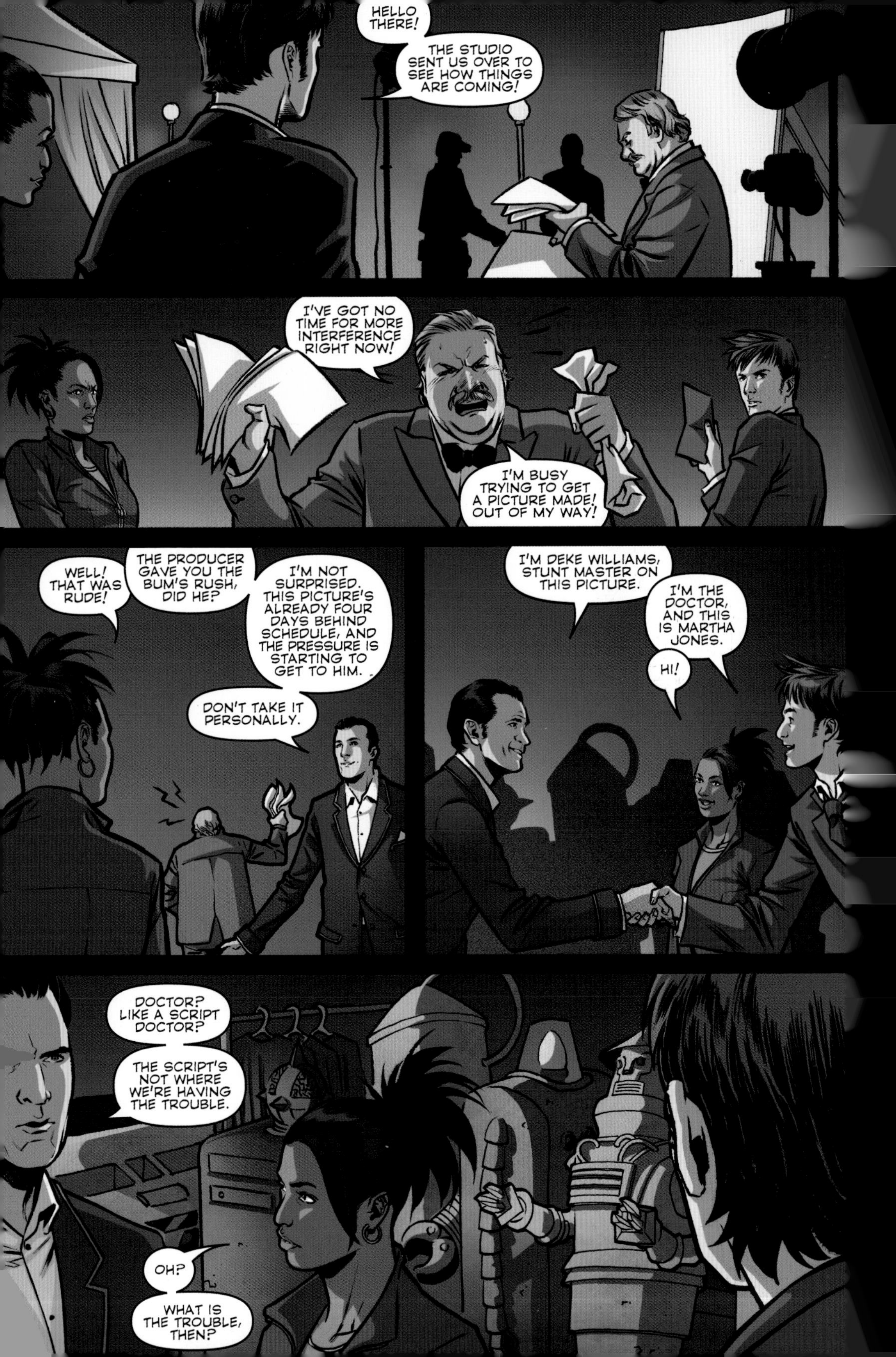
HELLO THERE!
THE STUDIO SENT US OVER TO SEE HOW THINGS ARE COMING!
I'VE GOT NO TIME FOR MORE INTERFERENCE RIGHT NOW!
I'M BUSY TRYING TO GET A PICTURE MADE! OUT OF MY WAY!
WELL! THAT WAS RUDE!
THE PRODUCER GAVE YOU THE BUM'S RUSH, DID HE?
I'M NOT SURPRISED. THIS PICTURE'S ALREADY FOUR DAYS BEHIND SCHEDULE, AND THE PRESSURE IS STARTING TO GET TO HIM.
DON'T TAKE IT PERSONALLY.
I'M DEKE WILLIAMS, STUNT MASTER ON THIS PICTURE.
I'M THE DOCTOR, AND THIS IS MARTHA JONES.
HI!
DOCTOR? LIKE A SCRIPT DOCTOR?
THE SCRIPT'S NOT WHERE WE'RE HAVING THE TROUBLE.
OH?
WHAT IS THE TROUBLE, THEN?

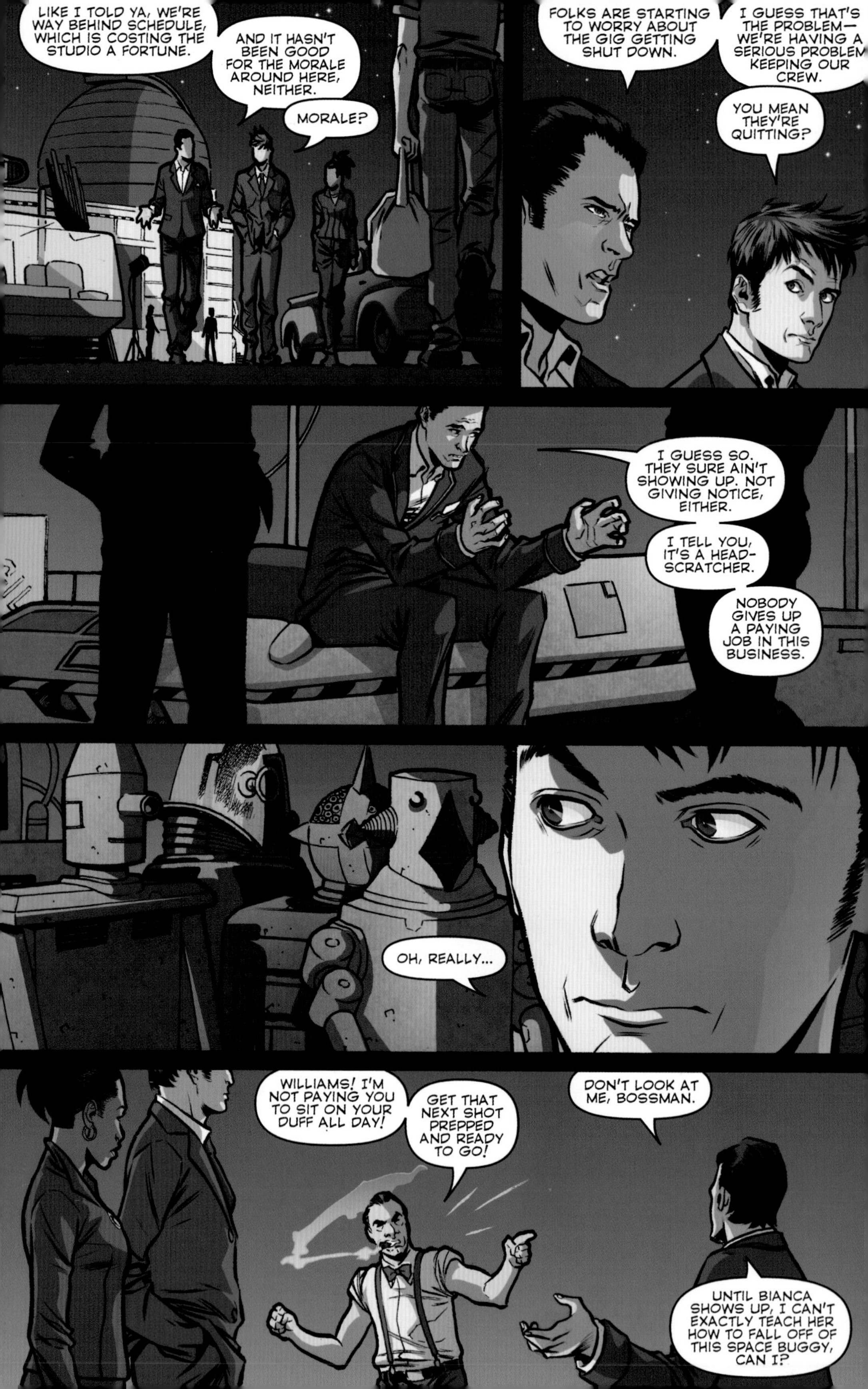

LIKE I TOLD YA, WE'RE WAY BEHIND SCHEDULE, WHICH IS COSTING THE STUDIO A FORTUNE.
AND IT HASN'T BEEN GOOD FOR THE MORALE AROUND HERE, NEITHER.
MORALE?
FOLKS ARE STARTING TO WORRY ABOUT THE GIG GETTING SHUT DOWN.
I GUESS THAT'S THE PROBLEM— WE'RE HAVING A SERIOUS PROBLEM KEEPING OUR CREW.
YOU MEAN THEY'RE QUITTING?
I GUESS SO. THEY SURE AIN'T SHOWING UP. NOT GIVING NOTICE, EITHER.
I TELL YOU, IT'S A HEAD-SCRATCHER.
NOBODY GIVES UP A PAYING JOB IN THIS BUSINESS.
OH, REALLY...
WILLIAMS! I'M NOT PAYING YOU TO SIT ON YOUR DUFF ALL DAY!
GET THAT NEXT SHOT PREPPED AND READY TO GO!
DON'T LOOK AT ME, BOSSMAN.
UNTIL BIANCA SHOWS UP, I CAN'T EXACTLY TEACH HER HOW TO FALL OFF OF THIS SPACE BUGGY, CAN I?

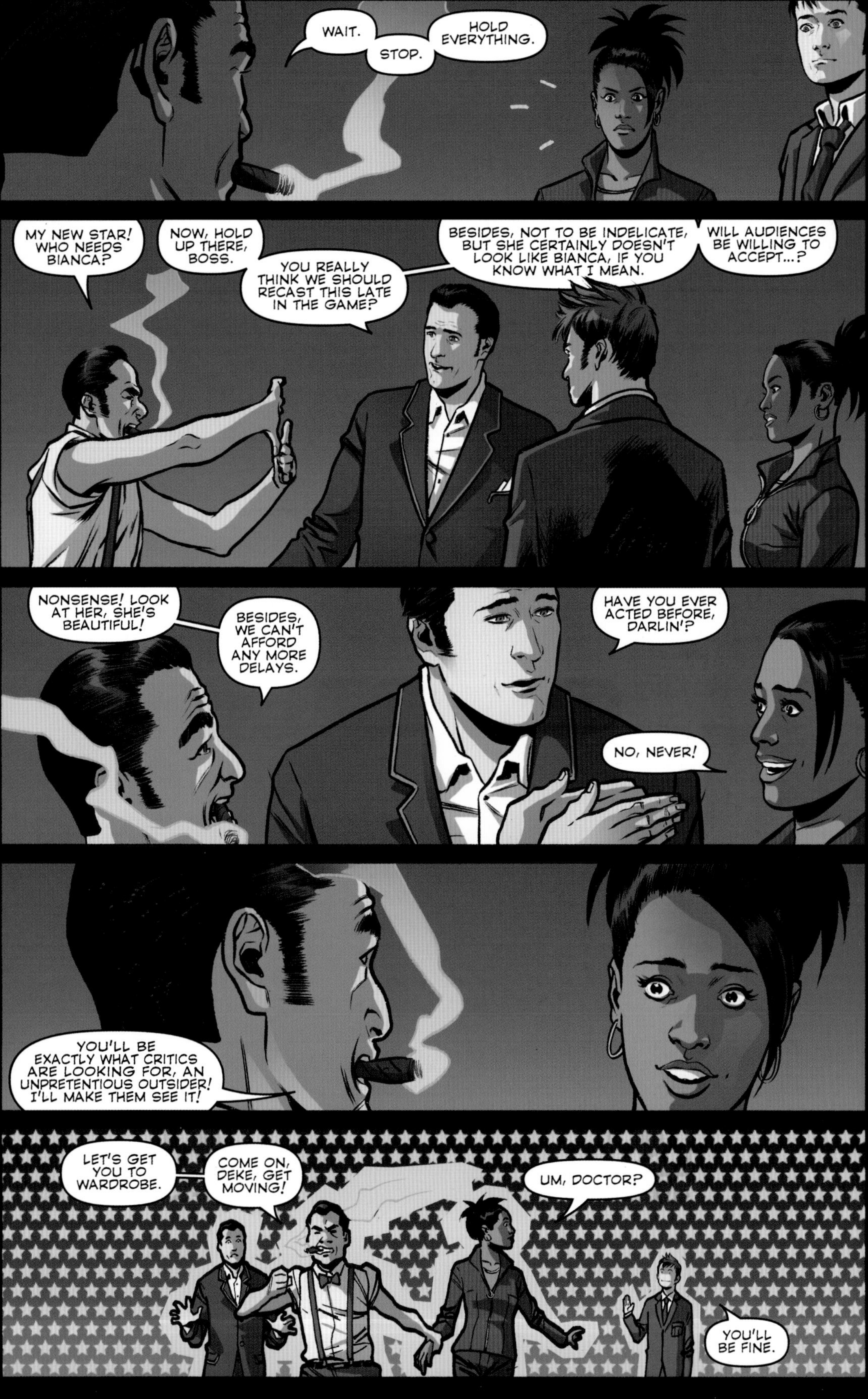
WAIT.
STOP.
HOLD EVERYTHING.
MY NEW STAR! WHO NEEDS BIANCA?
NOW, HOLD UP THERE, BOSS.
YOU REALLY THINK WE SHOULD RECAST THIS LATE IN THE GAME?
BESIDES, NOT TO BE INDELICATE, BUT SHE CERTAINLY DOESN'T LOOK LIKE BIANCA, IF YOU KNOW WHAT I MEAN.
WILL AUDIENCES BE WILLING TO ACCEPT...?
NONSENSE! LOOK AT HER, SHE'S BEAUTIFUL!
BESIDES, WE CAN'T AFFORD ANY MORE DELAYS.
HAVE YOU EVER ACTED BEFORE, DARLIN'?
NO, NEVER!
YOU'LL BE EXACTLY WHAT CRITICS ARE LOOKING FOR, AN UNPRETENTIOUS OUTSIDER! I'LL MAKE THEM SEE IT!
LET'S GET YOU TO WARDROBE.
COME ON, DEKE, GET MOVING!
UM, DOCTOR?
YOU'LL BE FINE.

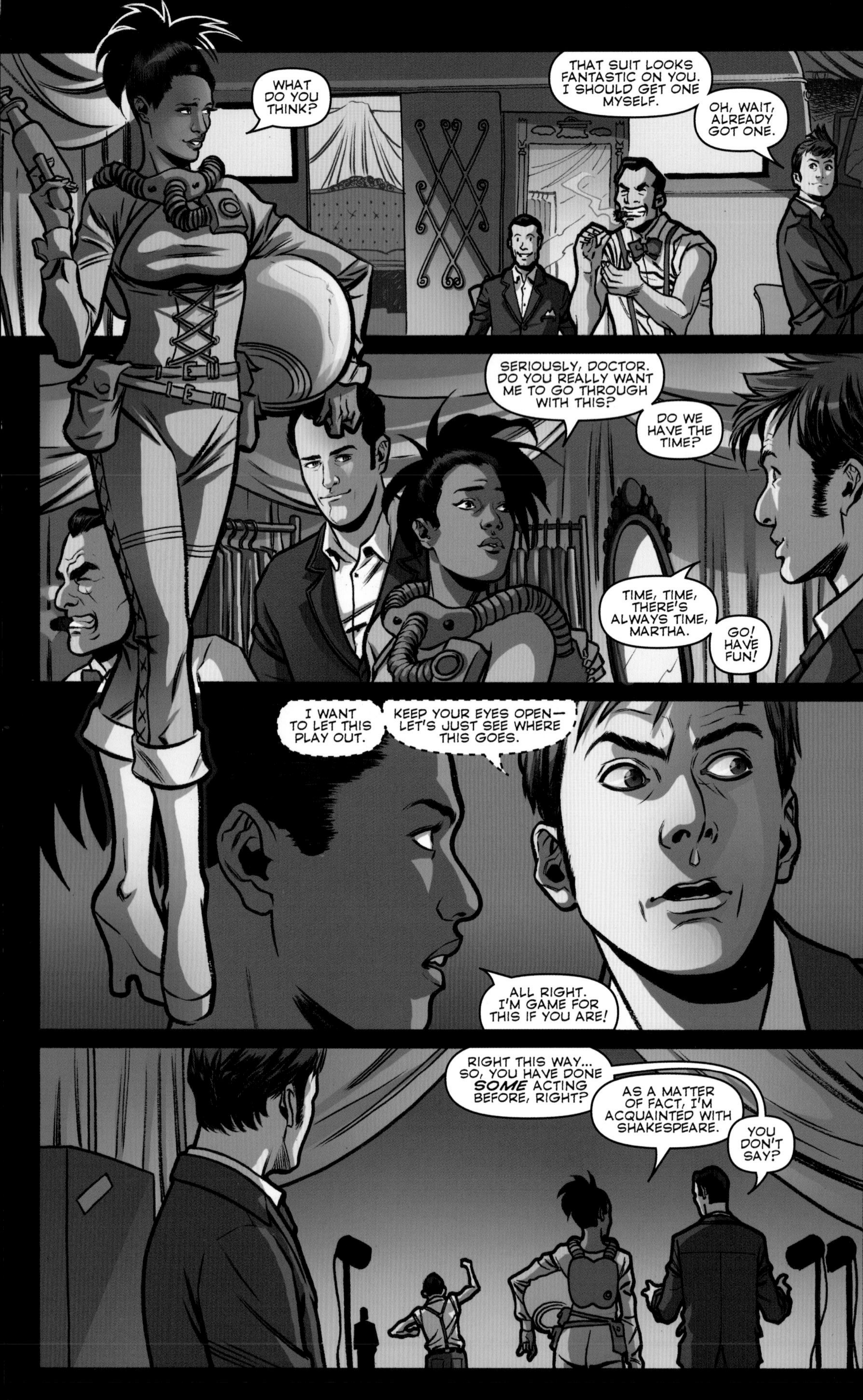
WHAT DO YOU THINK?
THAT SUIT LOOKS FANTASTIC ON YOU. I SHOULD GET ONE MYSELF.
OH, WAIT, ALREADY GOT ONE.
SERIOUSLY, DOCTOR. DO YOU REALLY WANT ME TO GO THROUGH WITH THIS?
DO WE HAVE THE TIME?
TIME, TIME, THERE'S ALWAYS TIME, MARTHA.
GO! HAVE FUN!
I WANT TO LET THIS PLAY OUT.
KEEP YOUR EYES OPEN— LET'S JUST SEE WHERE THIS GOES.
ALL RIGHT. I'M GAME FOR THIS IF YOU ARE!
RIGHT THIS WAY... SO, YOU HAVE DONE SOME ACTING BEFORE, RIGHT?
AS A MATTER OF FACT, I'M ACQUAINTED WITH SHAKESPEARE.
YOU DON'T SAY?

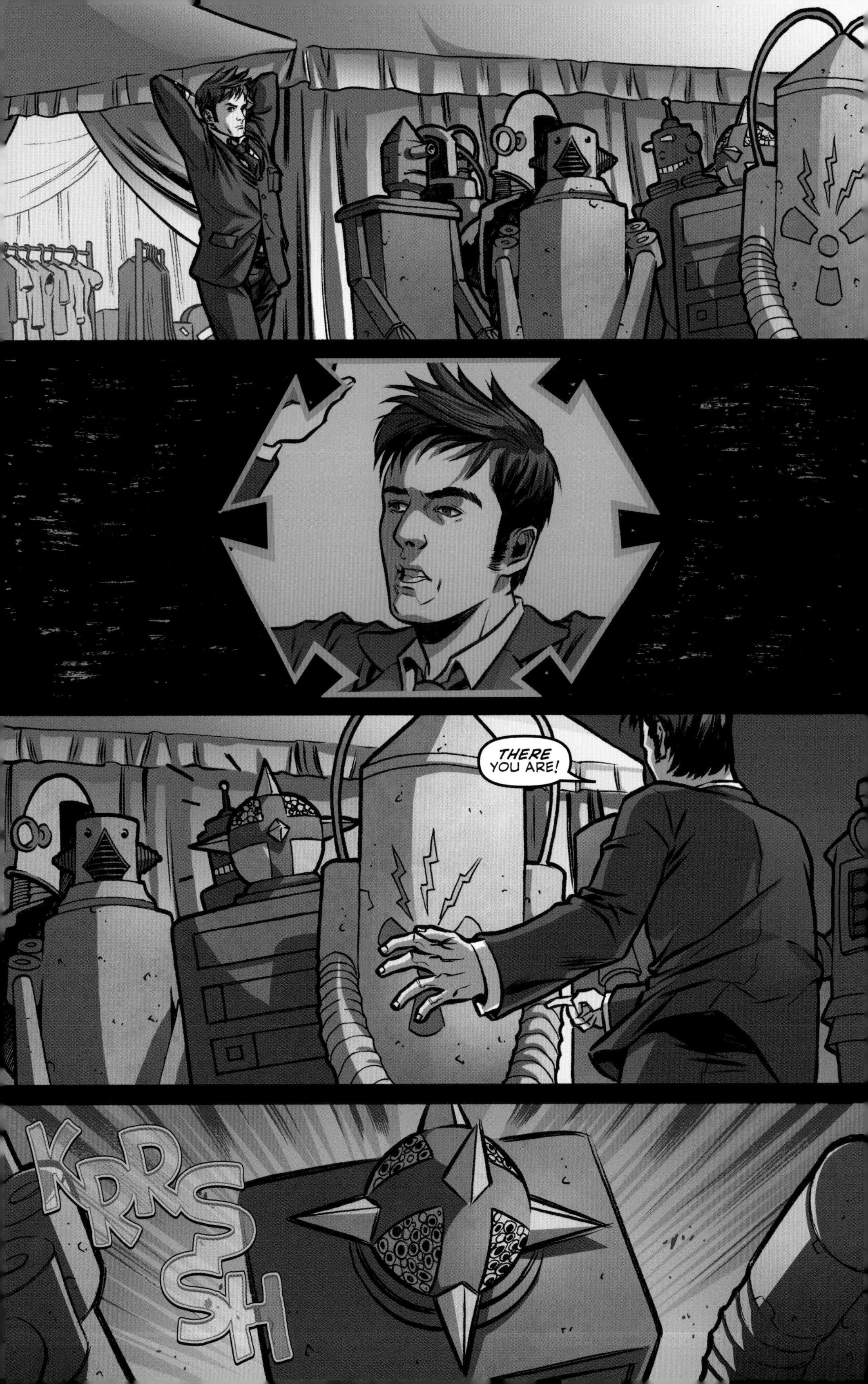
THERE YOU ARE!
KRRSSH

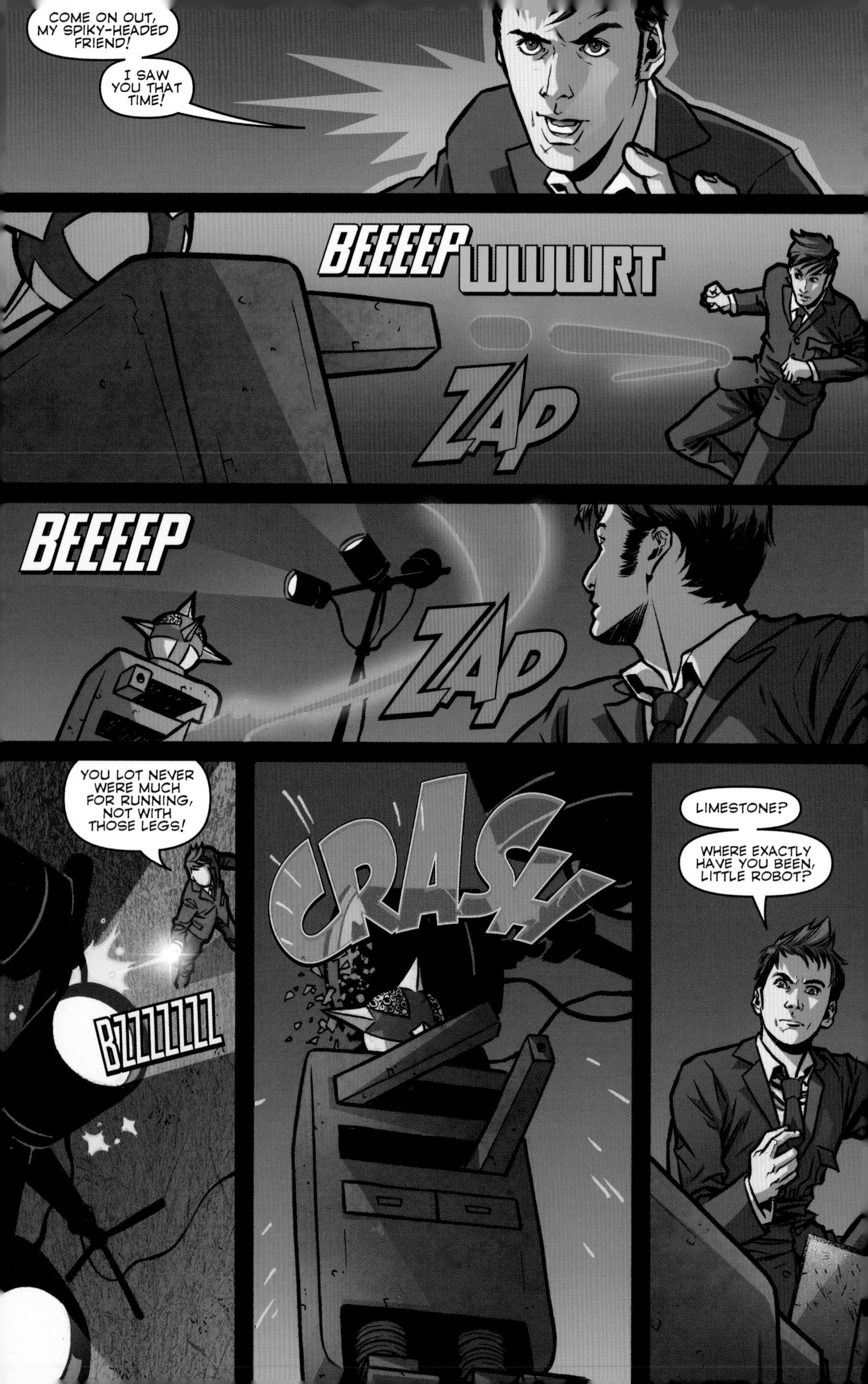
COME ON OUT, MY SPIKY-HEADED FRIEND!
I SAW YOU THAT TIME!
BEEEEP WWWRT
ZAP
BEEEEP
ZAP
YOU LOT NEVER WERE MUCH FOR RUNNING, NOT WITH THOSE LEGS!
BZZZZZZZ
CRASH
LIMESTONE?
WHERE EXACTLY HAVE YOU BEEN, LITTLE ROBOT?

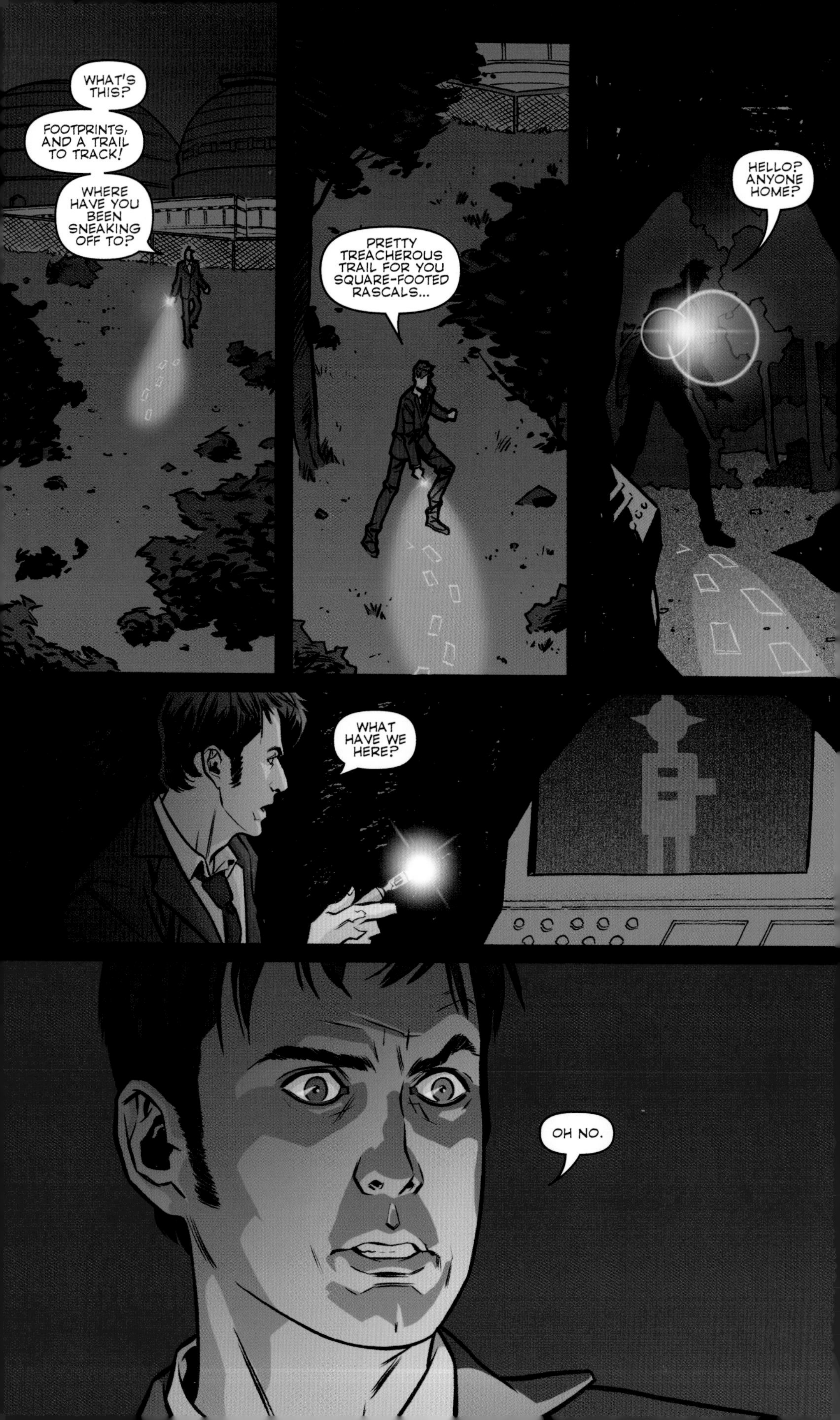
WHAT'S THIS?
FOOTPRINTS, AND A TRAIL TO TRACK!
WHERE HAVE YOU BEEN SNEAKING OFF TO?
PRETTY TREACHEROUS TRAIL FOR YOU SQUARE-FOOTED RASCALS...
HELLO? ANYONE HOME?
WHAT HAVE WE HERE?
OH NO.

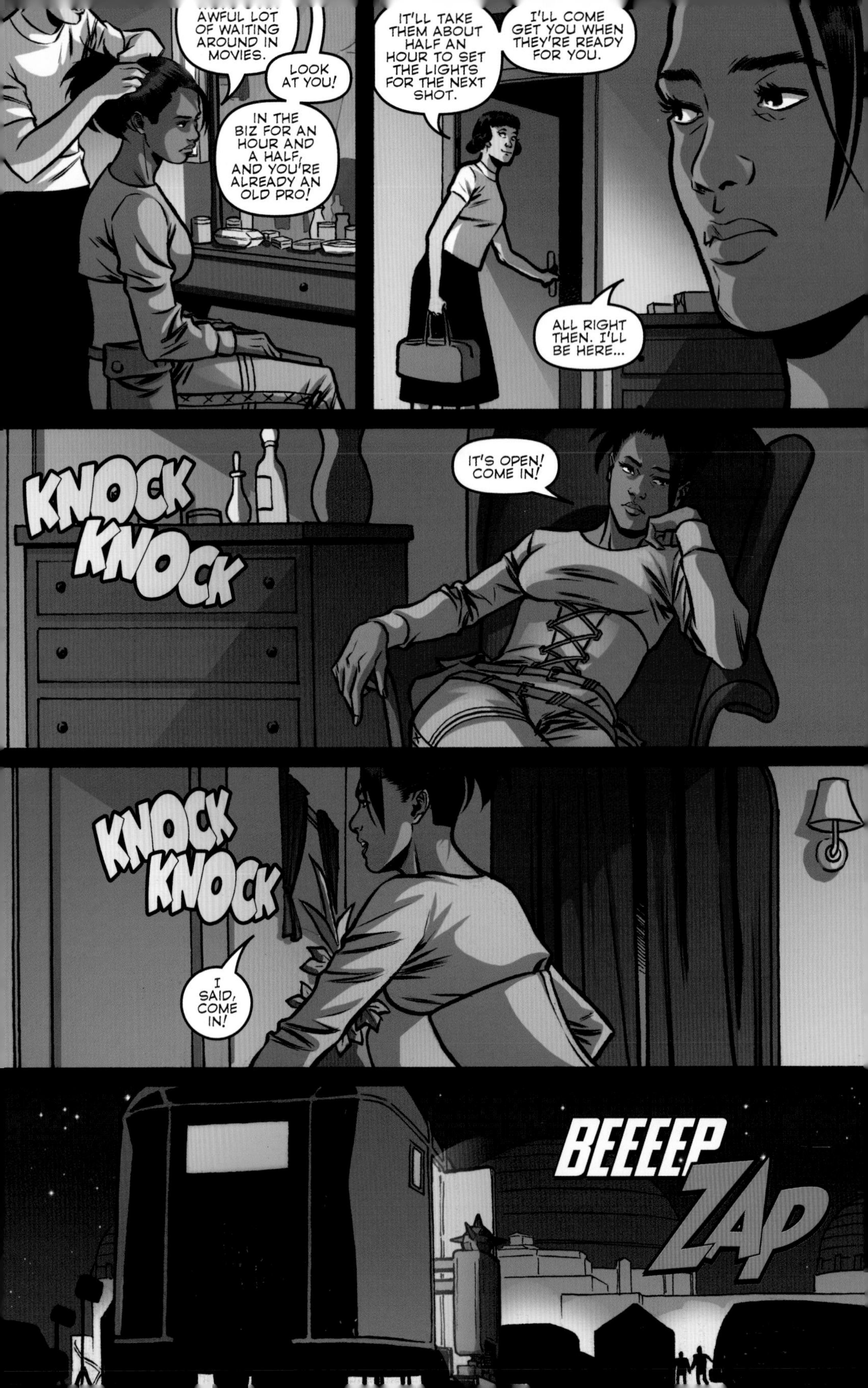
AWFUL LOT OF WAITING AROUND IN MOVIES.
LOOK AT YOU!
IN THE BIZ FOR AN HOUR AND A HALF, AND YOU'RE ALREADY AN OLD PRO!
IT'LL TAKE THEM ABOUT HALF AN HOUR TO SET THE LIGHTS FOR THE NEXT SHOT.
I'LL COME GET YOU WHEN THEY'RE READY FOR YOU.
ALL RIGHT THEN. I'LL BE HERE...
KNOCK KNOCK
IT'S OPEN! COME IN!
KNOCK KNOCK
I SAID, COME IN!
BEEEEP
ZAP

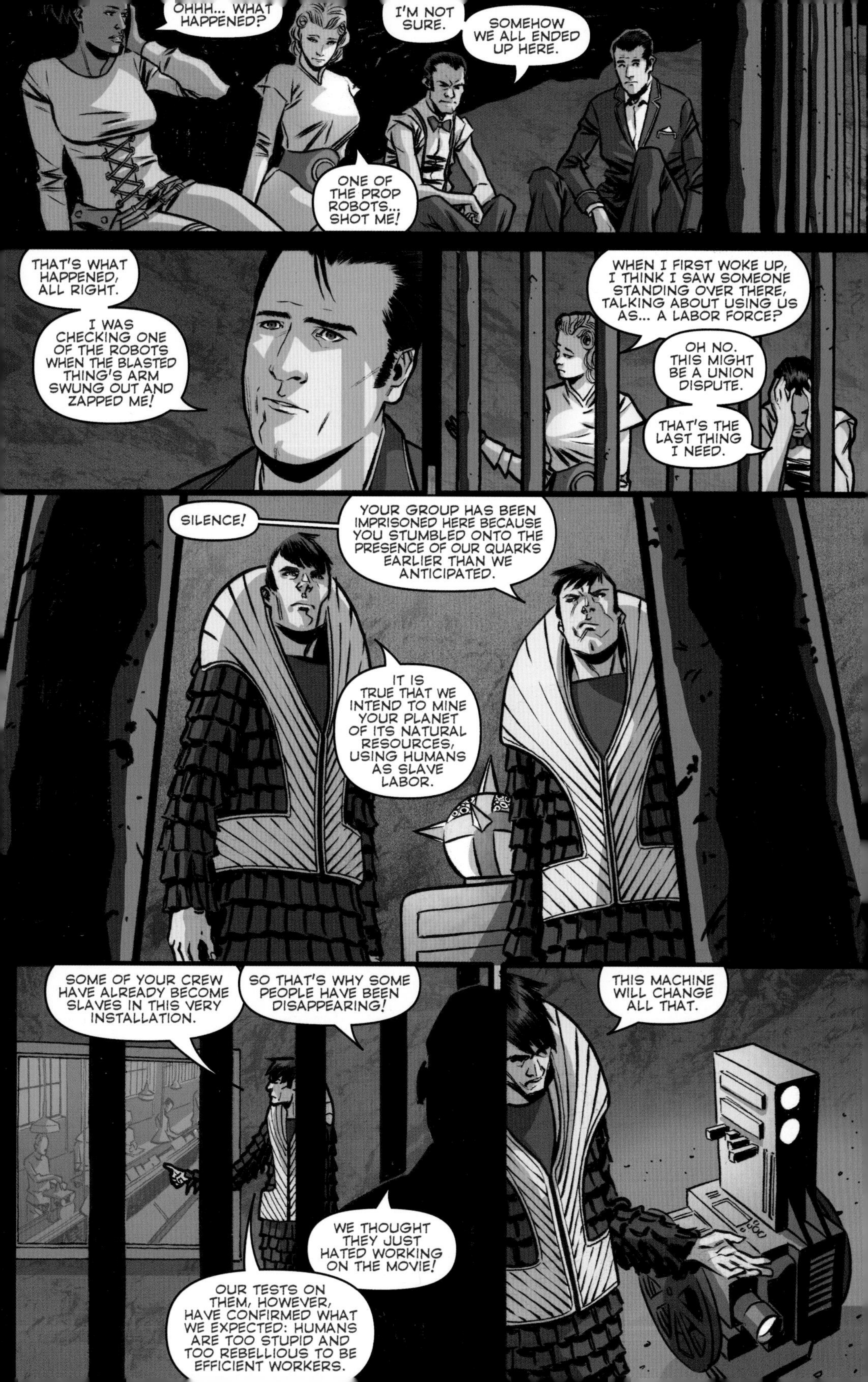
OHHH... WHAT HAPPENED?
I'M NOT SURE.
SOMEHOW WE ALL ENDED UP HERE.
ONE OF THE PROP ROBOTS... SHOT ME!
THAT'S WHAT HAPPENED, ALL RIGHT.
I WAS CHECKING ONE OF THE ROBOTS WHEN THE BLASTED THING'S ARM SWUNG OUT AND ZAPPED ME!
WHEN I FIRST WOKE UP, I THINK I SAW SOMEONE STANDING OVER THERE, TALKING ABOUT USING US AS... A LABOR FORCE?
OH NO. THIS MIGHT BE A UNION DISPUTE.
THAT'S THE LAST THING I NEED.
SILENCE!
YOUR GROUP HAS BEEN IMPRISONED HERE BECAUSE YOU STUMBLED ONTO THE PRESENCE OF OUR QUARKS EARLIER THAN WE ANTICIPATED.
IT IS TRUE THAT WE INTEND TO MINE YOUR PLANET OF ITS NATURAL RESOURCES, USING HUMANS AS SLAVE LABOR.
SOME OF YOUR CREW HAVE ALREADY BECOME SLAVES IN THIS VERY INSTALLATION.
SO THAT'S WHY SOME PEOPLE HAVE BEEN DISAPPEARING!
WE THOUGHT THEY JUST HATED WORKING ON THE MOVIE!
OUR TESTS ON THEM, HOWEVER, HAVE CONFIRMED WHAT WE EXPECTED: HUMANS ARE TOO STUPID AND TOO REBELLIOUS TO BE EFFICIENT WORKERS.
THIS MACHINE WILL CHANGE ALL THAT.

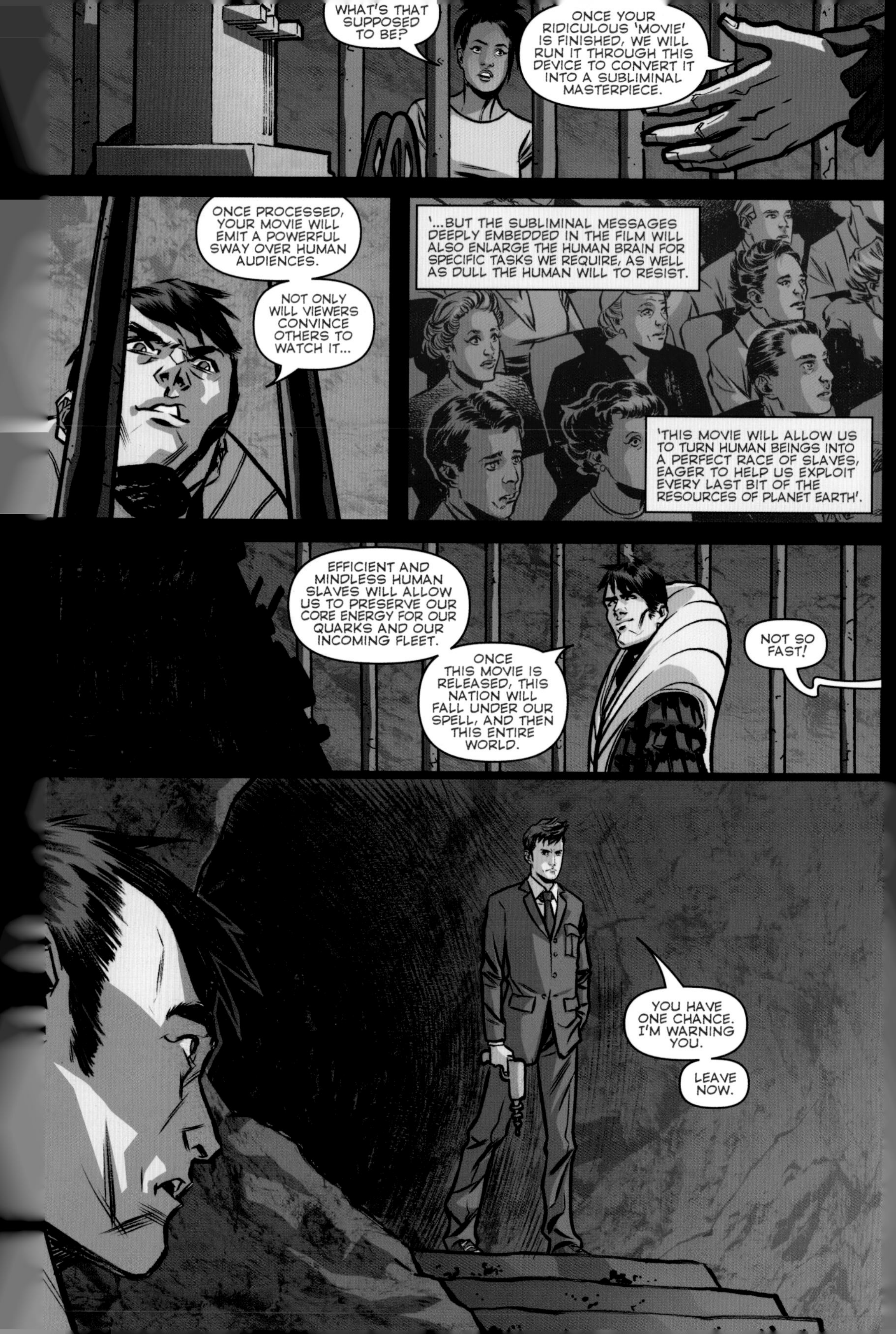
WHAT'S THAT SUPPOSED TO BE?
ONCE YOUR RIDICULOUS 'MOVIE' IS FINISHED, WE WILL RUN IT THROUGH THIS DEVICE TO CONVERT IT INTO A SUBLIMINAL MASTERPIECE.
ONCE PROCESSED, YOUR MOVIE WILL EMIT A POWERFUL SWAY OVER HUMAN AUDIENCES.
NOT ONLY WILL VIEWERS CONVINCE OTHERS TO WATCH IT...
'...BUT THE SUBLIMINAL MESSAGES DEEPLY EMBEDDED IN THE FILM WILL ALSO ENLARGE THE HUMAN BRAIN FOR SPECIFIC TASKS WE REQUIRE, AS WELL AS DULL THE HUMAN WILL TO RESIST.
'THIS MOVIE WILL ALLOW US TO TURN HUMAN BEINGS INTO A PERFECT RACE OF SLAVES, EAGER TO HELP US EXPLOIT EVERY LAST BIT OF THE RESOURCES OF PLANET EARTH'.
EFFICIENT AND MINDLESS HUMAN SLAVES WILL ALLOW US TO PRESERVE OUR CORE ENERGY FOR OUR QUARKS AND OUR INCOMING FLEET.
ONCE THIS MOVIE IS RELEASED, THIS NATION WILL FALL UNDER OUR SPELL, AND THEN THIS ENTIRE WORLD.
NOT SO FAST!
YOU HAVE ONE CHANCE. I'M WARNING YOU.
LEAVE NOW.

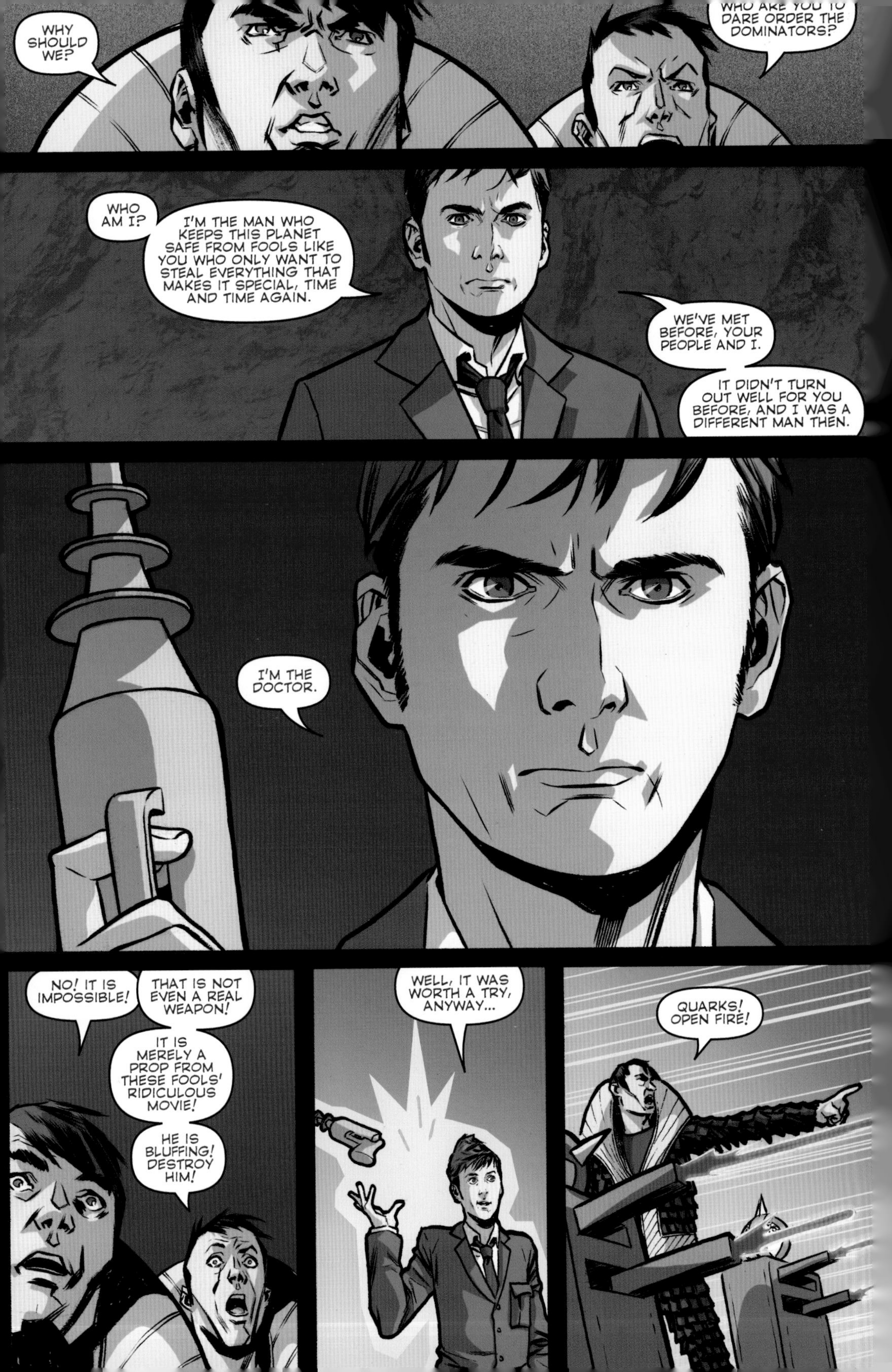
WHY SHOULD WE?
WHO ARE YOU TO DARE ORDER THE DOMINATORS?
WHO AM I?
I'M THE MAN WHO KEEPS THIS PLANET SAFE FROM FOOLS LIKE YOU WHO ONLY WANT TO STEAL EVERYTHING THAT MAKES IT SPECIAL, TIME AND TIME AGAIN.
WE'VE MET BEFORE, YOUR PEOPLE AND I.
IT DIDN'T TURN OUT WELL FOR YOU BEFORE, AND I WAS A DIFFERENT MAN THEN.
I'M THE DOCTOR.
NO! IT IS IMPOSSIBLE!
THAT IS NOT EVEN A REAL WEAPON!
IT IS MERELY A PROP FROM THESE FOOLS' RIDICULOUS MOVIE!
HE IS BLUFFING! DESTROY HIM!
WELL, IT WAS WORTH A TRY, ANYWAY...
QUARKS! OPEN FIRE!

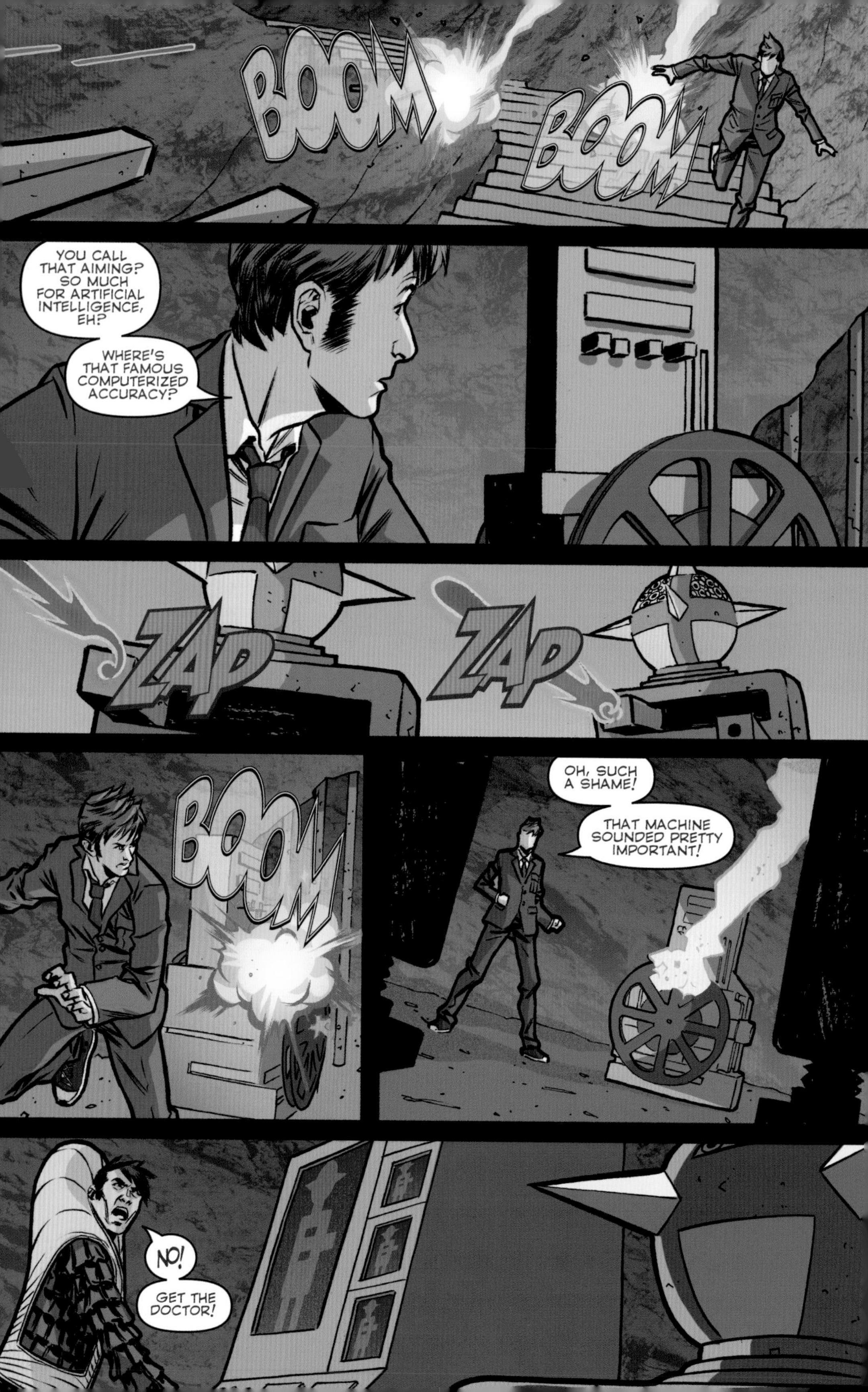
BOOM
BOOM
YOU CALL THAT AIMING? SO MUCH FOR ARTIFICIAL INTELLIGENCE, EH?
WHERE'S THAT FAMOUS COMPUTERIZED ACCURACY?
ZAP
ZAP
BOOM
OH, SUCH A SHAME!
THAT MACHINE SOUNDED PRETTY IMPORTANT!
NO!
GET THE DOCTOR!

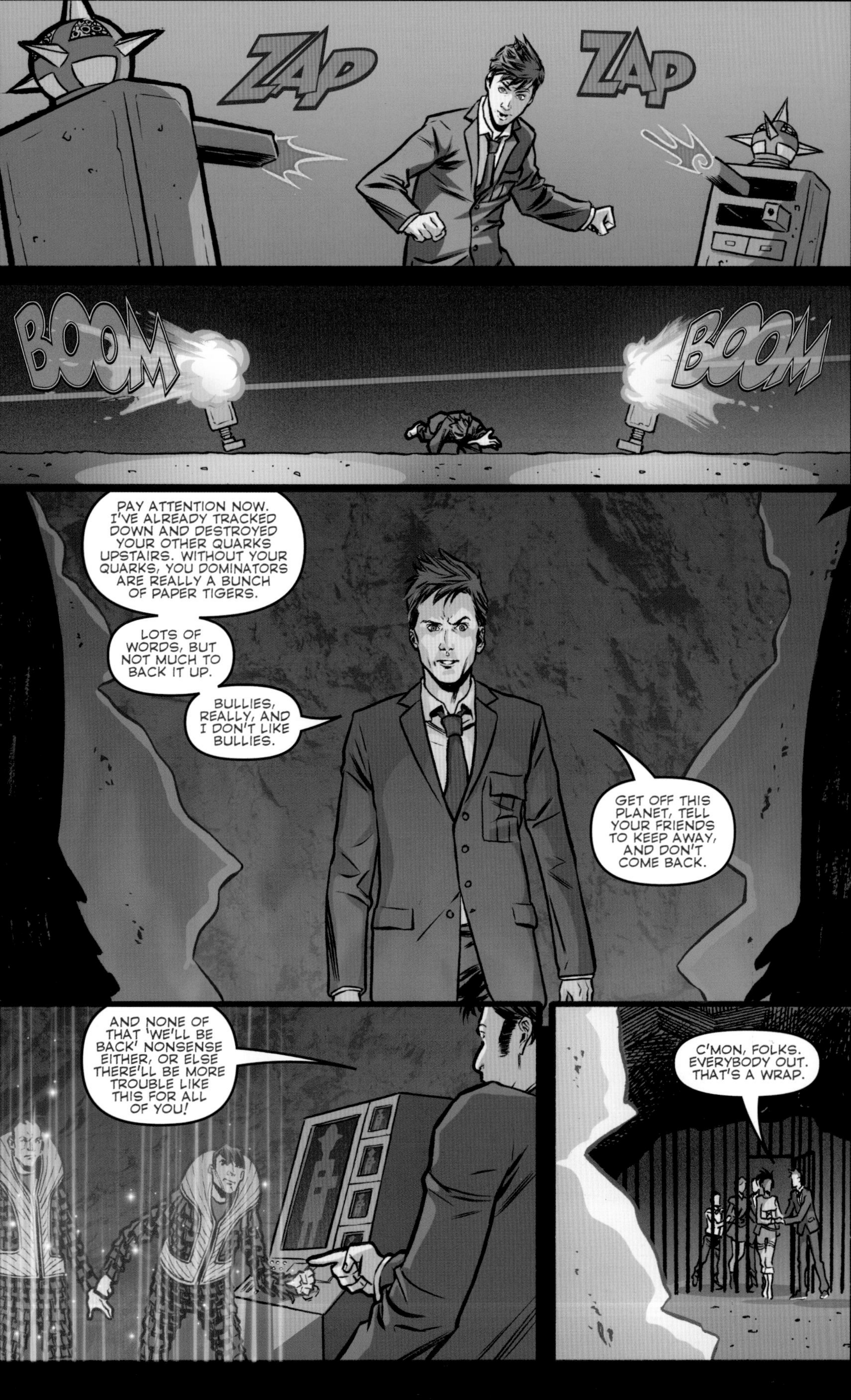
ZAP
ZAP
BOOM
BOOM
PAY ATTENTION NOW. I'VE ALREADY TRACKED DOWN AND DESTROYED YOUR OTHER QUARKS UPSTAIRS. WITHOUT YOUR QUARKS, YOU DOMINATORS ARE REALLY A BUNCH OF PAPER TIGERS.
LOTS OF WORDS, BUT NOT MUCH TO BACK IT UP.
BULLIES, REALLY, AND I DON'T LIKE BULLIES.
GET OFF THIS PLANET, TELL YOUR FRIENDS TO KEEP AWAY, AND DON'T COME BACK.
AND NONE OF THAT 'WE'LL BE BACK' NONSENSE EITHER, OR ELSE THERE'LL BE MORE TROUBLE LIKE THIS FOR ALL OF YOU!
C'MON, FOLKS. EVERYBODY OUT. THAT'S A WRAP.

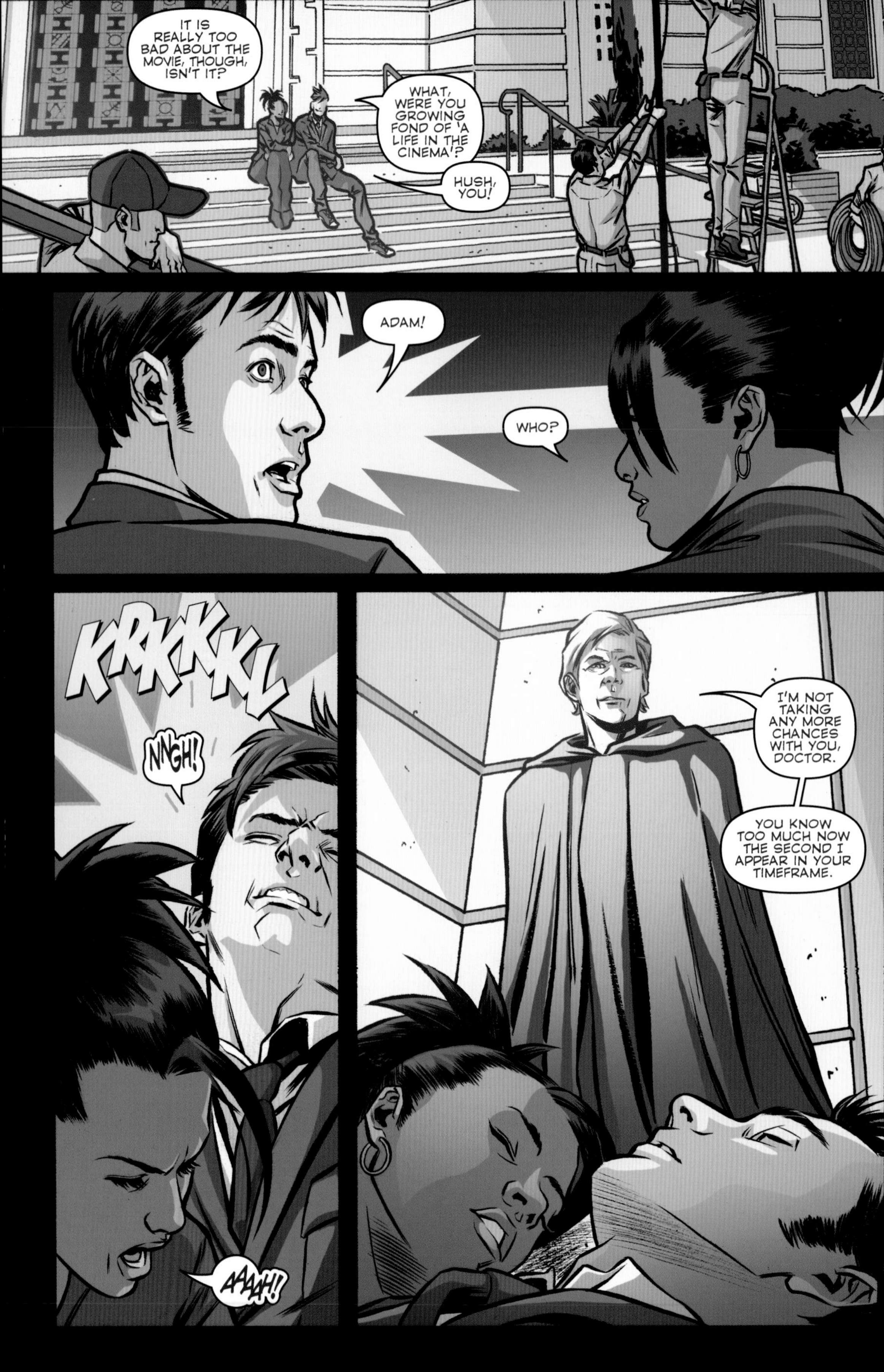
IT IS REALLY TOO BAD ABOUT THE MOVIE, THOUGH, ISN'T IT?
WHAT, WERE YOU GROWING FOND OF 'A LIFE IN THE CINEMA'?
HUSH, YOU!
ADAM!
WHO?
KRKKKL
NNGH!
AAAH!
I'M NOT TAKING ANY MORE CHANCES WITH YOU, DOCTOR.
YOU KNOW TOO MUCH NOW THE SECOND I APPEAR IN YOUR TIMEFRAME.

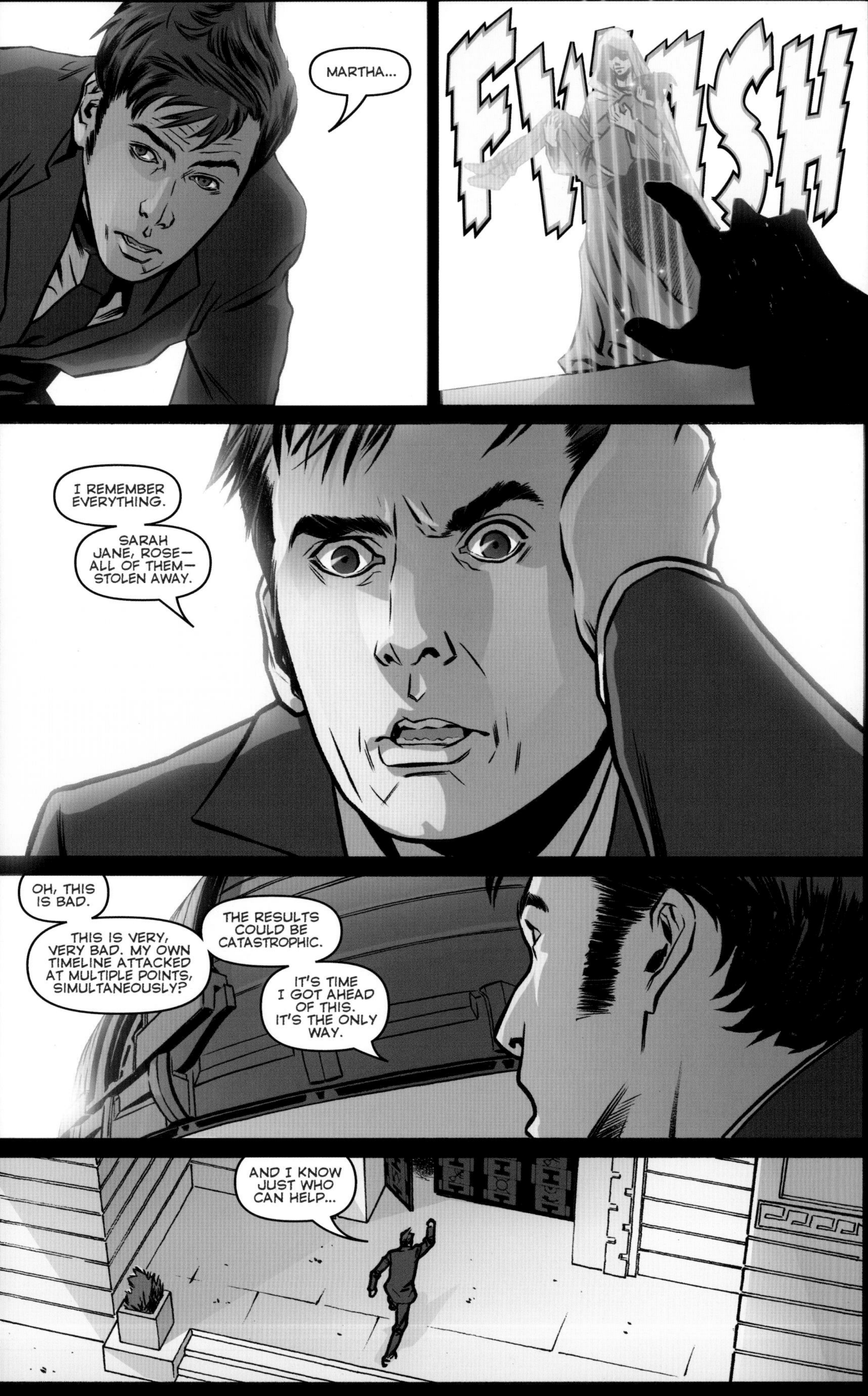

MARTHA...
FWOOSH
I REMEMBER EVERYTHING.
SARAH JANE, ROSE— ALL OF THEM— STOLEN AWAY.
OH, THIS IS BAD.
THIS IS VERY, VERY BAD. MY OWN TIMELINE ATTACKED AT MULTIPLE POINTS, SIMULTANEOUSLY?
THE RESULTS COULD BE CATASTROPHIC.
IT'S TIME I GOT AHEAD OF THIS. IT'S THE ONLY WAY.
AND I KNOW JUST WHO CAN HELP...

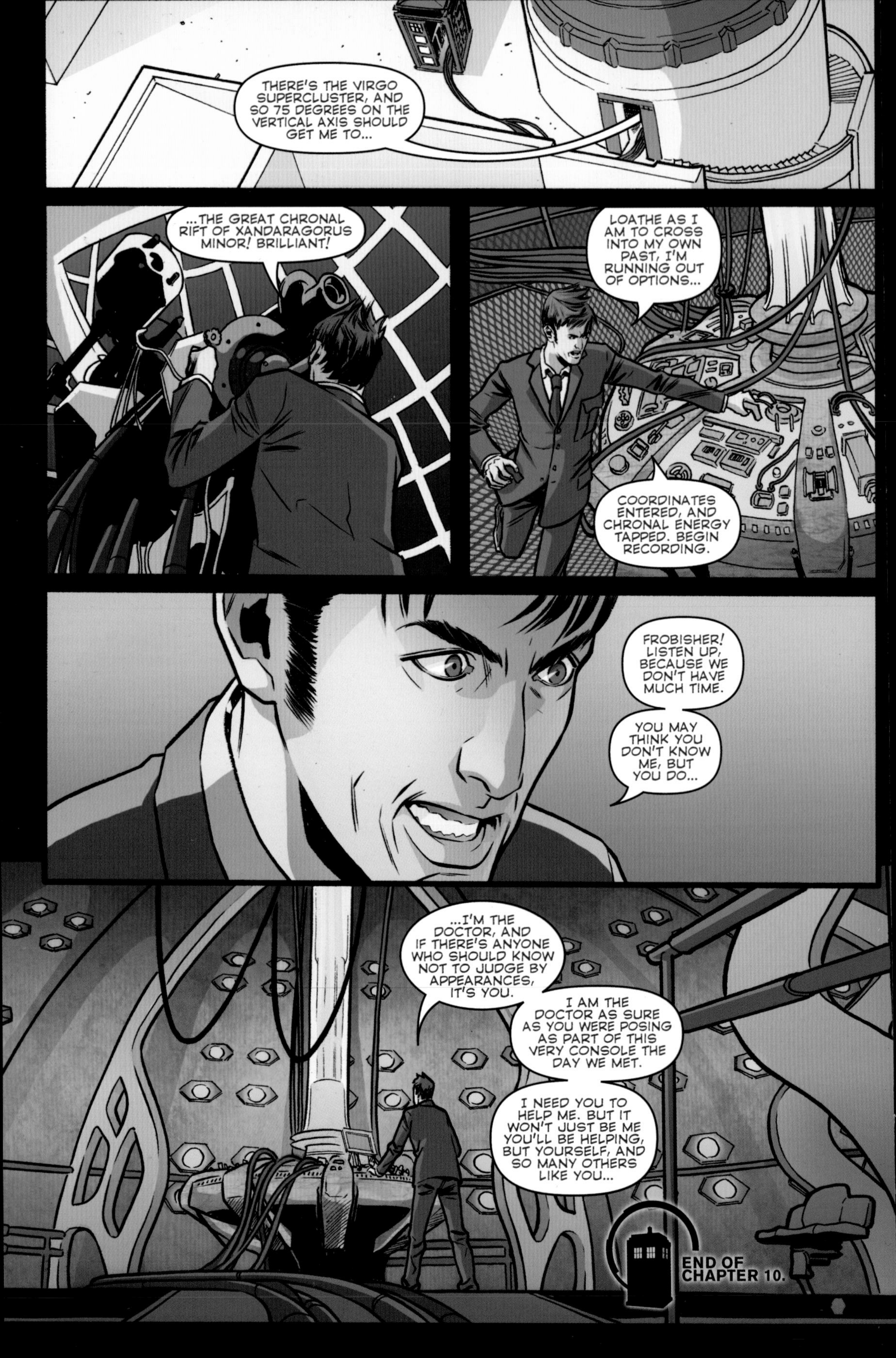
THERE'S THE VIRGO SUPERCLUSTER, AND SO 75 DEGREES ON THE VERTICAL AXIS SHOULD GET ME TO...
...THE GREAT CHRONAL RIFT OF XANDARAGORUS MINOR! BRILLIANT!
LOATHE AS I AM TO CROSS INTO MY OWN PAST, I'M RUNNING OUT OF OPTIONS...
COORDINATES ENTERED, AND CHRONAL ENERGY TAPPED. BEGIN RECORDING.
FROBISHER! LISTEN UP, BECAUSE WE DON'T HAVE MUCH TIME.
YOU MAY THINK YOU DON'T KNOW ME, BUT YOU DO...
...I'M THE DOCTOR, AND IF THERE'S ANYONE WHO SHOULD KNOW NOT TO JUDGE BY APPEARANCES, IT'S YOU.
I AM THE DOCTOR AS SURE AS YOU WERE POSING AS PART OF THIS VERY CONSOLE THE DAY WE MET.
I NEED YOU TO HELP ME. BUT IT WON'T JUST BE ME YOU'LL BE HELPING, BUT YOURSELF, AND SO MANY OTHERS LIKE YOU...
END OF CHAPTER 10.

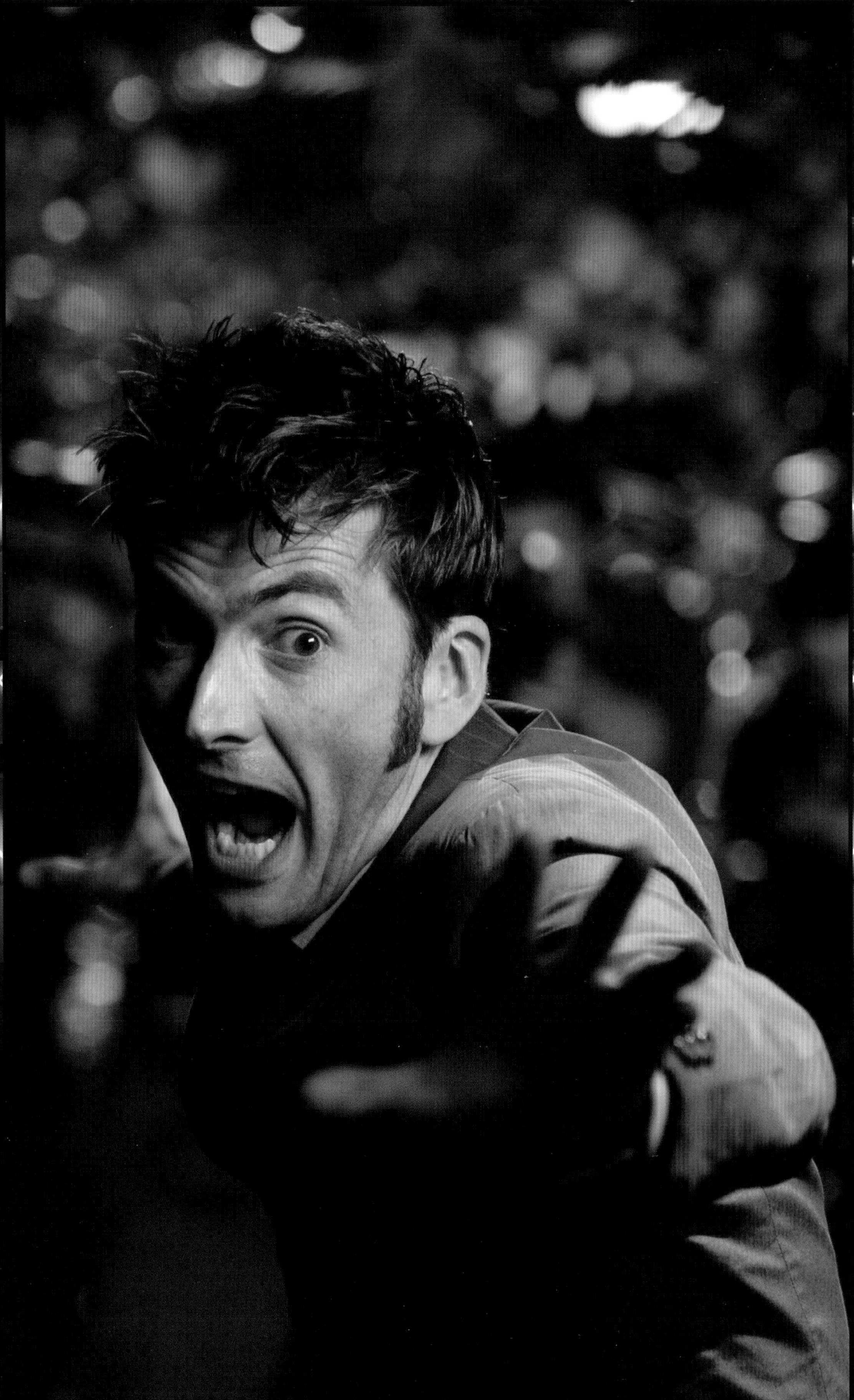

CHAPTER 11
"THE CHOICE"
Cover Art by Francesco Francavilla

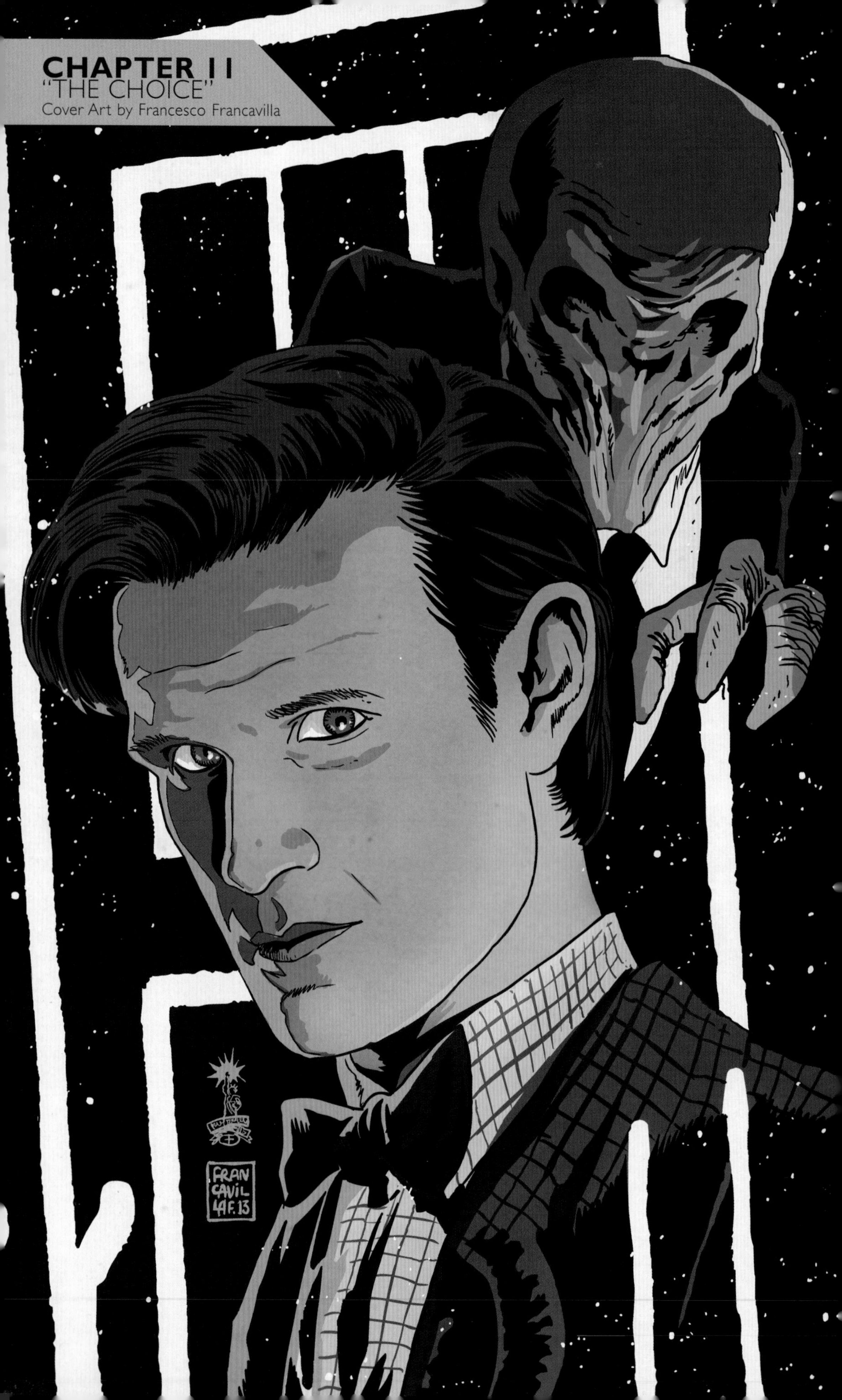
FRAN
CAVIL
LA F. 13

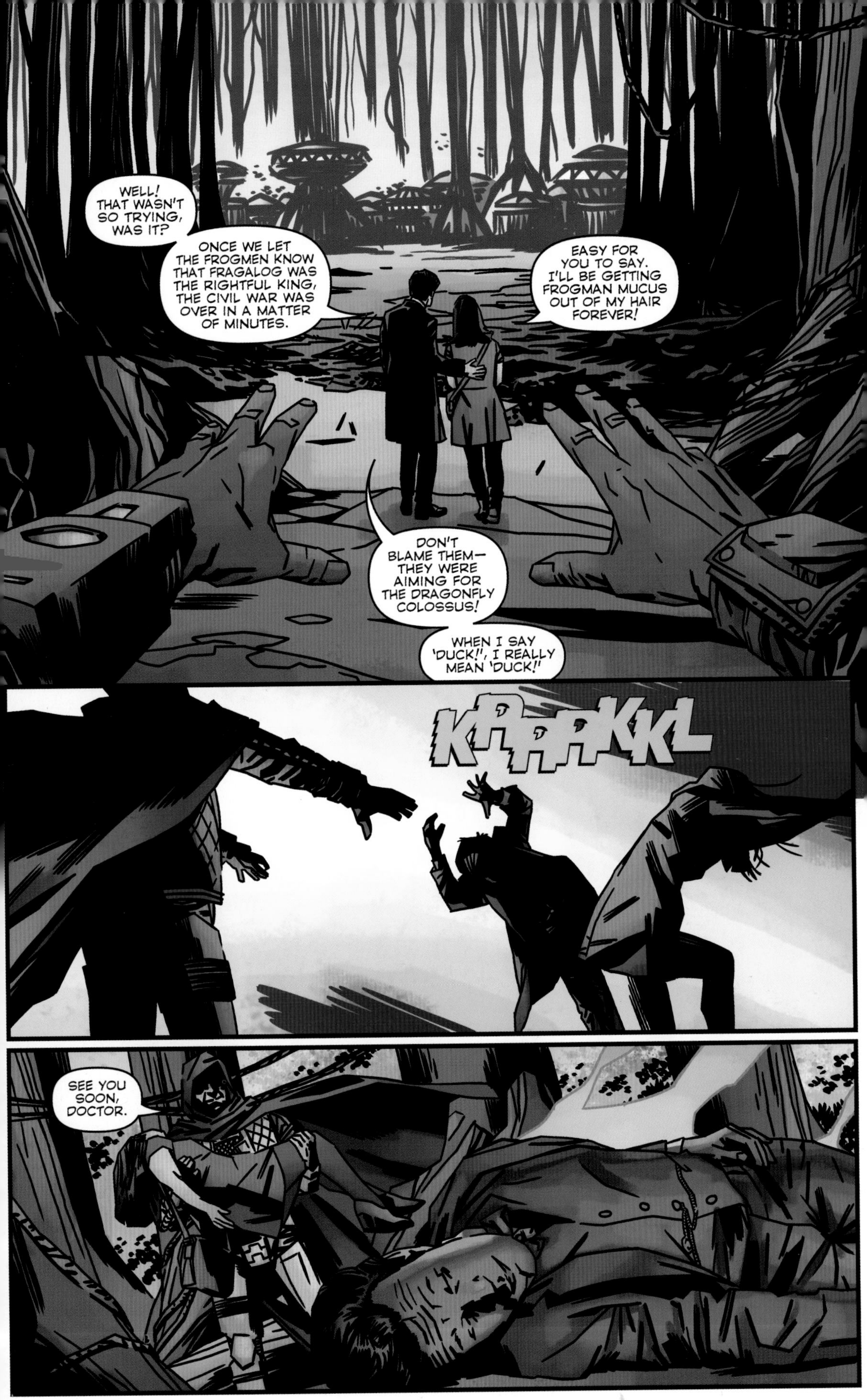
WELL! THAT WASN'T SO TRYING, WAS IT?
ONCE WE LET THE FROGMEN KNOW THAT FRAGALOG WAS THE RIGHTFUL KING, THE CIVIL WAR WAS OVER IN A MATTER OF MINUTES.
EASY FOR YOU TO SAY. I'LL BE GETTING FROGMAN MUCUS OUT OF MY HAIR FOREVER!
DON'T BLAME THEM— THEY WERE AIMING FOR THE DRAGONFLY COLOSSUS!
WHEN I SAY 'DUCK!', I REALLY MEAN 'DUCK!'
KRRRKKL
SEE YOU SOON, DOCTOR.

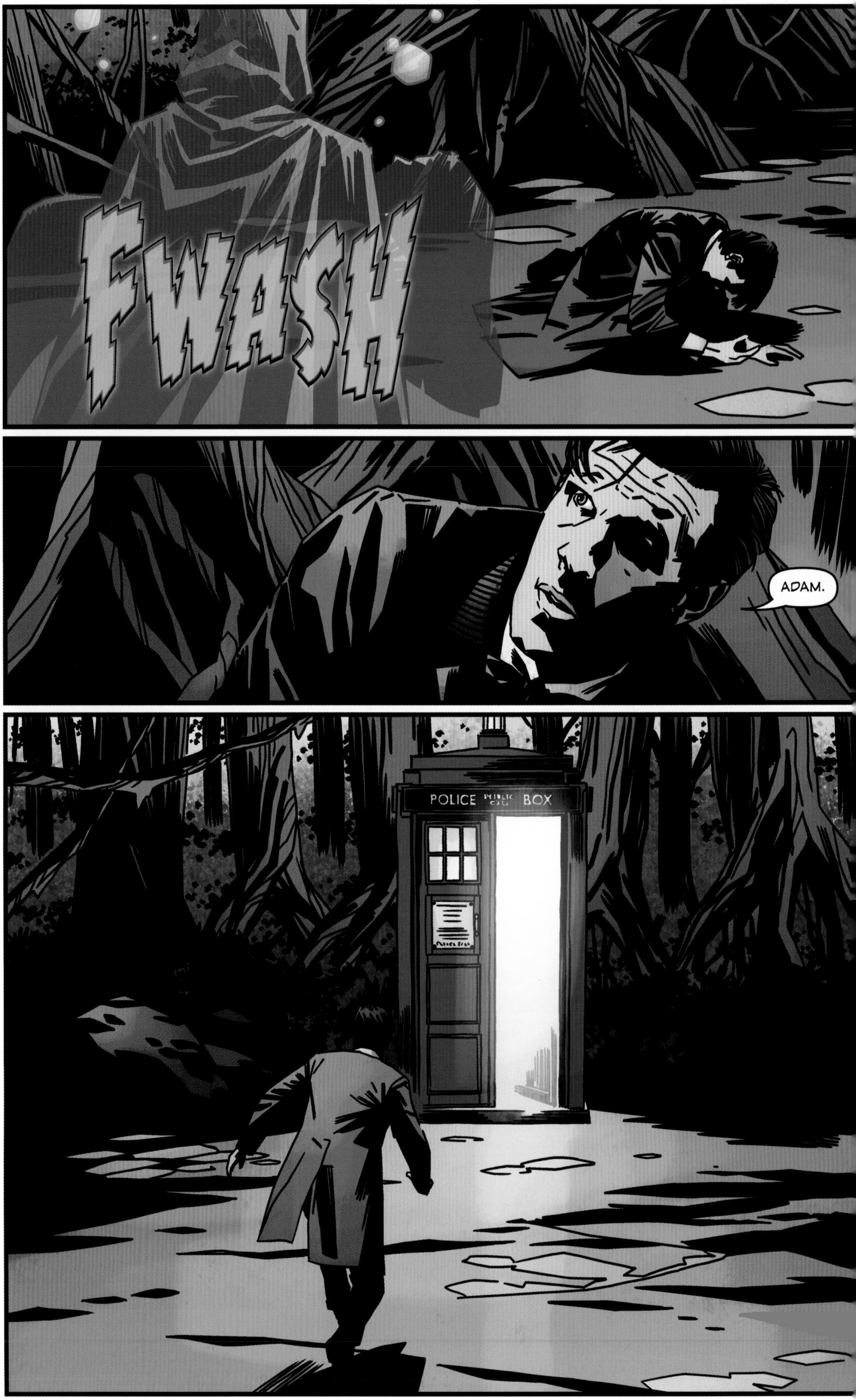
FWASH
ADAM.
POLICE BOX

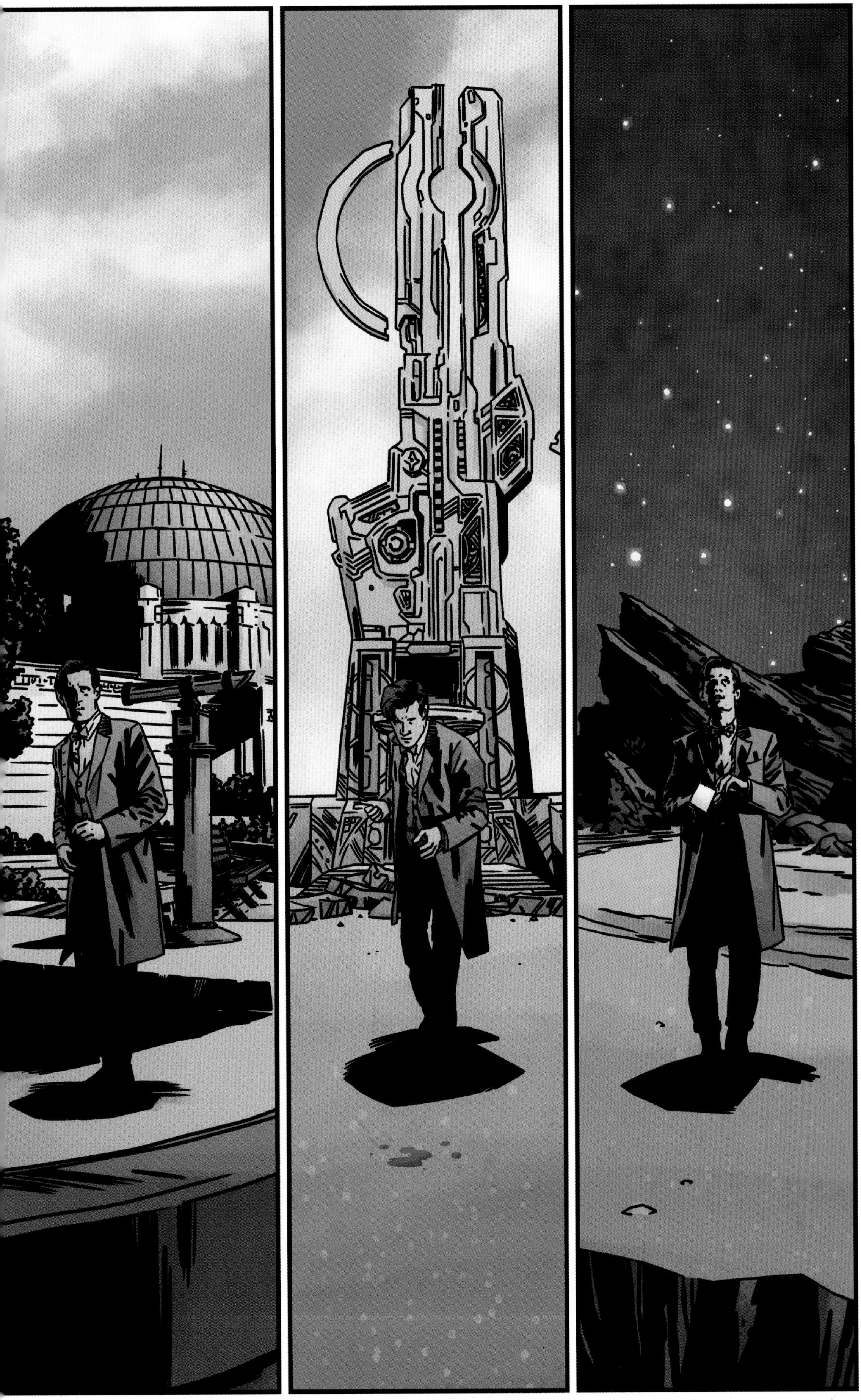

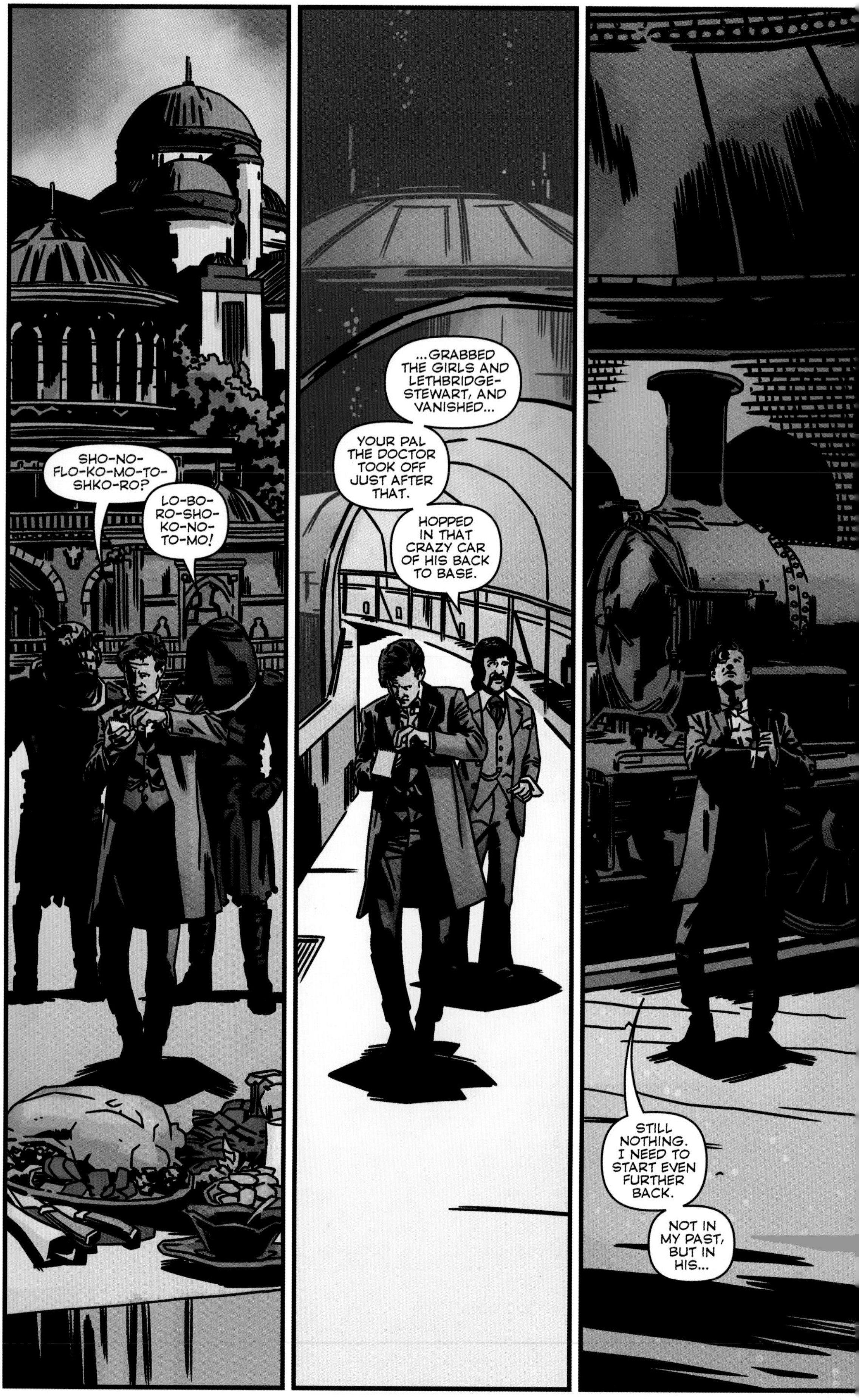
SHO-NO-FLO-KO-MO-TO-SHKO-RO?
LO-BO-RO-SHO-KO-NO-TO-MO!
...GRABBED THE GIRLS AND LETHBRIDGE-STEWART, AND VANISHED...
YOUR PAL THE DOCTOR TOOK OFF JUST AFTER THAT.
HOPPED IN THAT CRAZY CAR OF HIS BACK TO BASE.
STILL NOTHING. I NEED TO START EVEN FURTHER BACK.
NOT IN MY PAST, BUT IN HIS...

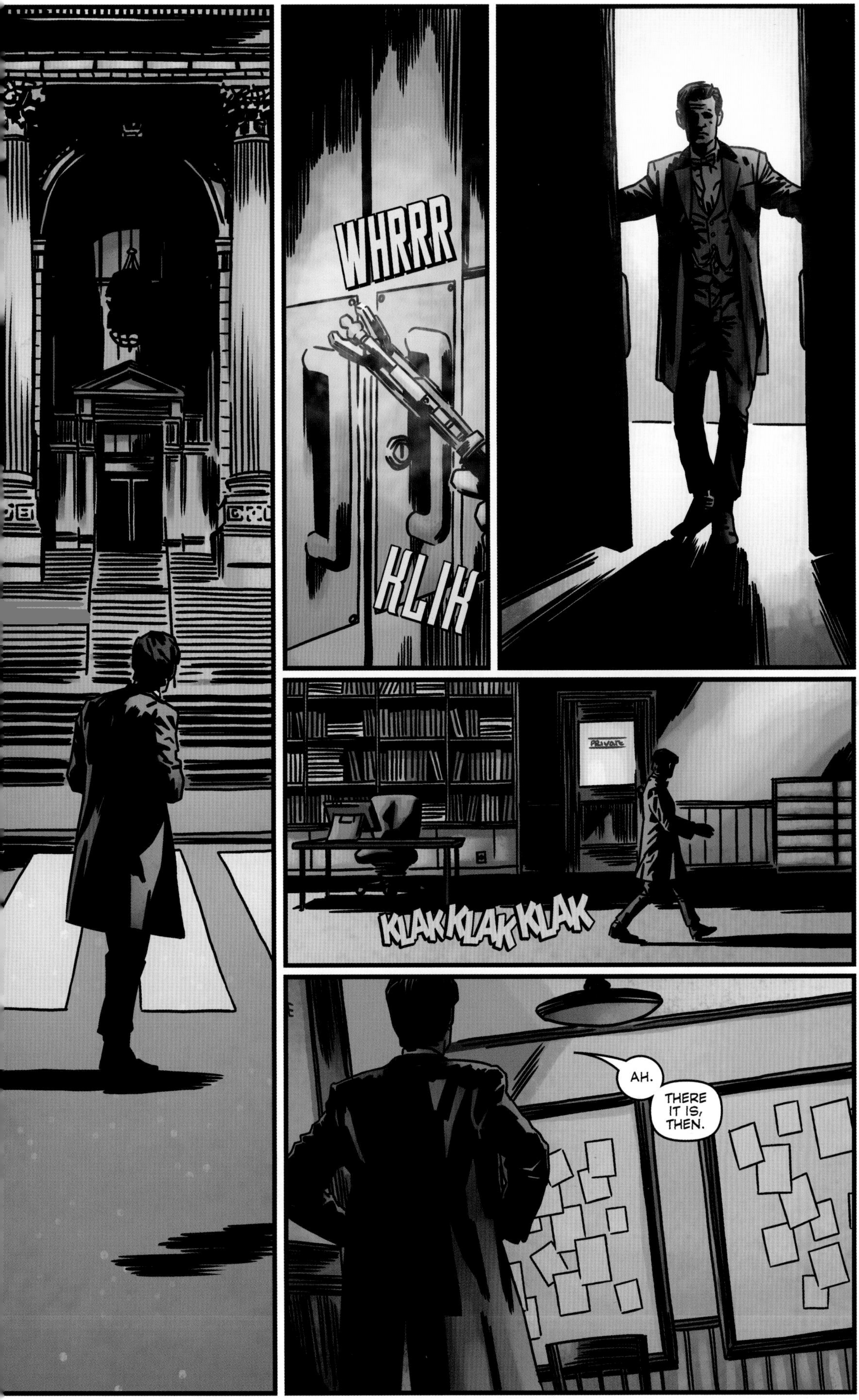
WHRRR
KLIK
PRIVATE
KLAK KLAK KLAK
AH.
THERE IT IS, THEN.

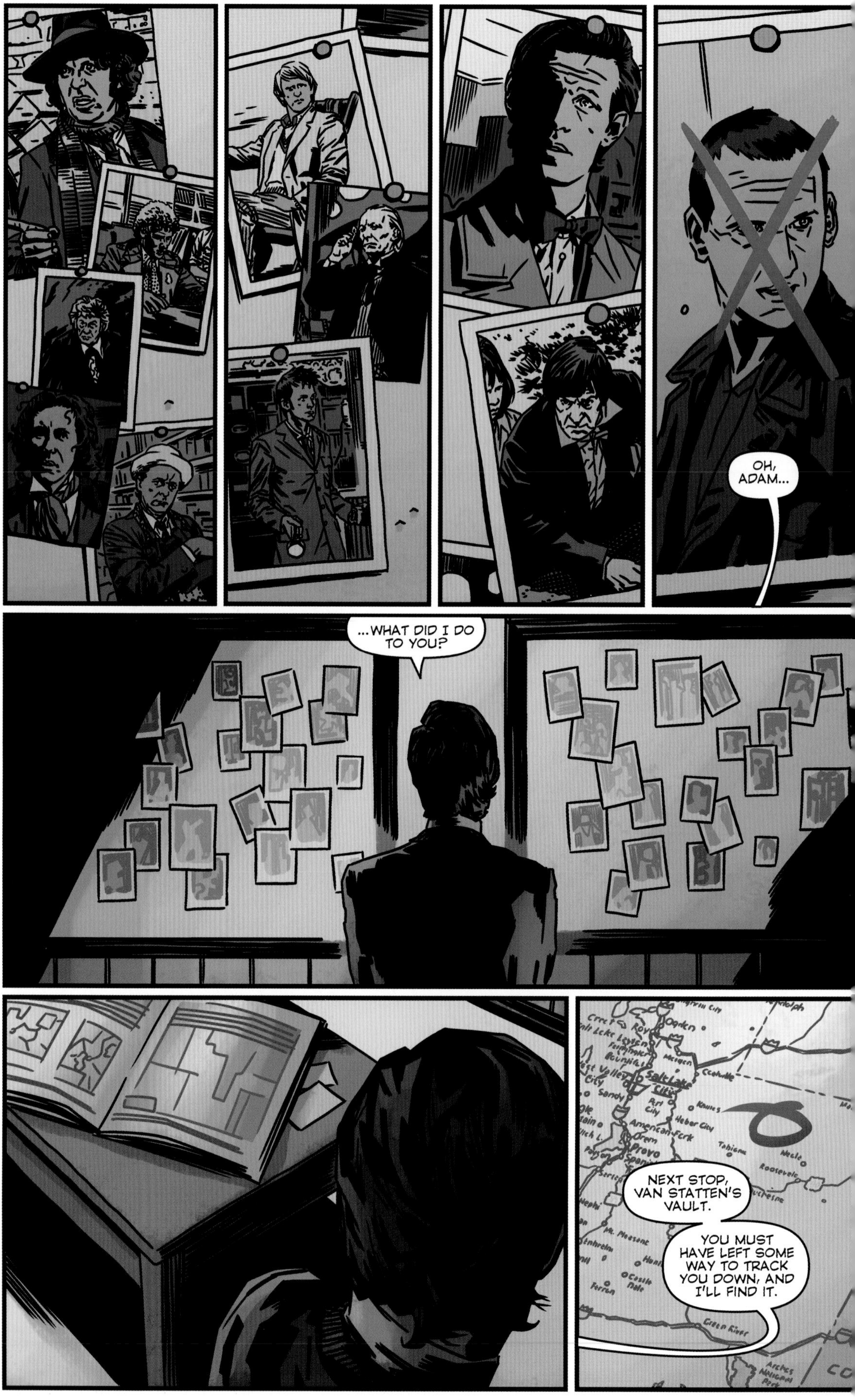
OH, ADAM...
...WHAT DID I DO TO YOU?
NEXT STOP, VAN STATTEN'S VAULT.
YOU MUST HAVE LEFT SOME WAY TO TRACK YOU DOWN, AND I'LL FIND IT.
Ogden
Salt Lake City
Provo
American Fork
Heber City
Roosevelt
Green River

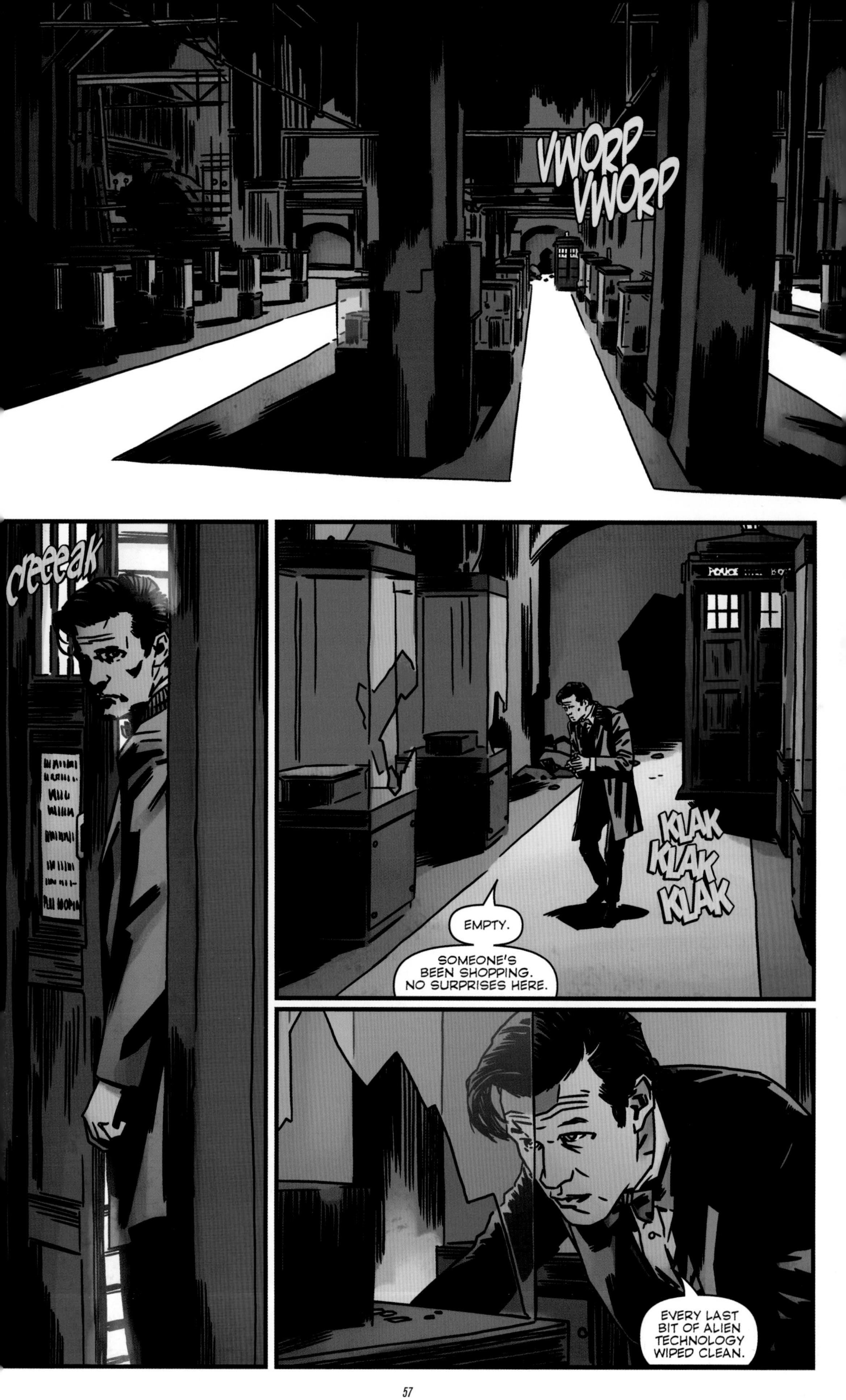
VWORP VWORP
CREEEAK
EMPTY.
SOMEONE'S BEEN SHOPPING. NO SURPRISES HERE.
KLAK KLAK KLAK
EVERY LAST BIT OF ALIEN TECHNOLOGY WIPED CLEAN.

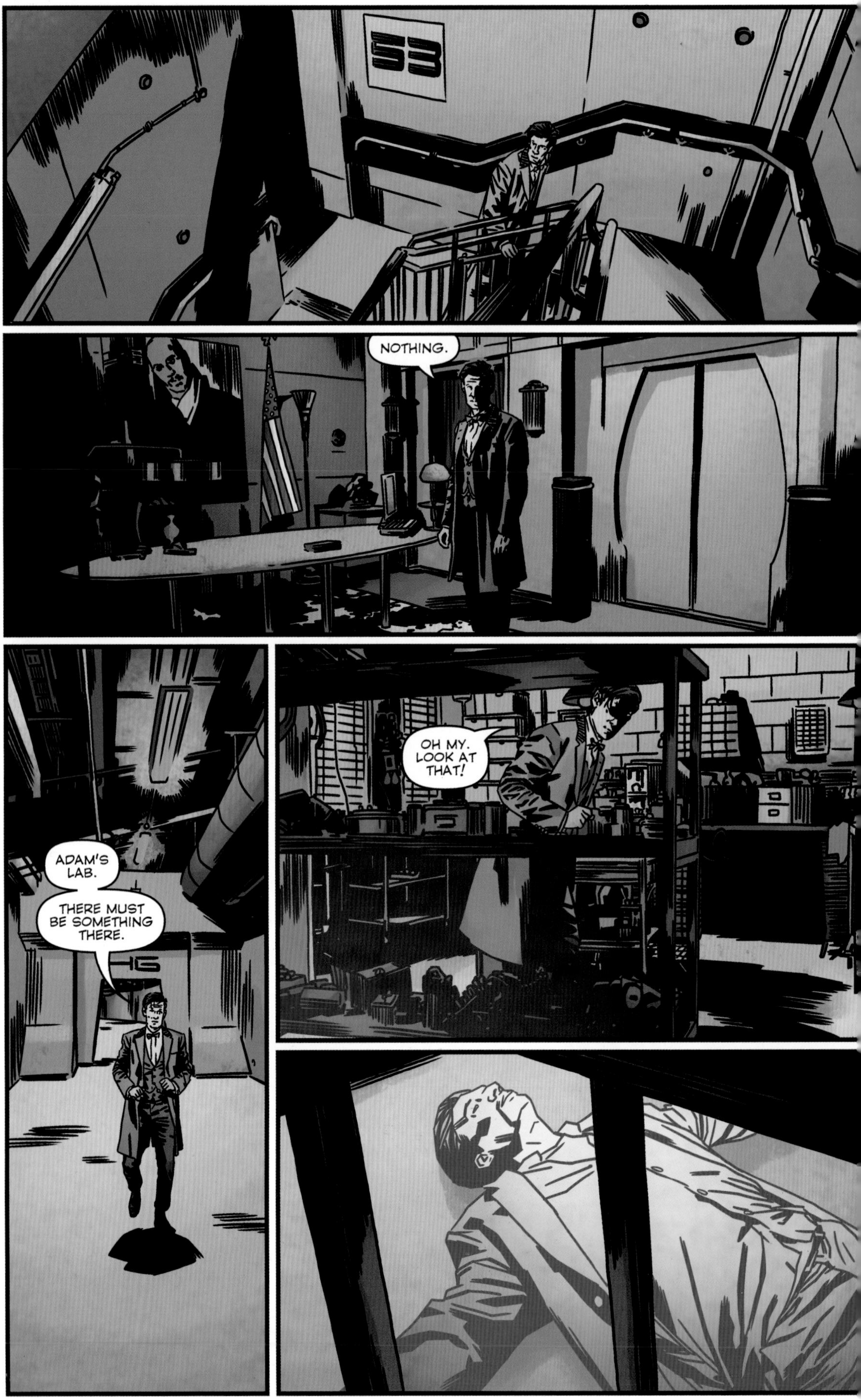
NOTHING.
ADAM'S LAB.
THERE MUST BE SOMETHING THERE.
OH MY. LOOK AT THAT!

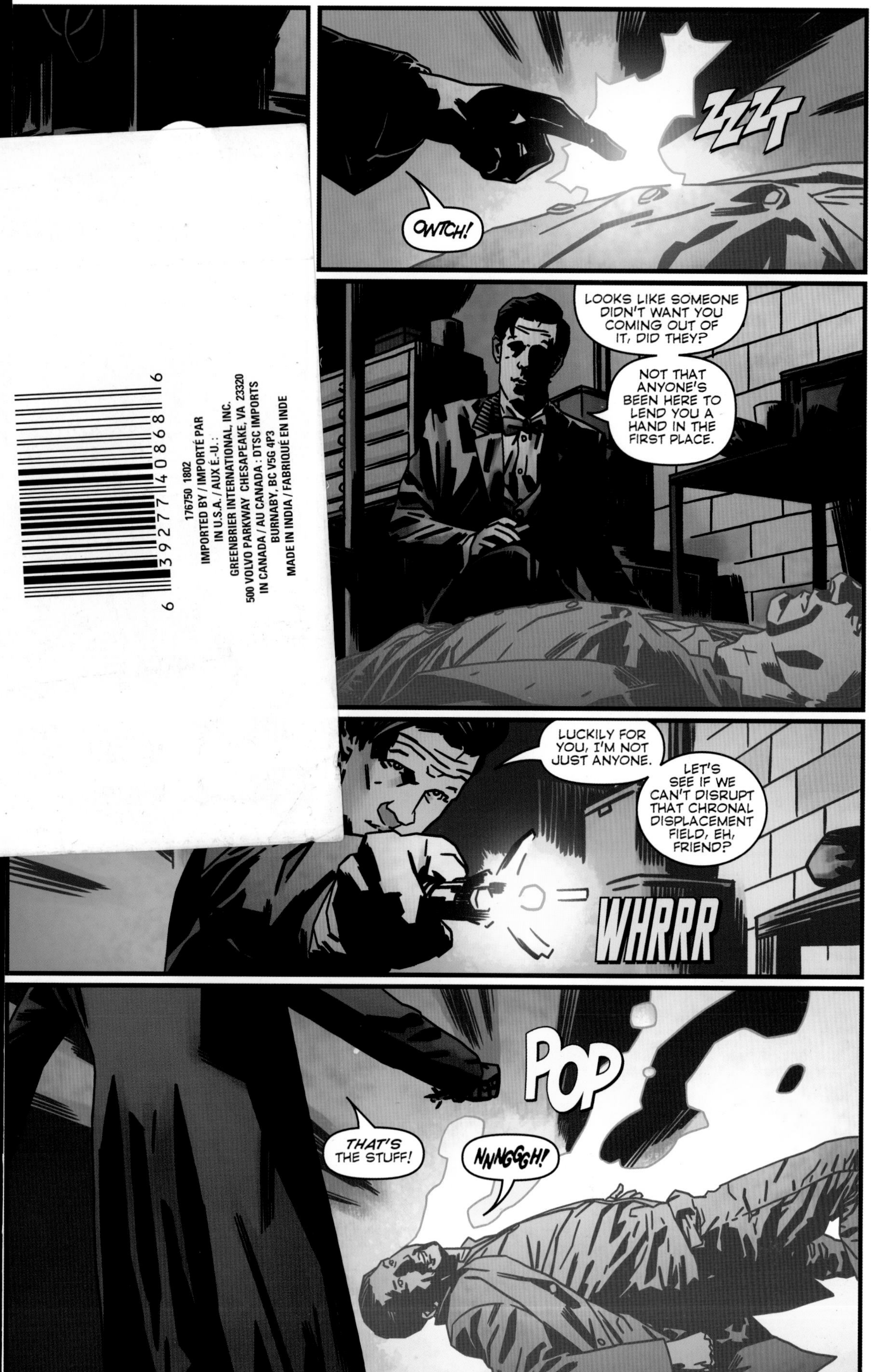
ZZZT
OWTCH!
LOOKS LIKE SOMEONE DIDN'T WANT YOU COMING OUT OF IT, DID THEY?
NOT THAT ANYONE'S BEEN HERE TO LEND YOU A HAND IN THE FIRST PLACE.
LUCKILY FOR YOU, I'M NOT JUST ANYONE.
LET'S SEE IF WE CAN'T DISRUPT THAT CHRONAL DISPLACEMENT FIELD, EH, FRIEND?
WHRRR
POP
THAT'S THE STUFF!
NNNGGGH!

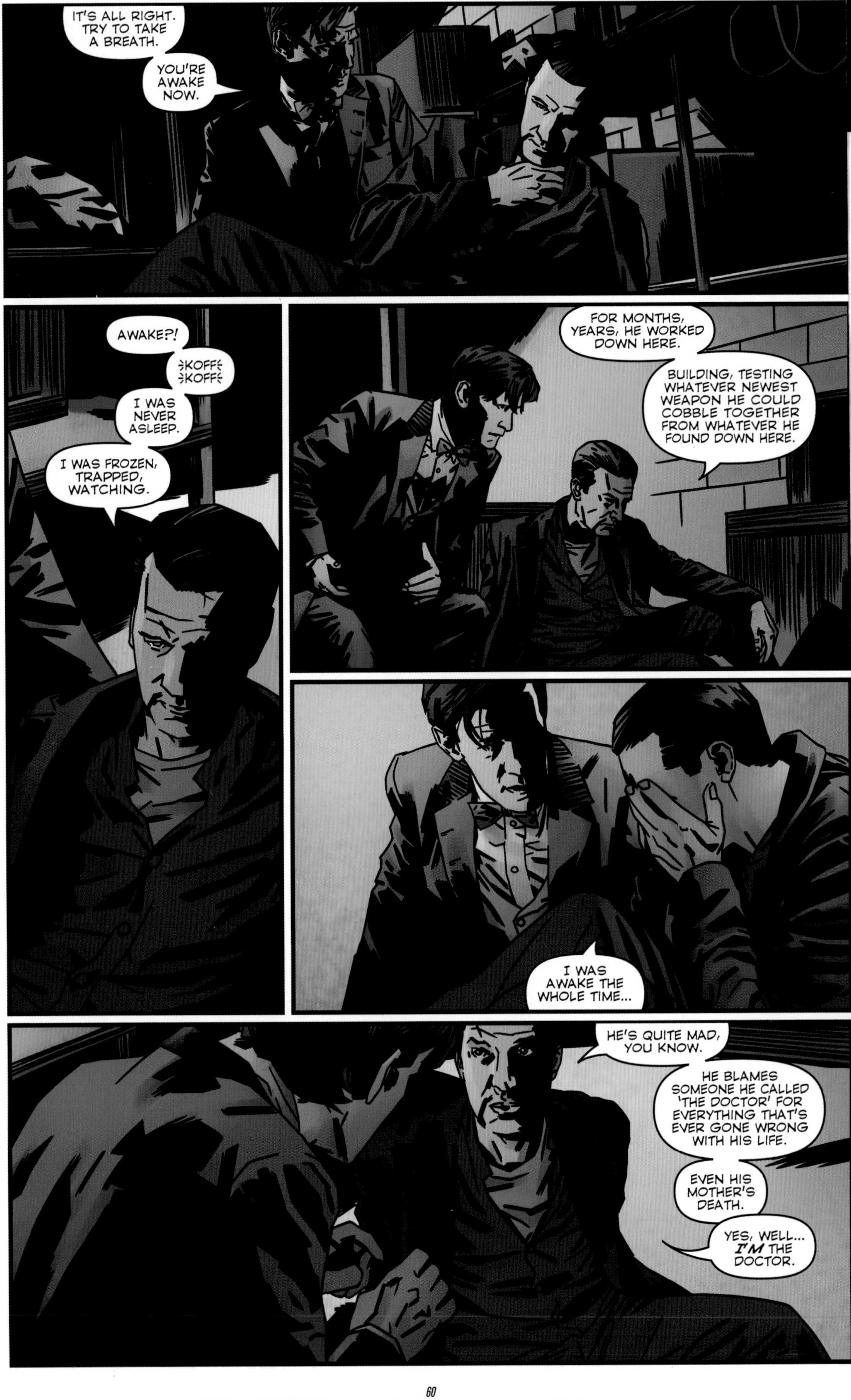
IT'S ALL RIGHT. TRY TO TAKE A BREATH.
YOU'RE AWAKE NOW.
AWAKE?!
KOFF KOFF
I WAS NEVER ASLEEP.
I WAS FROZEN, TRAPPED, WATCHING.
FOR MONTHS, YEARS, HE WORKED DOWN HERE.
BUILDING, TESTING WHATEVER NEWEST WEAPON HE COULD COBBLE TOGETHER FROM WHATEVER HE FOUND DOWN HERE.
I WAS AWAKE THE WHOLE TIME...
HE'S QUITE MAD, YOU KNOW.
HE BLAMES SOMEONE HE CALLED 'THE DOCTOR' FOR EVERYTHING THAT'S EVER GONE WRONG WITH HIS LIFE.
EVEN HIS MOTHER'S DEATH.
YES, WELL... *I'M* THE DOCTOR.

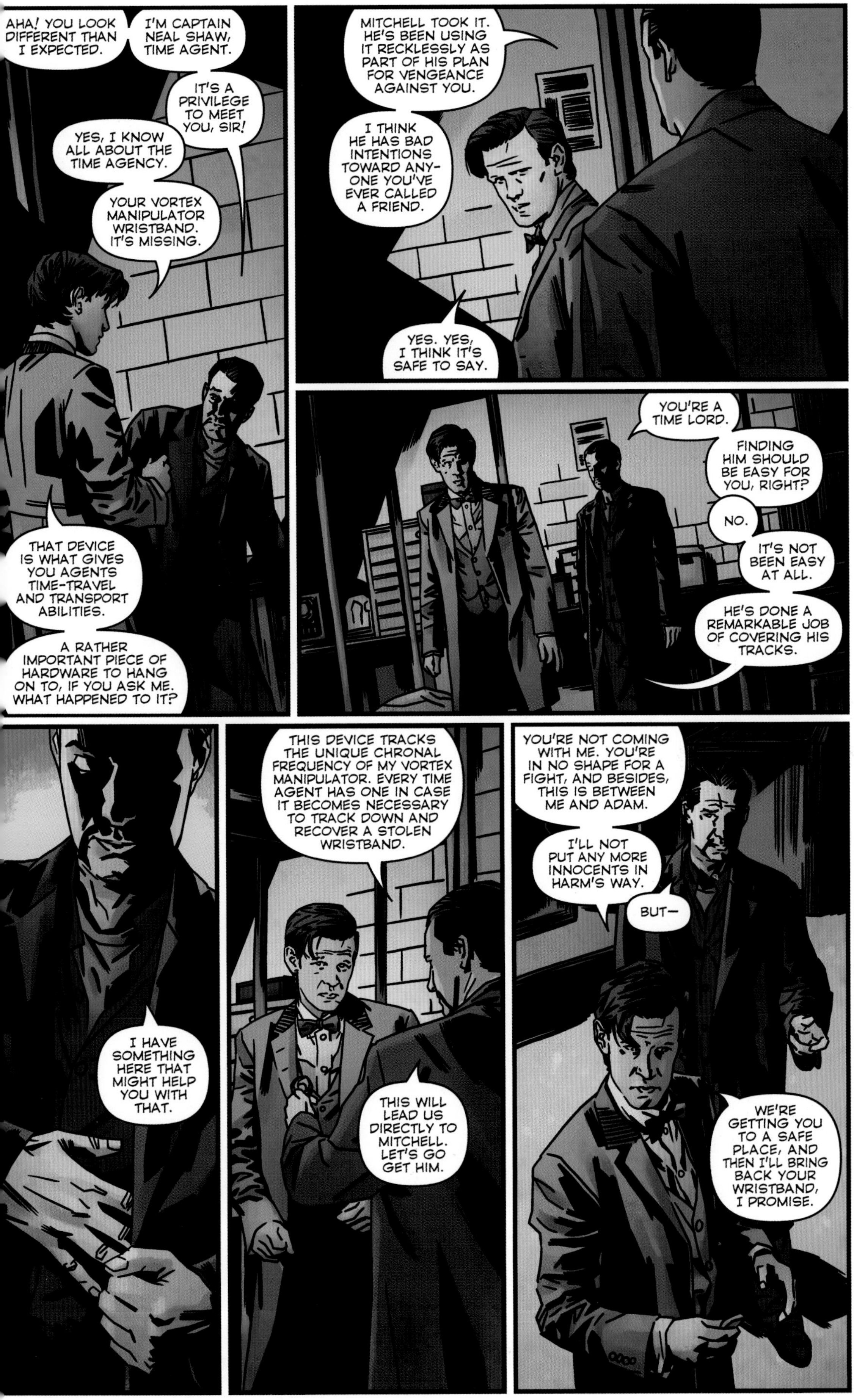
AHA! YOU LOOK DIFFERENT THAN I EXPECTED.
I'M CAPTAIN NEAL SHAW, TIME AGENT.
IT'S A PRIVILEGE TO MEET YOU, SIR!
YES, I KNOW ALL ABOUT THE TIME AGENCY.
YOUR VORTEX MANIPULATOR WRISTBAND. IT'S MISSING.
THAT DEVICE IS WHAT GIVES YOU AGENTS TIME-TRAVEL AND TRANSPORT ABILITIES.
A RATHER IMPORTANT PIECE OF HARDWARE TO HANG ON TO, IF YOU ASK ME. WHAT HAPPENED TO IT?
MITCHELL TOOK IT. HE'S BEEN USING IT RECKLESSLY AS PART OF HIS PLAN FOR VENGEANCE AGAINST YOU.
I THINK HE HAS BAD INTENTIONS TOWARD ANYONE YOU'VE EVER CALLED A FRIEND.
YES. YES, I THINK IT'S SAFE TO SAY.
YOU'RE A TIME LORD.
FINDING HIM SHOULD BE EASY FOR YOU, RIGHT?
NO.
IT'S NOT BEEN EASY AT ALL.
HE'S DONE A REMARKABLE JOB OF COVERING HIS TRACKS.
I HAVE SOMETHING HERE THAT MIGHT HELP YOU WITH THAT.
THIS DEVICE TRACKS THE UNIQUE CHRONAL FREQUENCY OF MY VORTEX MANIPULATOR. EVERY TIME AGENT HAS ONE IN CASE IT BECOMES NECESSARY TO TRACK DOWN AND RECOVER A STOLEN WRISTBAND.
THIS WILL LEAD US DIRECTLY TO MITCHELL. LET'S GO GET HIM.
YOU'RE NOT COMING WITH ME. YOU'RE IN NO SHAPE FOR A FIGHT, AND BESIDES, THIS IS BETWEEN ME AND ADAM.
I'LL NOT PUT ANY MORE INNOCENTS IN HARM'S WAY.
BUT—
WE'RE GETTING YOU TO A SAFE PLACE, AND THEN I'LL BRING BACK YOUR WRISTBAND, I PROMISE.

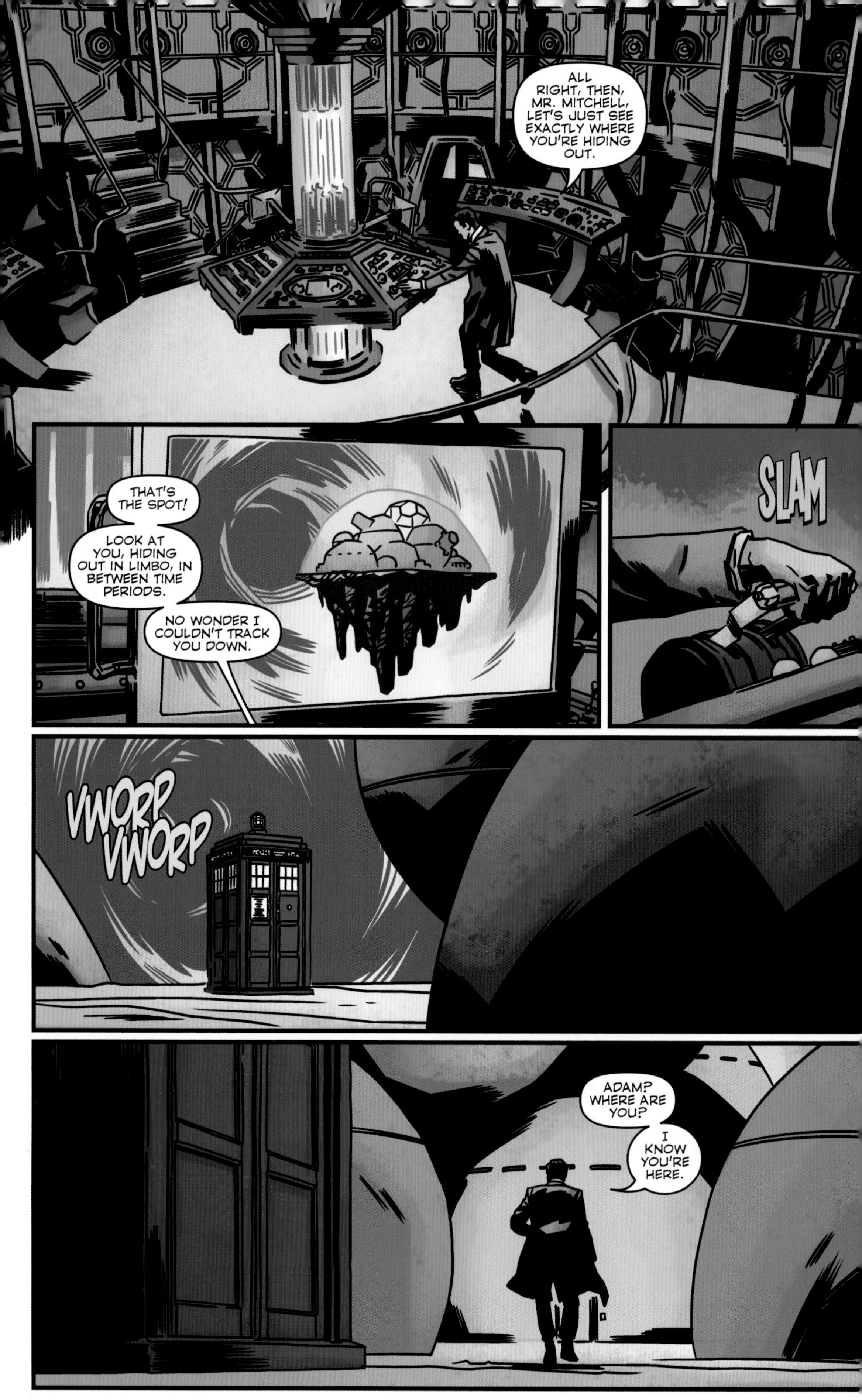

ALL RIGHT, THEN, MR. MITCHELL, LET'S JUST SEE EXACTLY WHERE YOU'RE HIDING OUT.
THAT'S THE SPOT!
LOOK AT YOU, HIDING OUT IN LIMBO, IN BETWEEN TIME PERIODS.
NO WONDER I COULDN'T TRACK YOU DOWN.
SLAM
VWORP VWORP
ADAM? WHERE ARE YOU?
I KNOW YOU'RE HERE.

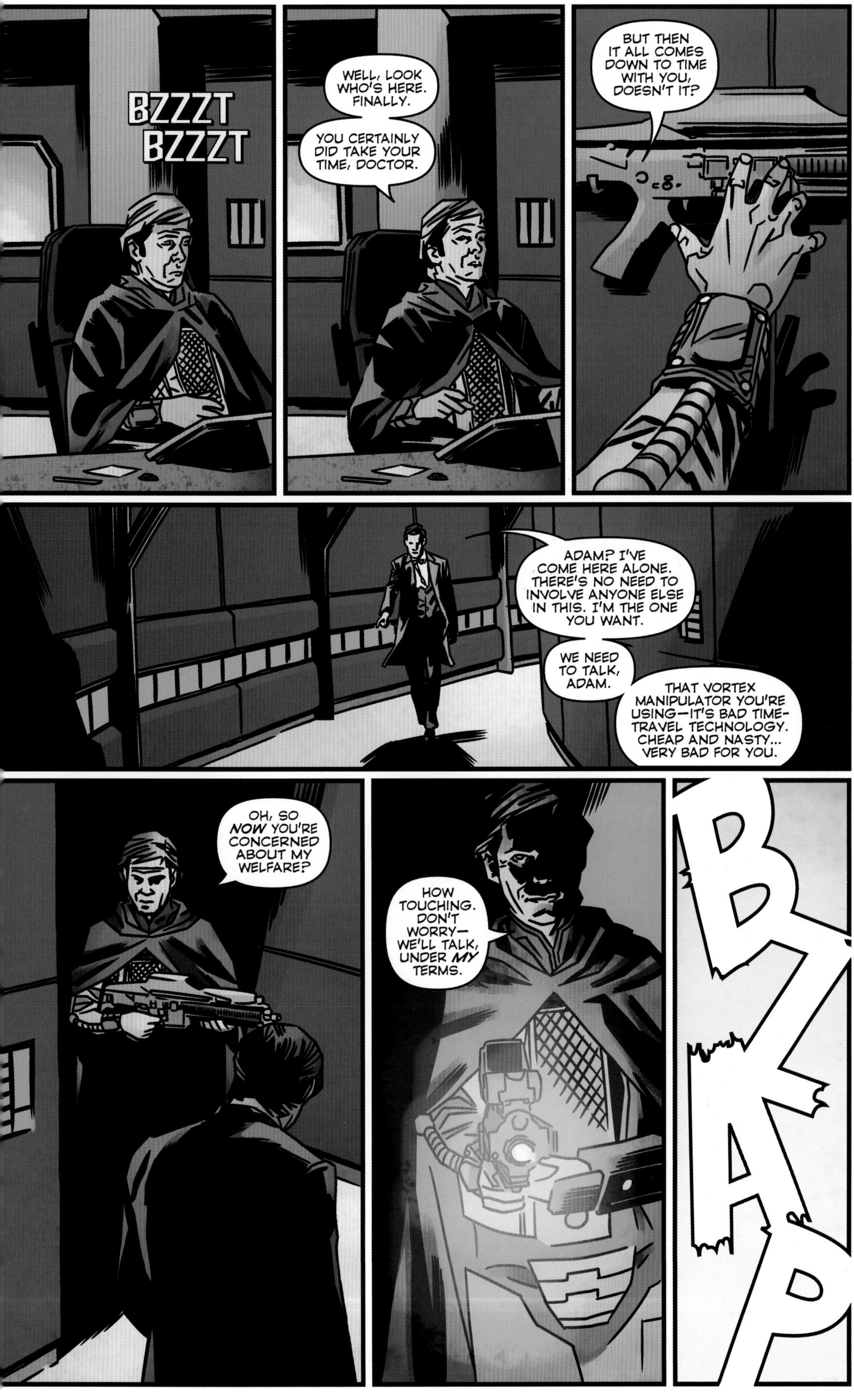
BZZZT BZZZT
WELL, LOOK WHO'S HERE. FINALLY.
YOU CERTAINLY DID TAKE YOUR TIME, DOCTOR.
BUT THEN IT ALL COMES DOWN TO TIME WITH YOU, DOESN'T IT?
ADAM? I'VE COME HERE ALONE. THERE'S NO NEED TO INVOLVE ANYONE ELSE IN THIS. I'M THE ONE YOU WANT.
WE NEED TO TALK, ADAM.
THAT VORTEX MANIPULATOR YOU'RE USING—IT'S BAD TIME-TRAVEL TECHNOLOGY. CHEAP AND NASTY... VERY BAD FOR YOU.
OH, SO NOW YOU'RE CONCERNED ABOUT MY WELFARE?
HOW TOUCHING. DON'T WORRY—WE'LL TALK, UNDER MY TERMS.
BZKAP

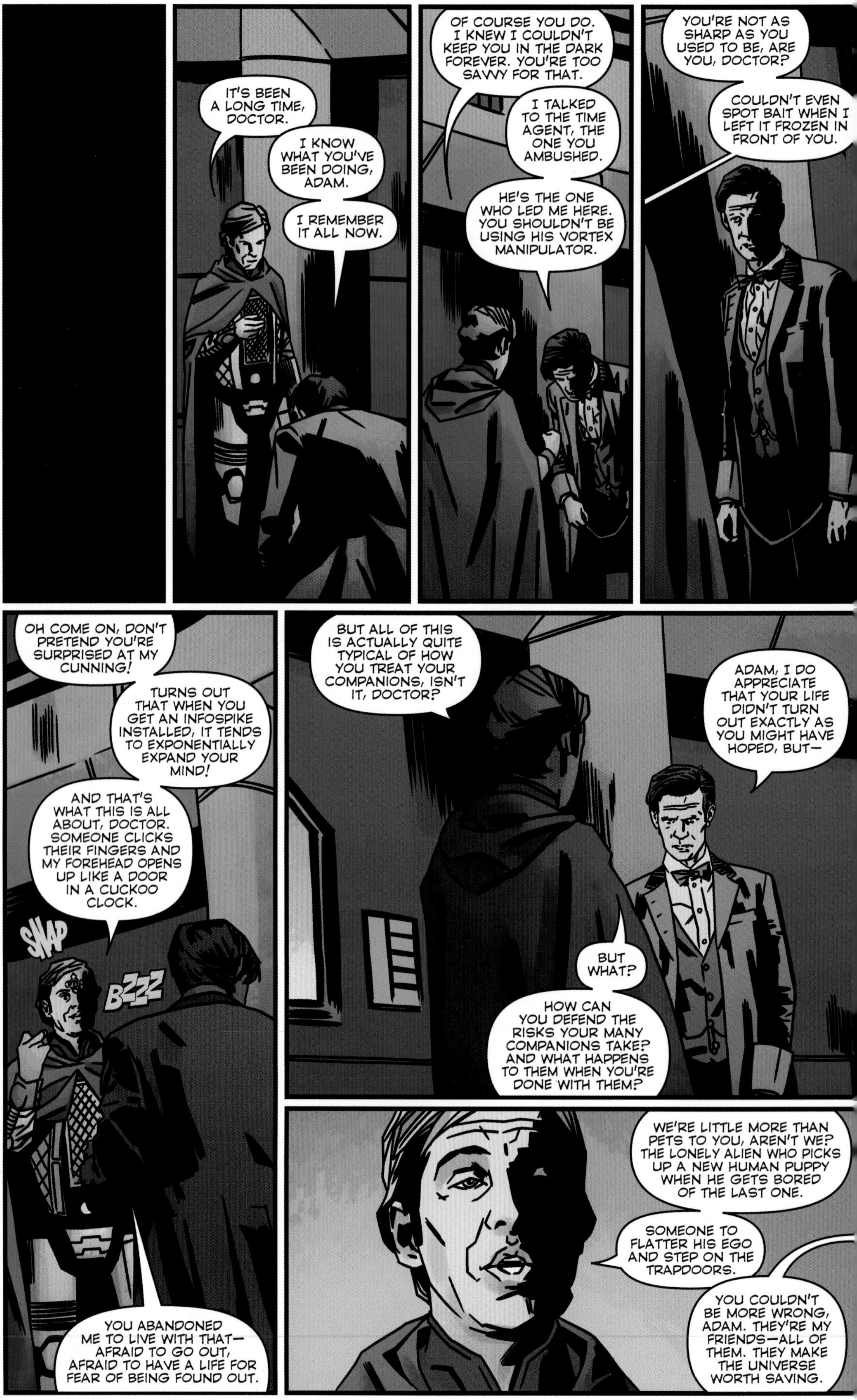
IT'S BEEN A LONG TIME, DOCTOR.
I KNOW WHAT YOU'VE BEEN DOING, ADAM.
I REMEMBER IT ALL NOW.
OF COURSE YOU DO. I KNEW I COULDN'T KEEP YOU IN THE DARK FOREVER. YOU'RE TOO SAVVY FOR THAT.
I TALKED TO THE TIME AGENT, THE ONE YOU AMBUSHED.
HE'S THE ONE WHO LED ME HERE. YOU SHOULDN'T BE USING HIS VORTEX MANIPULATOR.
YOU'RE NOT AS SHARP AS YOU USED TO BE, ARE YOU, DOCTOR?
COULDN'T EVEN SPOT BAIT WHEN I LEFT IT FROZEN IN FRONT OF YOU.
OH COME ON, DON'T PRETEND YOU'RE SURPRISED AT MY CUNNING!
TURNS OUT THAT WHEN YOU GET AN INFOSPIKE INSTALLED, IT TENDS TO EXPONENTIALLY EXPAND YOUR MIND!
AND THAT'S WHAT THIS IS ALL ABOUT, DOCTOR. SOMEONE CLICKS THEIR FINGERS AND MY FOREHEAD OPENS UP LIKE A DOOR IN A CUCKOO CLOCK.
SNAP
BZZZ
YOU ABANDONED ME TO LIVE WITH THAT— AFRAID TO GO OUT, AFRAID TO HAVE A LIFE FOR FEAR OF BEING FOUND OUT.
BUT ALL OF THIS IS ACTUALLY QUITE TYPICAL OF HOW YOU TREAT YOUR COMPANIONS, ISN'T IT, DOCTOR?
ADAM, I DO APPRECIATE THAT YOUR LIFE DIDN'T TURN OUT EXACTLY AS YOU MIGHT HAVE HOPED, BUT—
BUT WHAT?
HOW CAN YOU DEFEND THE RISKS YOUR MANY COMPANIONS TAKE? AND WHAT HAPPENS TO THEM WHEN YOU'RE DONE WITH THEM?
WE'RE LITTLE MORE THAN PETS TO YOU, AREN'T WE? THE LONELY ALIEN WHO PICKS UP A NEW HUMAN PUPPY WHEN HE GETS BORED OF THE LAST ONE.
SOMEONE TO FLATTER HIS EGO AND STEP ON THE TRAPDOORS.
YOU COULDN'T BE MORE WRONG, ADAM. THEY'RE MY FRIENDS—ALL OF THEM. THEY MAKE THE UNIVERSE WORTH SAVING.

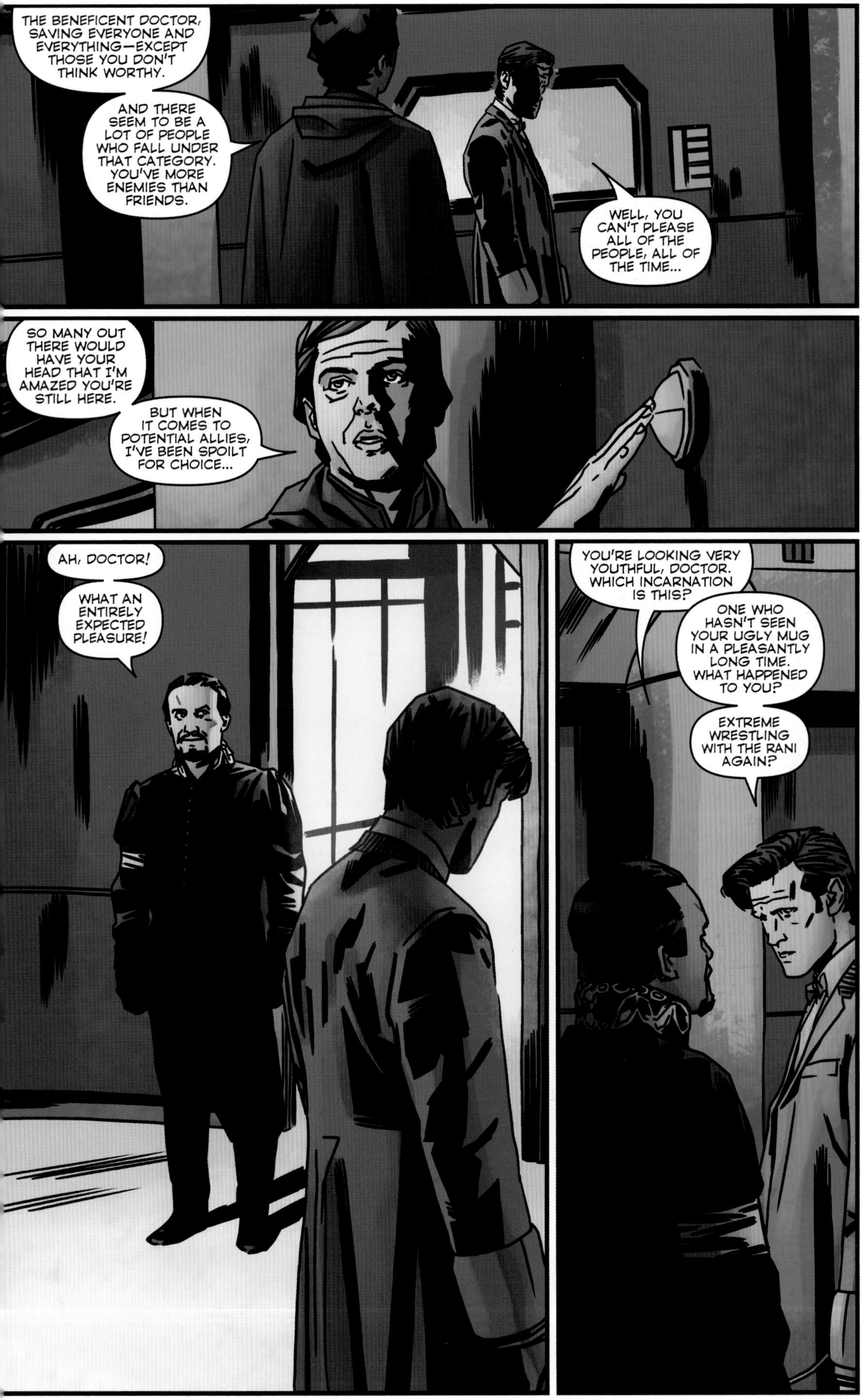
THE BENEFICENT DOCTOR, SAVING EVERYONE AND EVERYTHING—EXCEPT THOSE YOU DON'T THINK WORTHY.
AND THERE SEEM TO BE A LOT OF PEOPLE WHO FALL UNDER THAT CATEGORY. YOU'VE MORE ENEMIES THAN FRIENDS.
WELL, YOU CAN'T PLEASE ALL OF THE PEOPLE, ALL OF THE TIME...
SO MANY OUT THERE WOULD HAVE YOUR HEAD THAT I'M AMAZED YOU'RE STILL HERE.
BUT WHEN IT COMES TO POTENTIAL ALLIES, I'VE BEEN SPOILT FOR CHOICE...
AH, DOCTOR!
WHAT AN ENTIRELY EXPECTED PLEASURE!
YOU'RE LOOKING VERY YOUTHFUL, DOCTOR. WHICH INCARNATION IS THIS?
ONE WHO HASN'T SEEN YOUR UGLY MUG IN A PLEASANTLY LONG TIME. WHAT HAPPENED TO YOU?
EXTREME WRESTLING WITH THE RANI AGAIN?

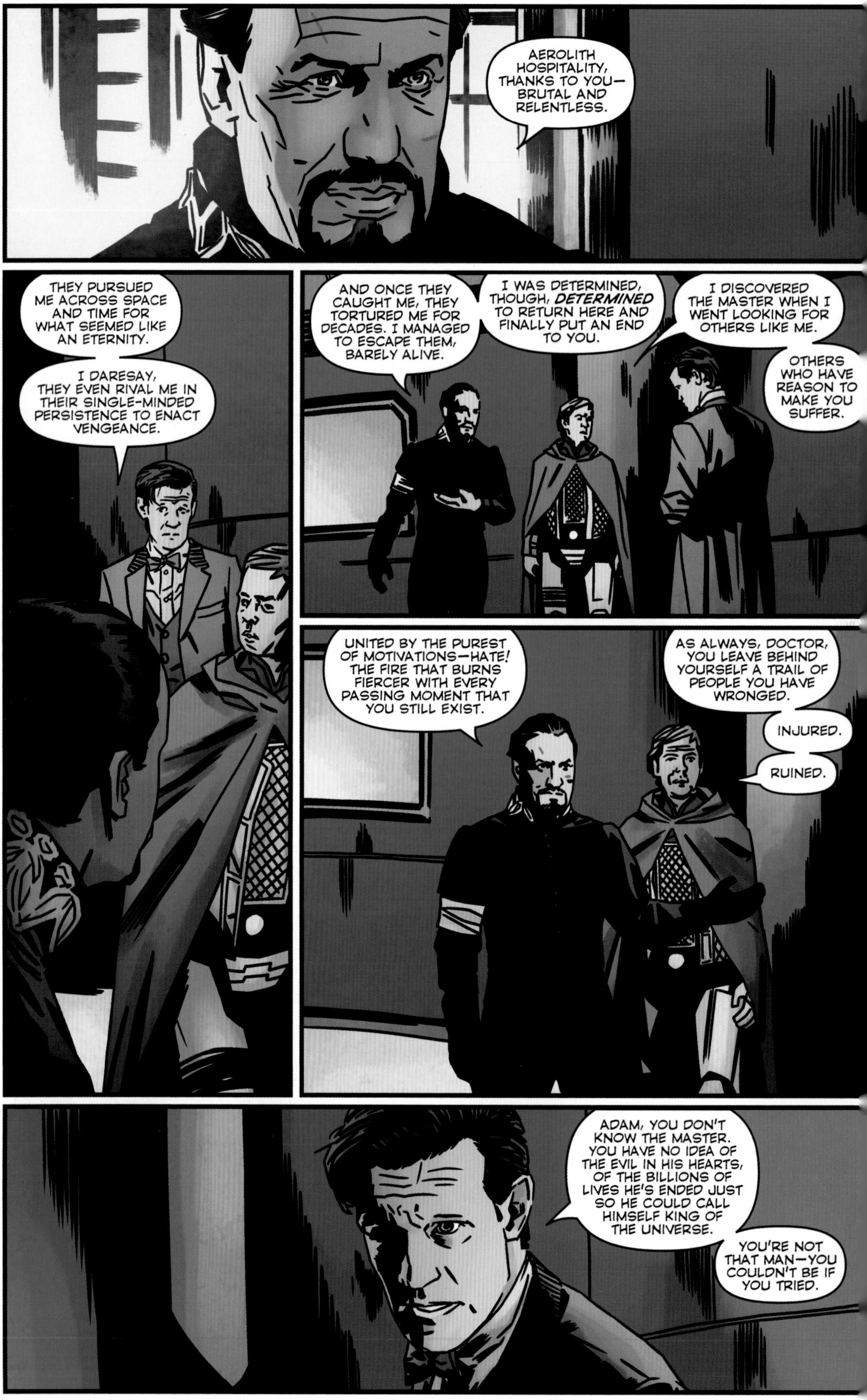

AEROLITH HOSPITALITY, THANKS TO YOU—BRUTAL AND RELENTLESS.
THEY PURSUED ME ACROSS SPACE AND TIME FOR WHAT SEEMED LIKE AN ETERNITY.
I DARESAY, THEY EVEN RIVAL ME IN THEIR SINGLE-MINDED PERSISTENCE TO ENACT VENGEANCE.
AND ONCE THEY CAUGHT ME, THEY TORTURED ME FOR DECADES. I MANAGED TO ESCAPE THEM, BARELY ALIVE.
I WAS DETERMINED, THOUGH, *DETERMINED* TO RETURN HERE AND FINALLY PUT AN END TO YOU.
I DISCOVERED THE MASTER WHEN I WENT LOOKING FOR OTHERS LIKE ME.
OTHERS WHO HAVE REASON TO MAKE YOU SUFFER.
UNITED BY THE PUREST OF MOTIVATIONS—HATE! THE FIRE THAT BURNS FIERCER WITH EVERY PASSING MOMENT THAT YOU STILL EXIST.
AS ALWAYS, DOCTOR, YOU LEAVE BEHIND YOURSELF A TRAIL OF PEOPLE YOU HAVE WRONGED.
INJURED.
RUINED.
ADAM, YOU DON'T KNOW THE MASTER. YOU HAVE NO IDEA OF THE EVIL IN HIS HEARTS, OF THE BILLIONS OF LIVES HE'S ENDED JUST SO HE COULD CALL HIMSELF KING OF THE UNIVERSE.
YOU'RE NOT THAT MAN—YOU COULDN'T BE IF YOU TRIED.

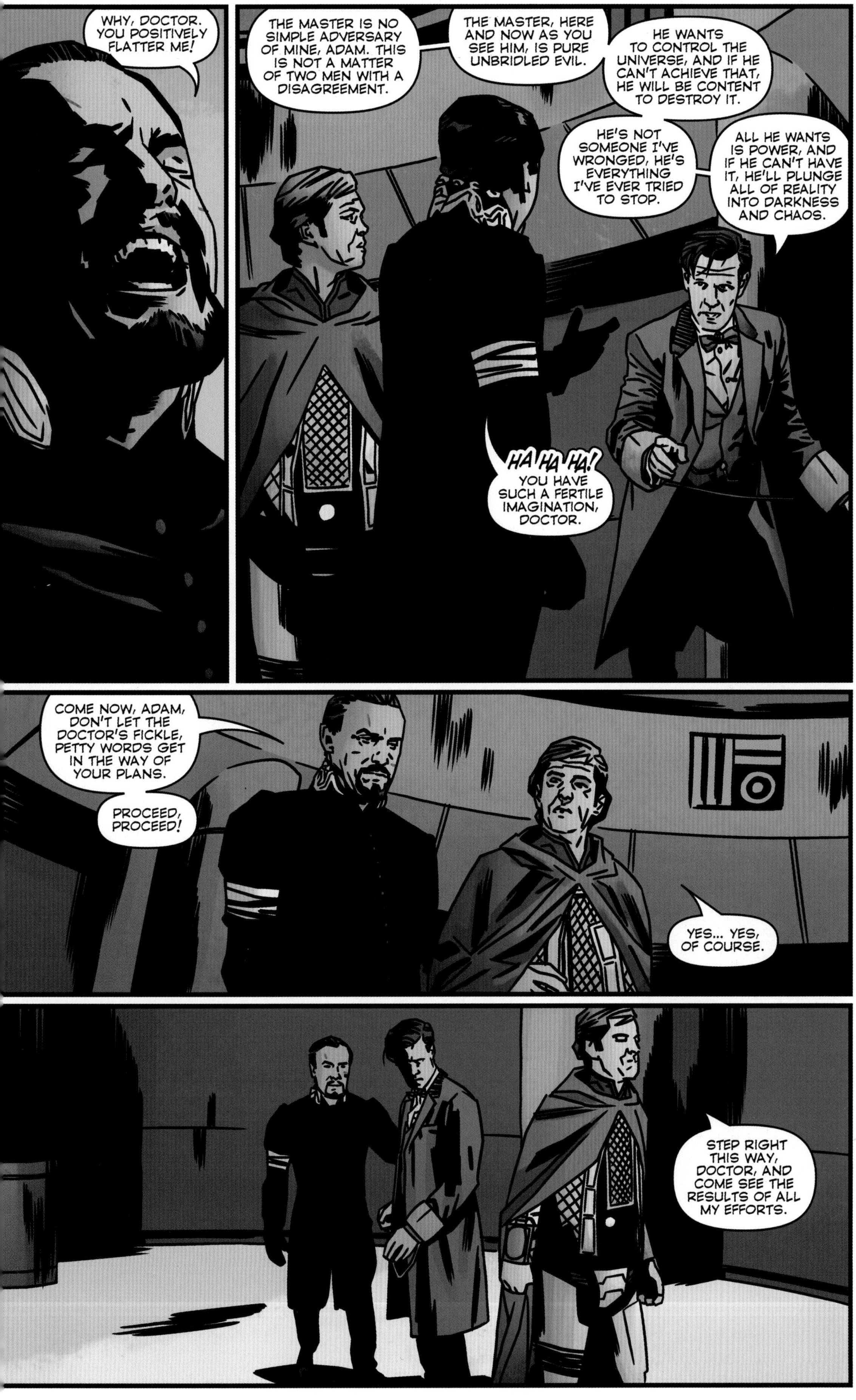
WHY, DOCTOR. YOU POSITIVELY FLATTER ME!
THE MASTER IS NO SIMPLE ADVERSARY OF MINE, ADAM. THIS IS NOT A MATTER OF TWO MEN WITH A DISAGREEMENT.
THE MASTER, HERE AND NOW AS YOU SEE HIM, IS PURE UNBRIDLED EVIL.
HE WANTS TO CONTROL THE UNIVERSE, AND IF HE CAN'T ACHIEVE THAT, HE WILL BE CONTENT TO DESTROY IT.
HE'S NOT SOMEONE I'VE WRONGED, HE'S EVERYTHING I'VE EVER TRIED TO STOP.
ALL HE WANTS IS POWER, AND IF HE CAN'T HAVE IT, HE'LL PLUNGE ALL OF REALITY INTO DARKNESS AND CHAOS.
HA HA HA! YOU HAVE SUCH A FERTILE IMAGINATION, DOCTOR.
COME NOW, ADAM, DON'T LET THE DOCTOR'S FICKLE, PETTY WORDS GET IN THE WAY OF YOUR PLANS.
PROCEED, PROCEED!
YES... YES, OF COURSE.
STEP RIGHT THIS WAY, DOCTOR, AND COME SEE THE RESULTS OF ALL MY EFFORTS.

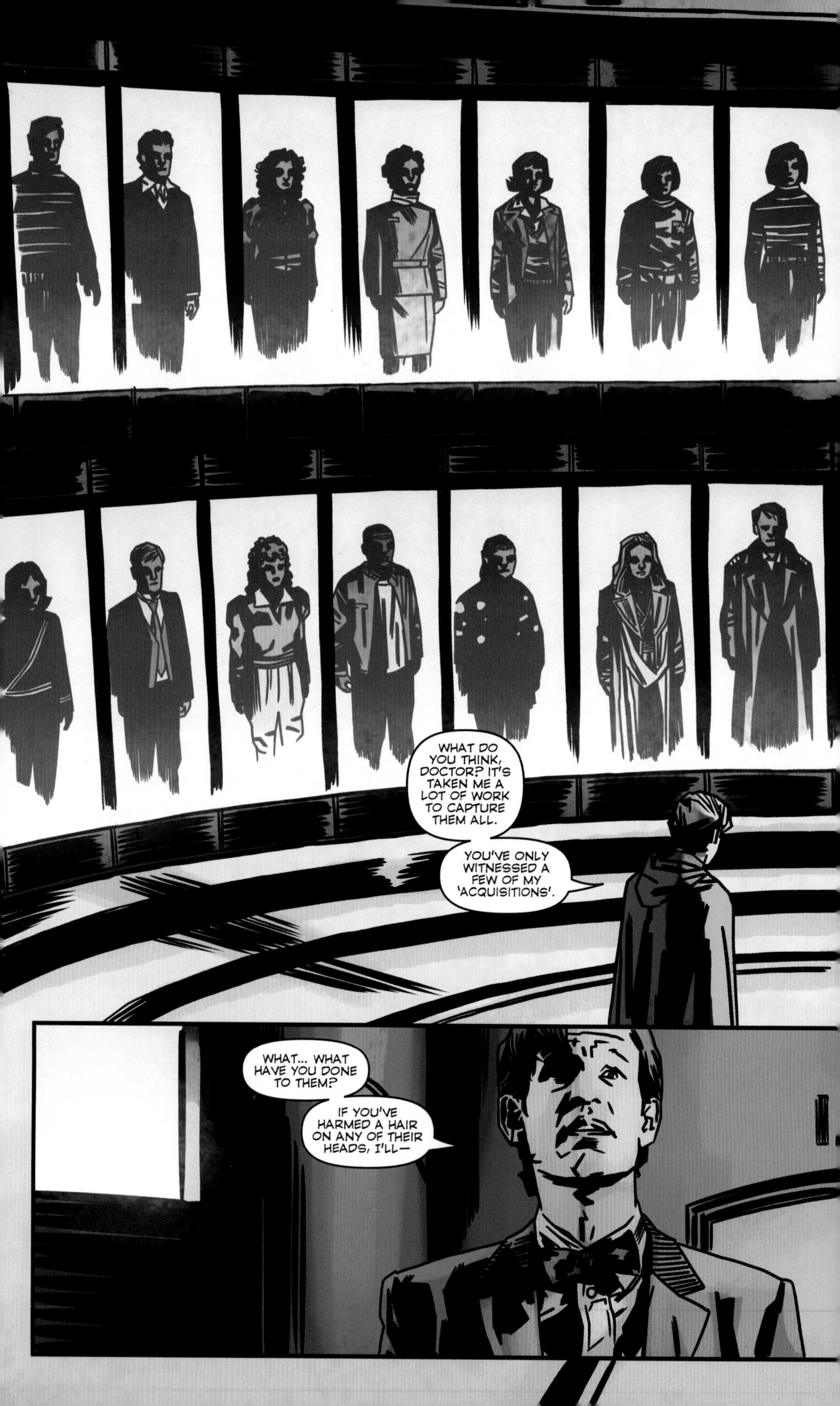
WHAT DO YOU THINK, DOCTOR? IT'S TAKEN ME A LOT OF WORK TO CAPTURE THEM ALL.
YOU'VE ONLY WITNESSED A FEW OF MY 'ACQUISITIONS'.
WHAT... WHAT HAVE YOU DONE TO THEM?
IF YOU'VE HARMED A HAIR ON ANY OF THEIR HEADS, I'LL—

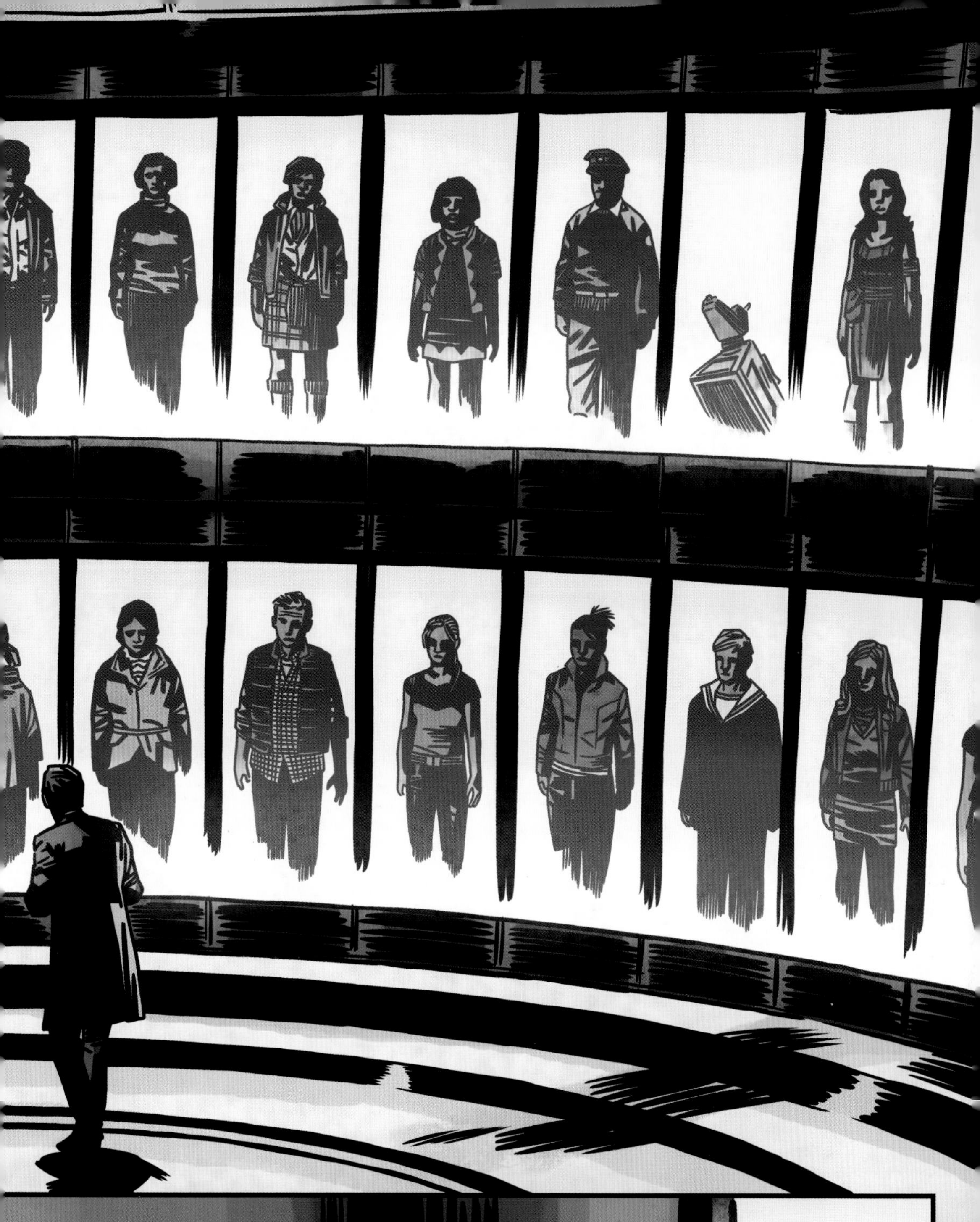

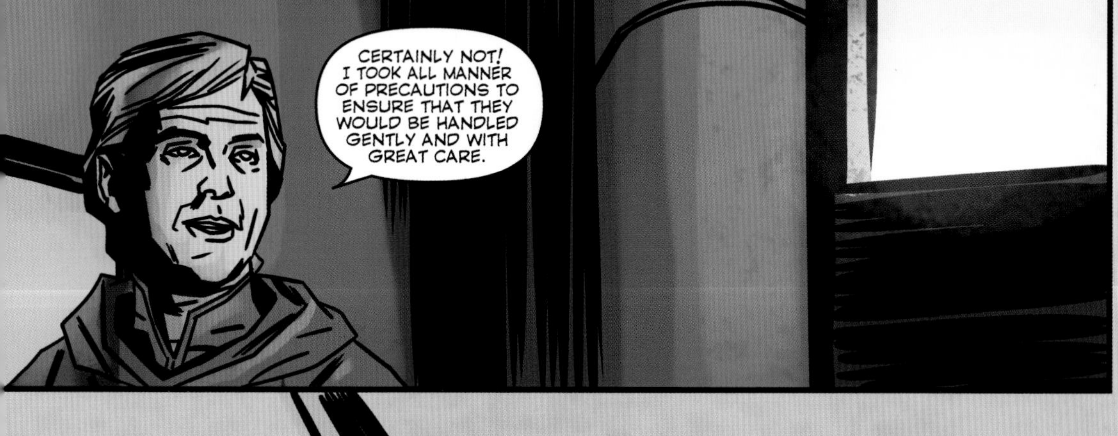
CERTAINLY NOT! I TOOK ALL MANNER OF PRECAUTIONS TO ENSURE THAT THEY WOULD BE HANDLED GENTLY AND WITH GREAT CARE.

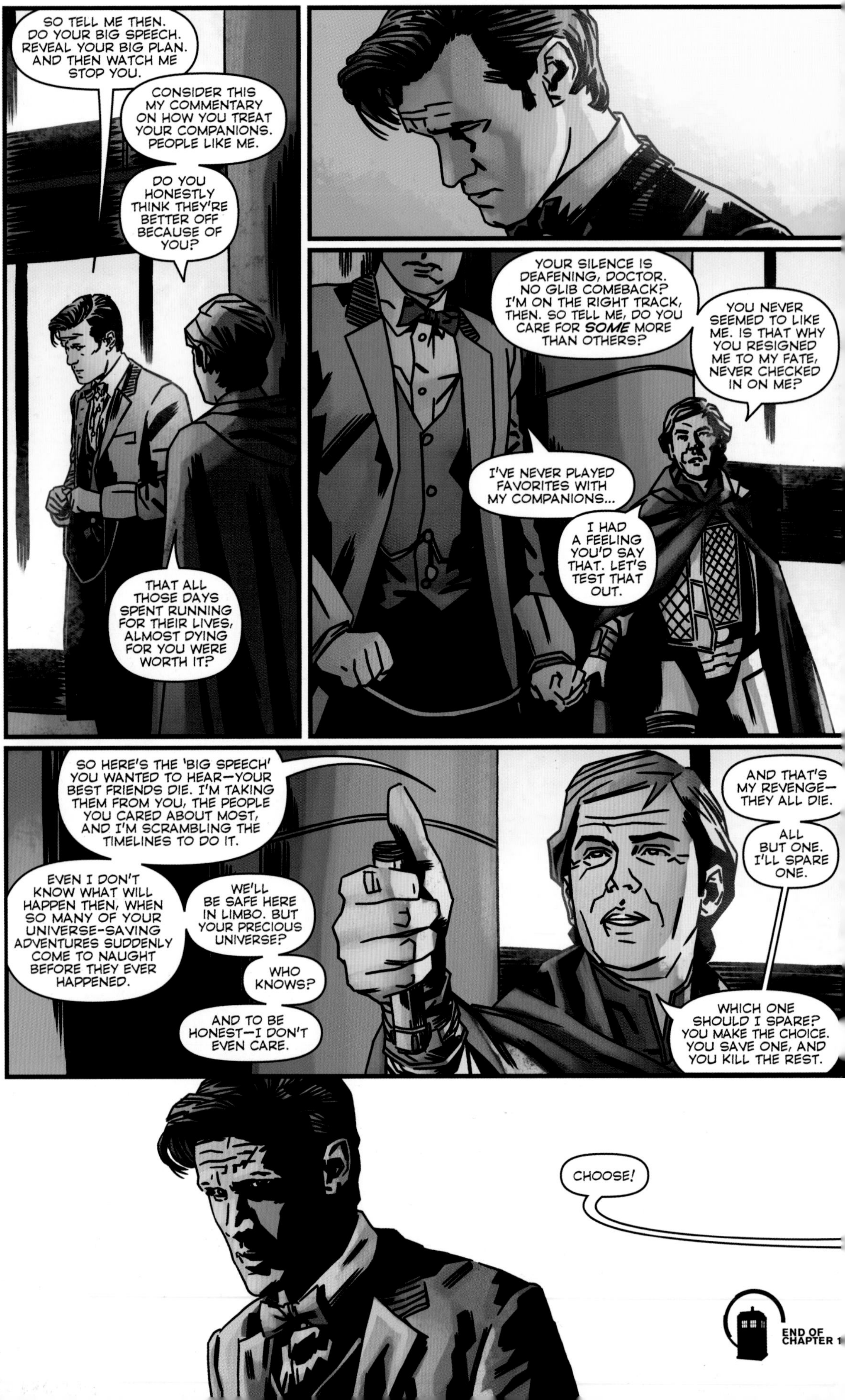
SO TELL ME THEN. DO YOUR BIG SPEECH. REVEAL YOUR BIG PLAN. AND THEN WATCH ME STOP YOU.
CONSIDER THIS MY COMMENTARY ON HOW YOU TREAT YOUR COMPANIONS. PEOPLE LIKE ME.
DO YOU HONESTLY THINK THEY'RE BETTER OFF BECAUSE OF YOU?
THAT ALL THOSE DAYS SPENT RUNNING FOR THEIR LIVES, ALMOST DYING FOR YOU WERE WORTH IT?
YOUR SILENCE IS DEAFENING, DOCTOR. NO GLIB COMEBACK? I'M ON THE RIGHT TRACK, THEN. SO TELL ME, DO YOU CARE FOR *SOME* MORE THAN OTHERS?
YOU NEVER SEEMED TO LIKE ME. IS THAT WHY YOU RESIGNED ME TO MY FATE, NEVER CHECKED IN ON ME?
I'VE NEVER PLAYED FAVORITES WITH MY COMPANIONS...
I HAD A FEELING YOU'D SAY THAT. LET'S TEST THAT OUT.
SO HERE'S THE 'BIG SPEECH' YOU WANTED TO HEAR—YOUR BEST FRIENDS DIE. I'M TAKING THEM FROM YOU, THE PEOPLE YOU CARED ABOUT MOST, AND I'M SCRAMBLING THE TIMELINES TO DO IT.
EVEN I DON'T KNOW WHAT WILL HAPPEN THEN, WHEN SO MANY OF YOUR UNIVERSE-SAVING ADVENTURES SUDDENLY COME TO NAUGHT BEFORE THEY EVER HAPPENED.
WE'LL BE SAFE HERE IN LIMBO. BUT YOUR PRECIOUS UNIVERSE?
WHO KNOWS?
AND TO BE HONEST—I DON'T EVEN CARE.
AND THAT'S MY REVENGE—THEY ALL DIE.
ALL BUT ONE. I'LL SPARE ONE.
WHICH ONE SHOULD I SPARE? YOU MAKE THE CHOICE. YOU SAVE ONE, AND YOU KILL THE REST.
CHOOSE!
END OF CHAPTER 1

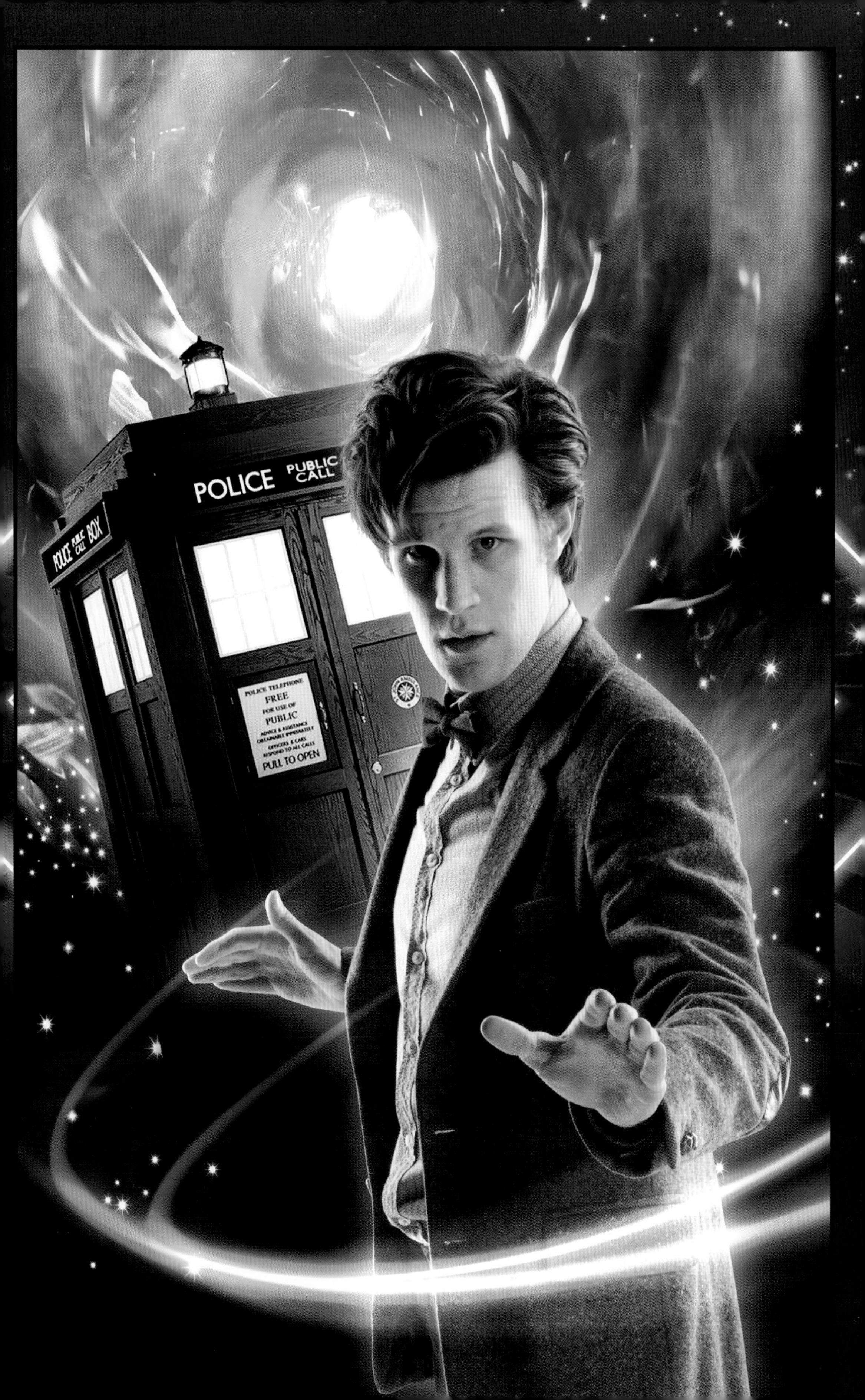
POLICE PUBLIC CALL BOX
POLICE PUBLIC CALL
POLICE TELEPHONE
FREE
FOR USE OF
PUBLIC
ADVICE & ASSISTANCE OBTAINABLE IMMEDIATELY
OFFICERS & CARS RESPOND TO ALL CALLS
PULL TO OPEN

CHAPTER 12
"ENDGAME"

Cover Art by Francesco Francavilla

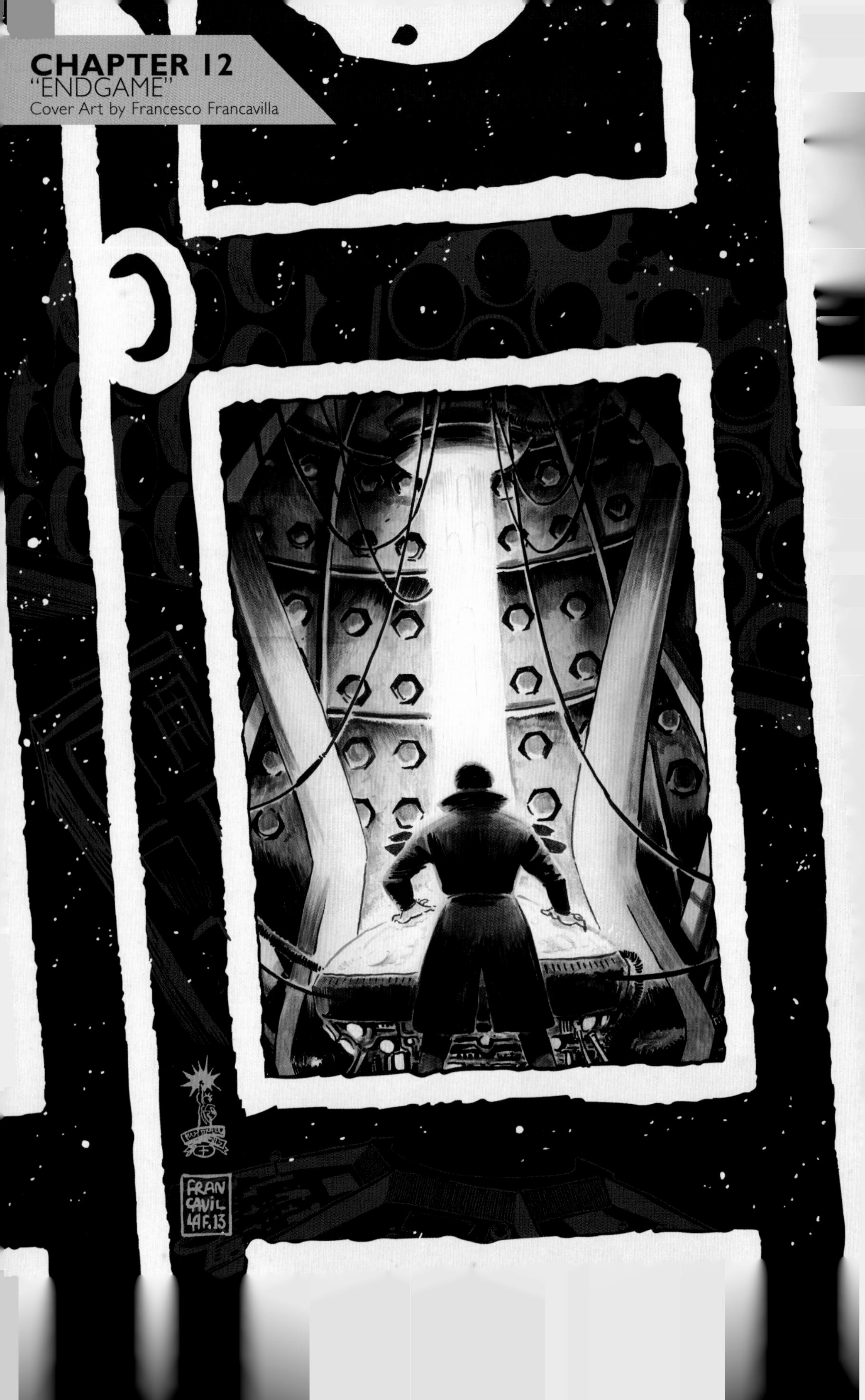
FRAN
CAVIL
LA F.13

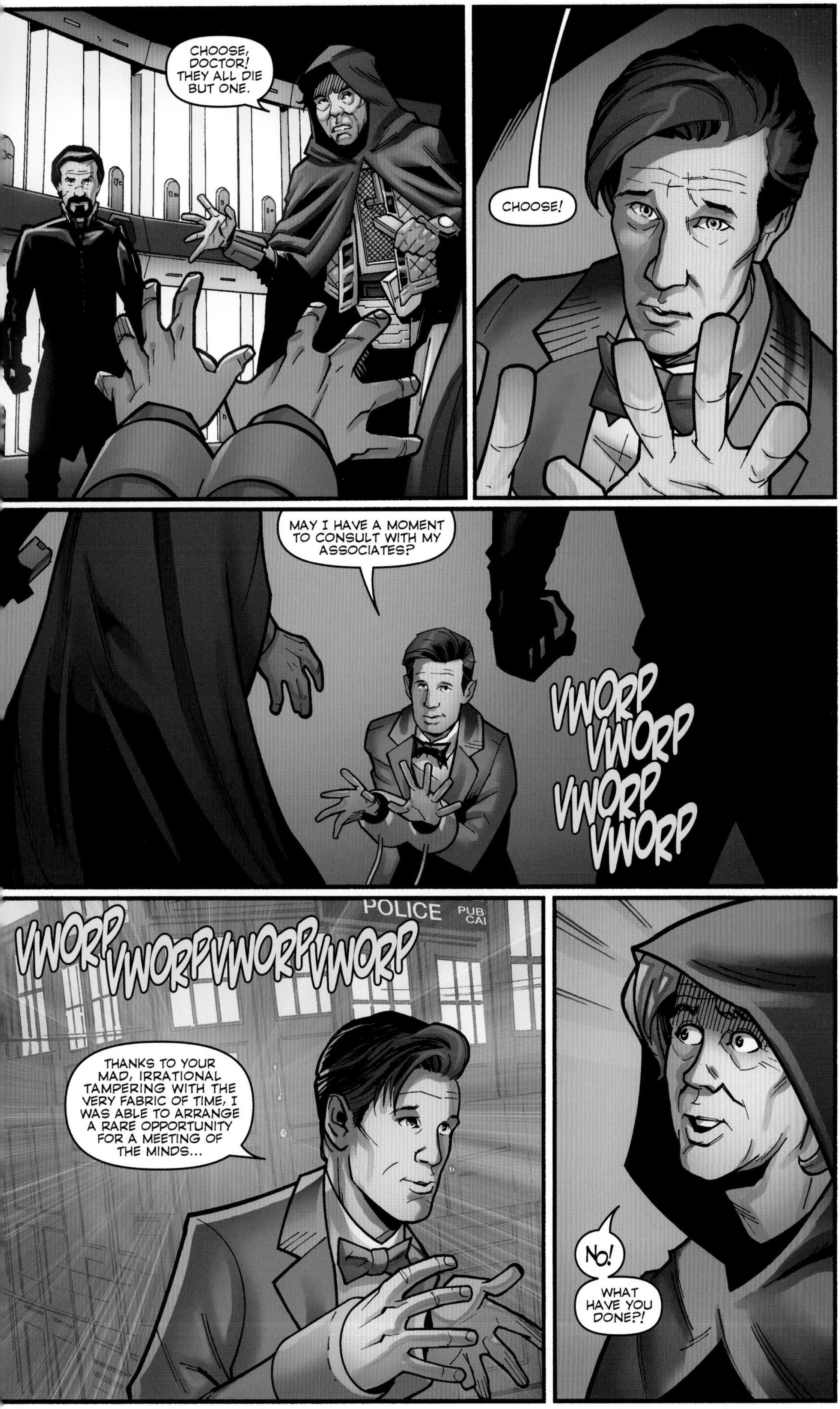
CHOOSE, DOCTOR! THEY ALL DIE BUT ONE.
CHOOSE!
MAY I HAVE A MOMENT TO CONSULT WITH MY ASSOCIATES?
VWORP VWORP VWORP VWORP
VWORP VWORP VWORP VWORP
POLICE PUB CAL
THANKS TO YOUR MAD, IRRATIONAL TAMPERING WITH THE VERY FABRIC OF TIME, I WAS ABLE TO ARRANGE A RARE OPPORTUNITY FOR A MEETING OF THE MINDS...
NO!
WHAT HAVE YOU DONE?!

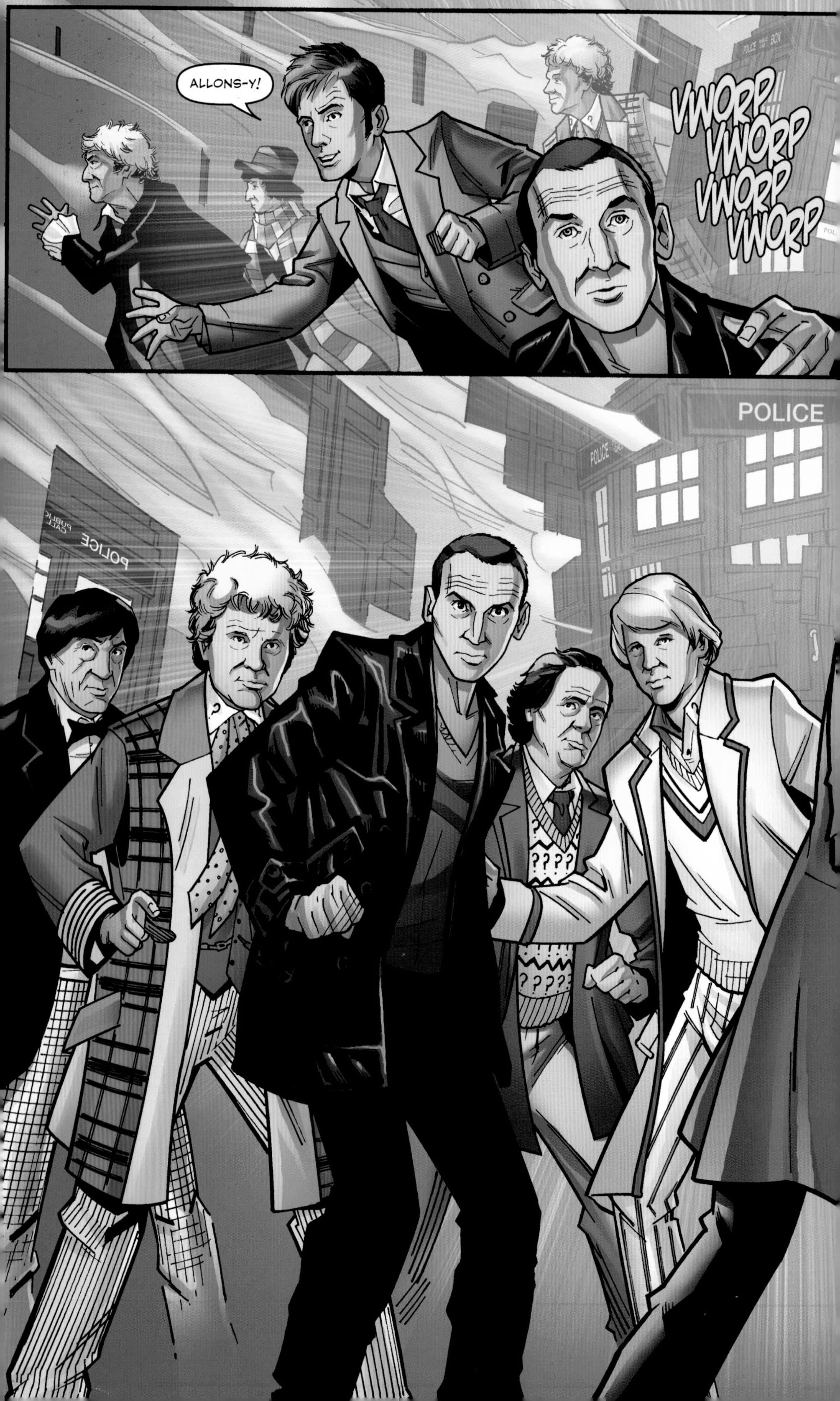
ALLONS-Y!
POLICE PUBLIC CALL BOX
VWORP VWORP VWORP VWORP
POLICE

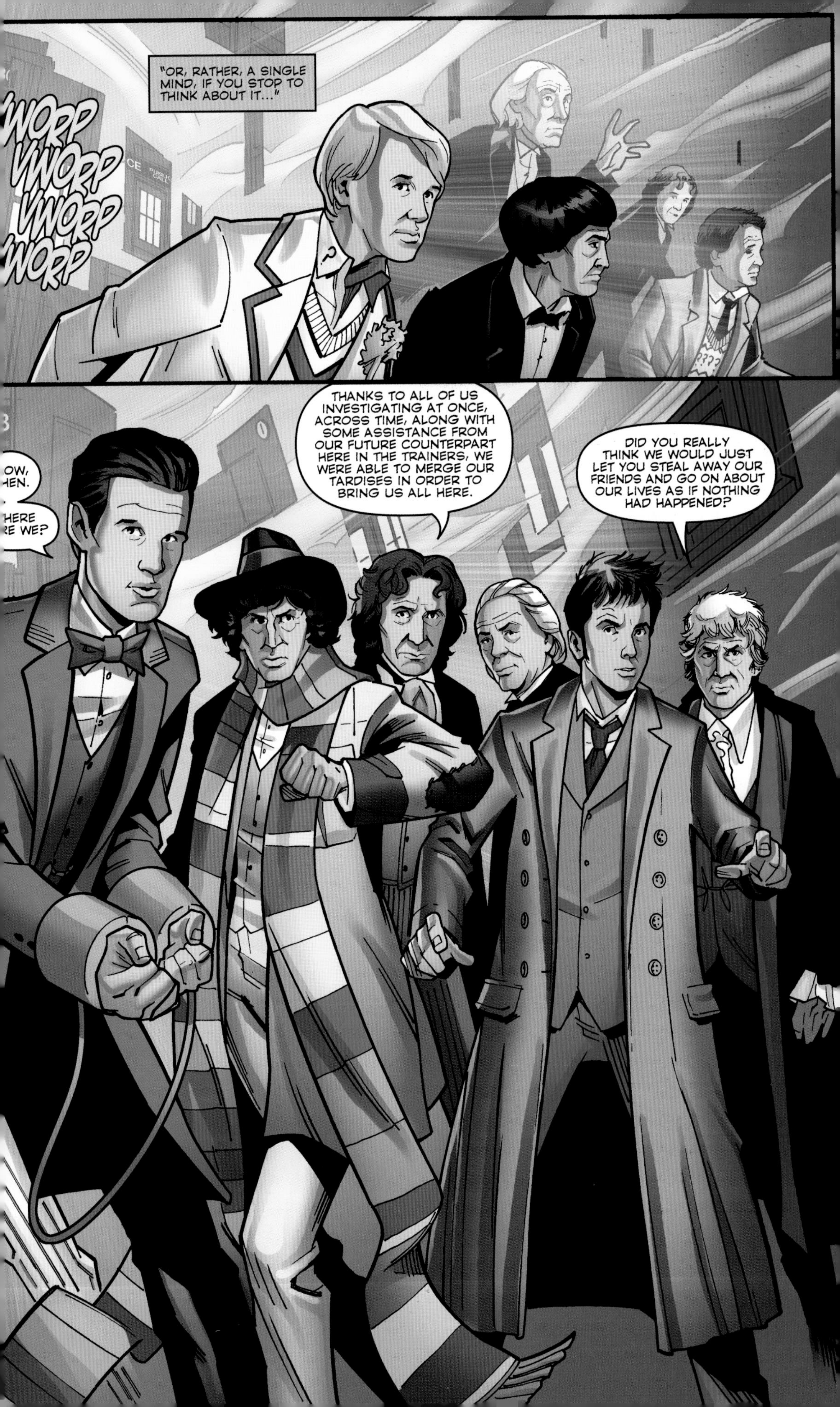

"OR, RATHER, A SINGLE MIND, IF YOU STOP TO THINK ABOUT IT..."
WORP
VWORP
VWORP
WORP
THANKS TO ALL OF US INVESTIGATING AT ONCE, ACROSS TIME, ALONG WITH SOME ASSISTANCE FROM OUR FUTURE COUNTERPART HERE IN THE TRAINERS, WE WERE ABLE TO MERGE OUR TARDISES IN ORDER TO BRING US ALL HERE.
DID YOU REALLY THINK WE WOULD JUST LET YOU STEAL AWAY OUR FRIENDS AND GO ON ABOUT OUR LIVES AS IF NOTHING HAD HAPPENED?

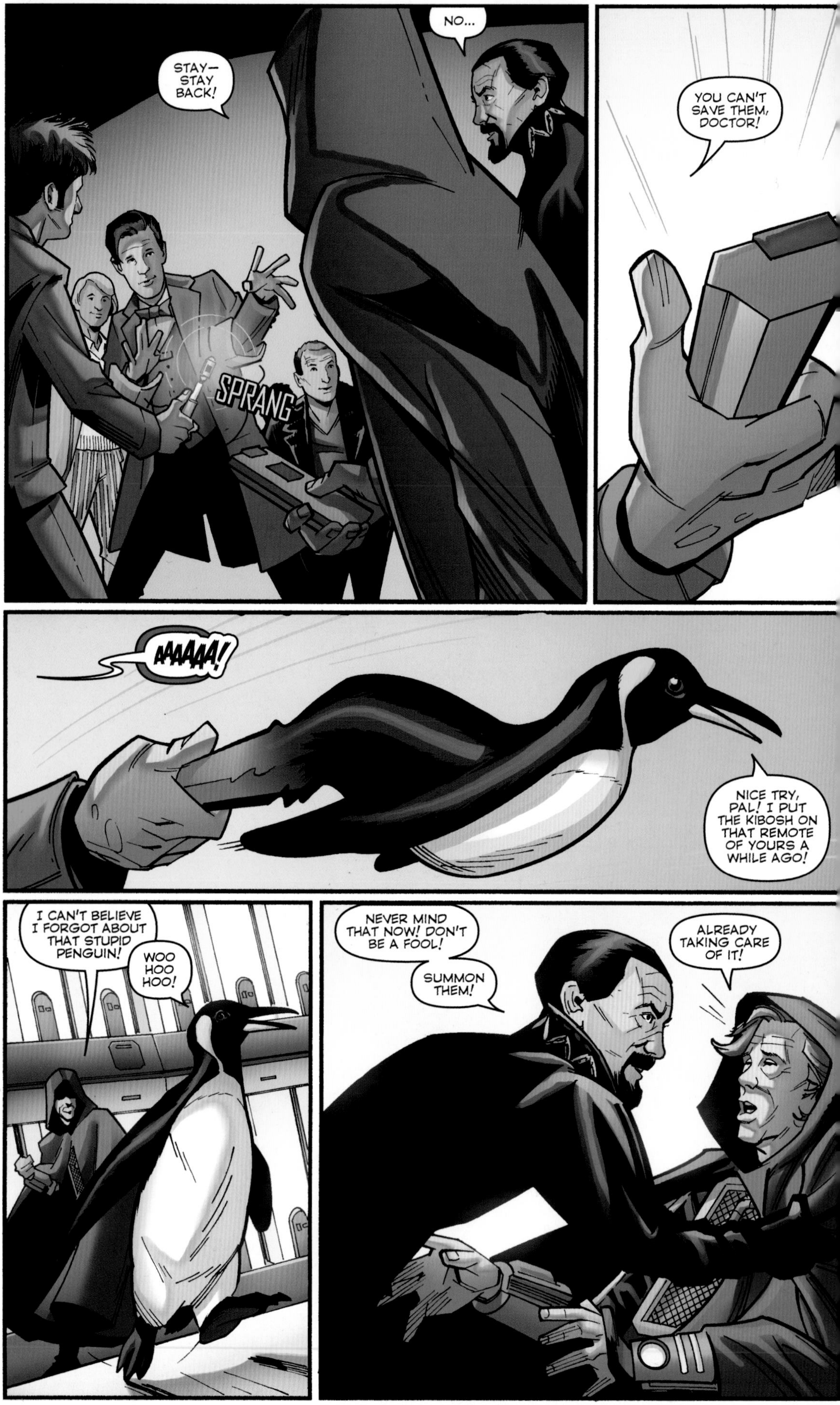
STAY—
STAY
BACK!
NO...
SPRANG
YOU CAN'T
SAVE THEM,
DOCTOR!
AAAAAA!
NICE TRY,
PAL! I PUT
THE KIBOSH ON
THAT REMOTE
OF YOURS A
WHILE AGO!
I CAN'T BELIEVE
I FORGOT ABOUT
THAT STUPID
PENGUIN!
WOO
HOO
HOO!
NEVER MIND
THAT NOW! DON'T
BE A FOOL!
SUMMON
THEM!
ALREADY
TAKING CARE
OF IT!

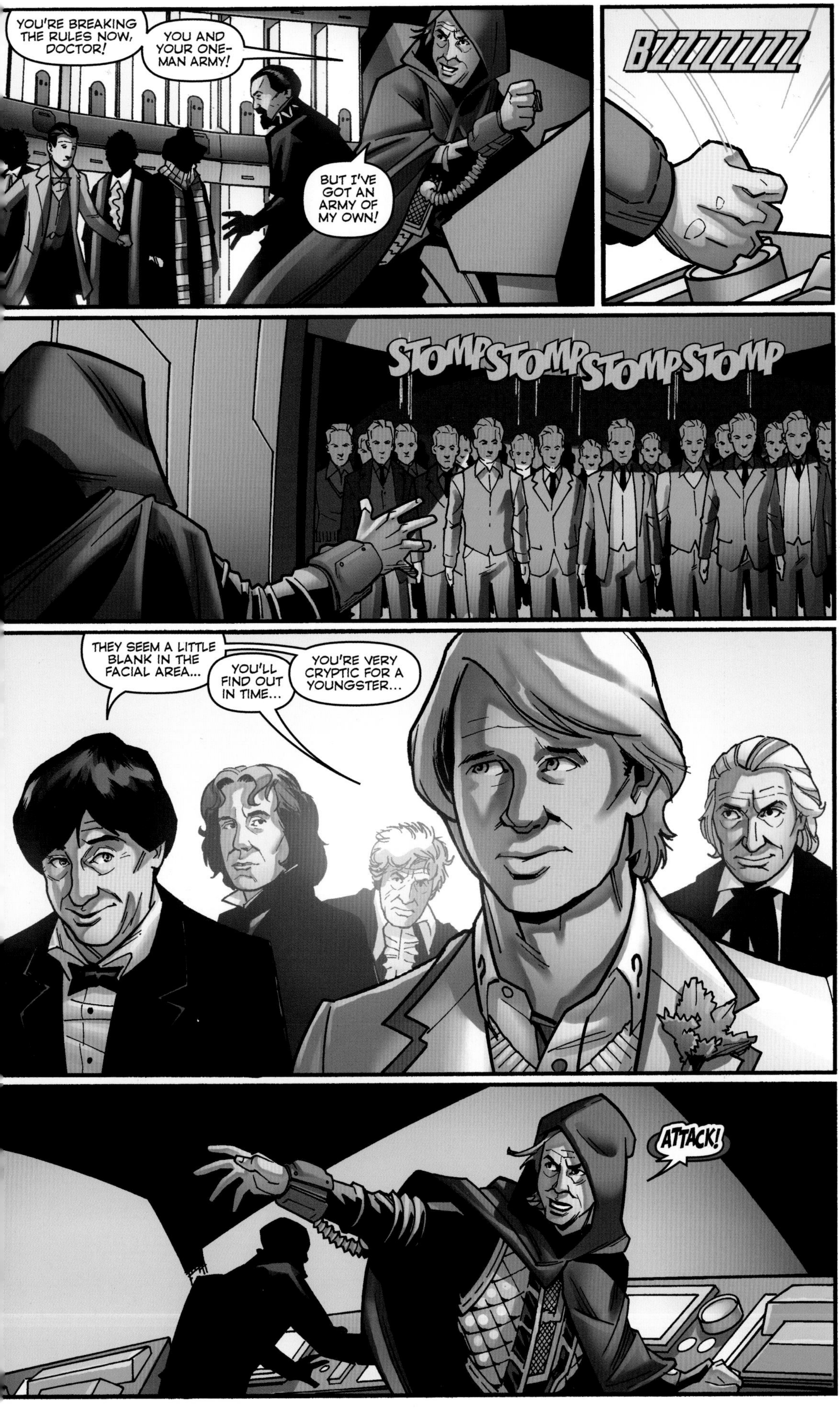
YOU'RE BREAKING THE RULES NOW, DOCTOR!
YOU AND YOUR ONE-MAN ARMY!
BUT I'VE GOT AN ARMY OF MY OWN!
BZZZZZZZ
STOMP STOMP STOMP STOMP
THEY SEEM A LITTLE BLANK IN THE FACIAL AREA...
YOU'LL FIND OUT IN TIME...
YOU'RE VERY CRYPTIC FOR A YOUNGSTER...
ATTACK!

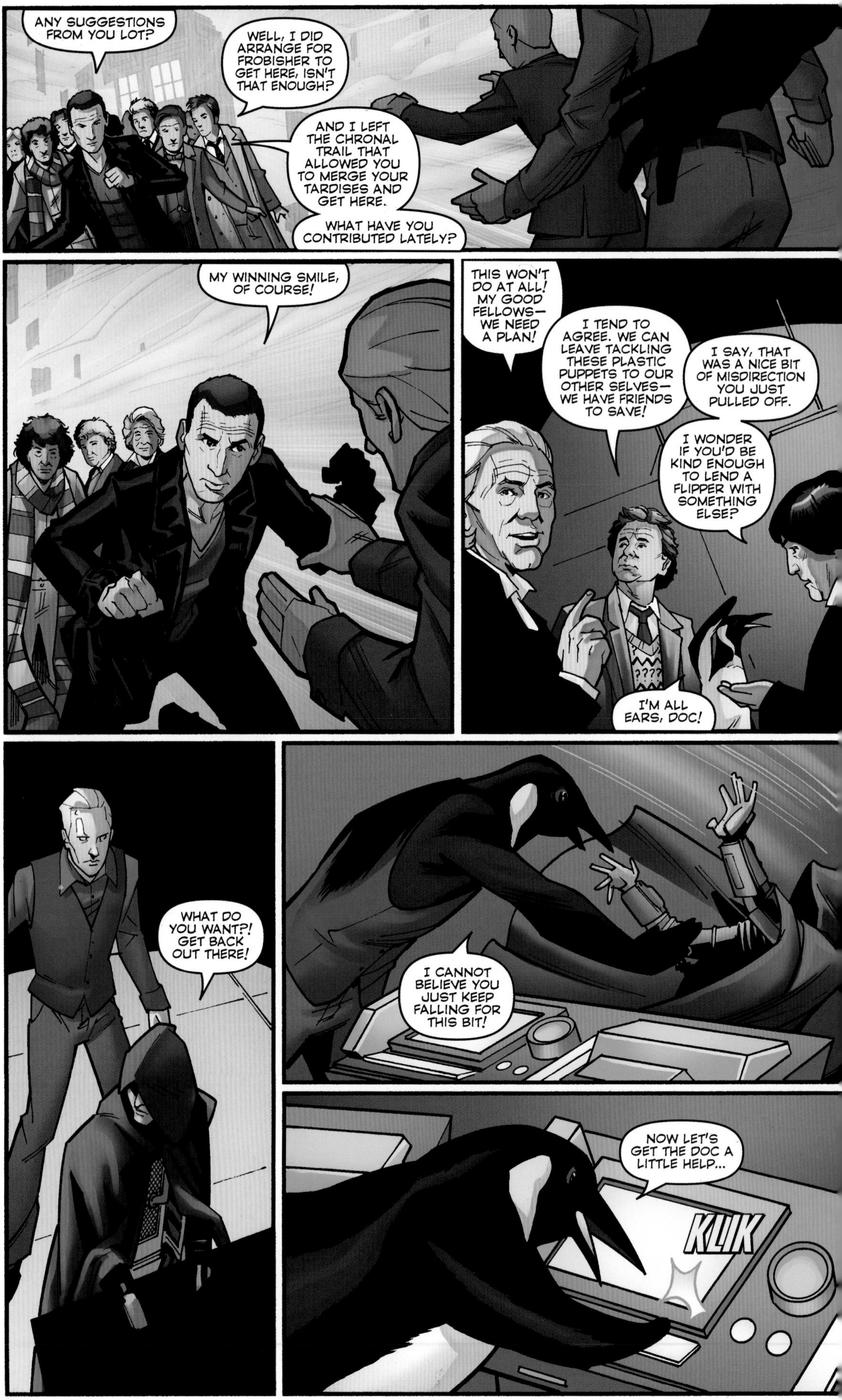
ANY SUGGESTIONS FROM YOU LOT?
WELL, I DID ARRANGE FOR FROBISHER TO GET HERE, ISN'T THAT ENOUGH?
AND I LEFT THE CHRONAL TRAIL THAT ALLOWED YOU TO MERGE YOUR TARDISES AND GET HERE.
WHAT HAVE YOU CONTRIBUTED LATELY?
MY WINNING SMILE, OF COURSE!
THIS WON'T DO AT ALL! MY GOOD FELLOWS— WE NEED A PLAN!
I TEND TO AGREE. WE CAN LEAVE TACKLING THESE PLASTIC PUPPETS TO OUR OTHER SELVES— WE HAVE FRIENDS TO SAVE!
I SAY, THAT WAS A NICE BIT OF MISDIRECTION YOU JUST PULLED OFF.
I WONDER IF YOU'D BE KIND ENOUGH TO LEND A FLIPPER WITH SOMETHING ELSE?
I'M ALL EARS, DOC!
WHAT DO YOU WANT?! GET BACK OUT THERE!
I CANNOT BELIEVE YOU JUST KEEP FALLING FOR THIS BIT!
NOW LET'S GET THE DOC A LITTLE HELP...
KLIK

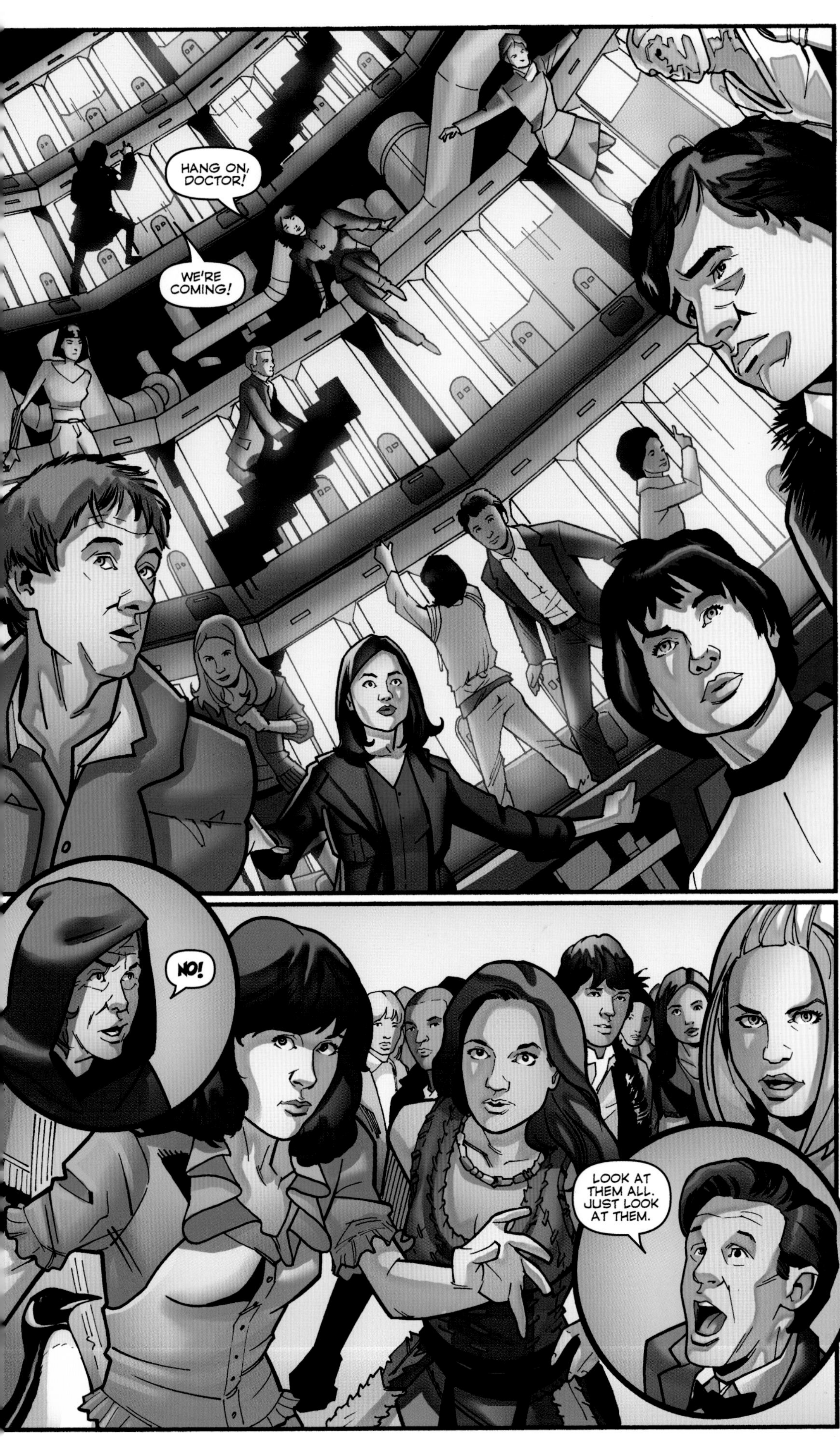
HANG ON, DOCTOR!
WE'RE COMING!
NO!
LOOK AT THEM ALL. JUST LOOK AT THEM.

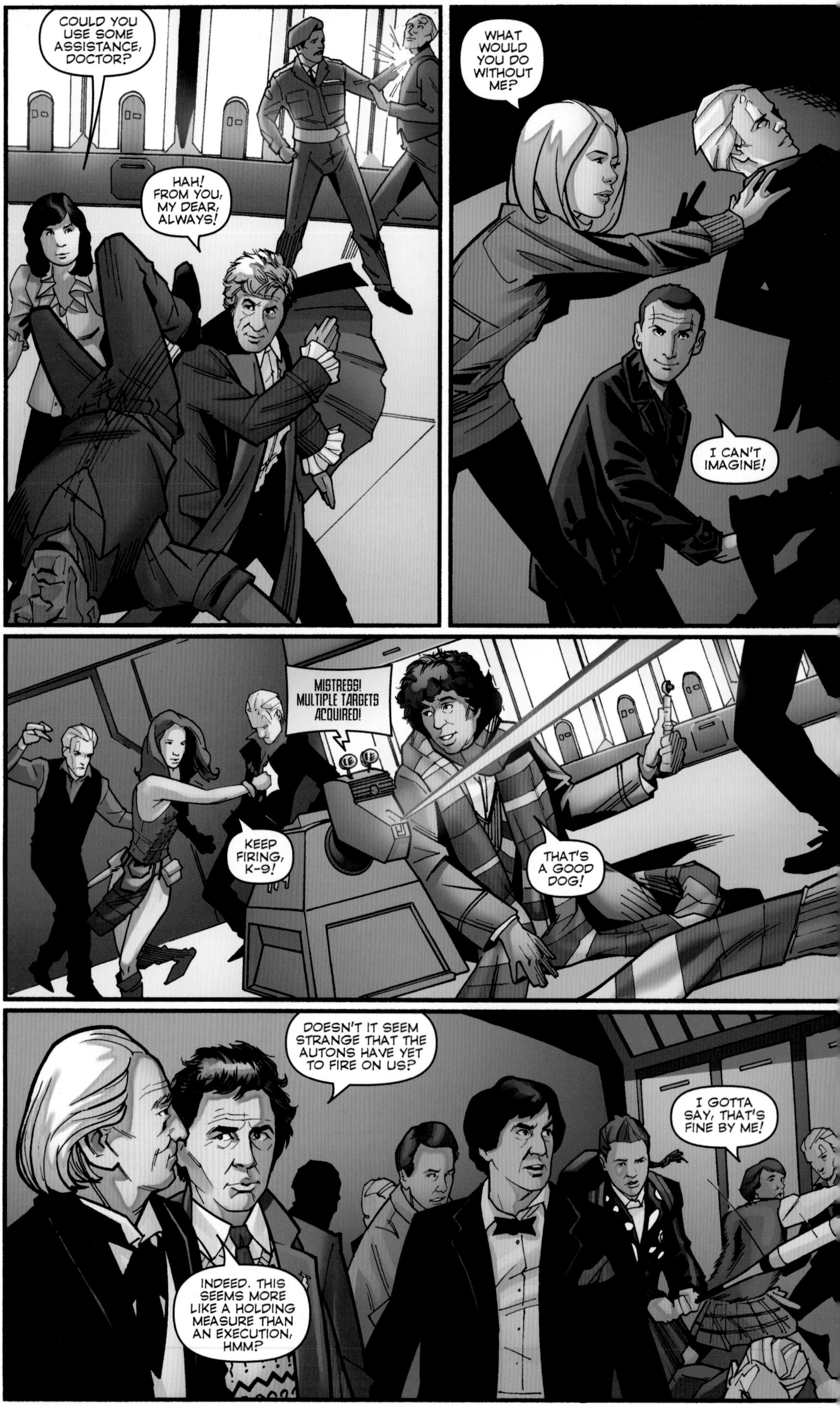
COULD YOU USE SOME ASSISTANCE, DOCTOR?
HAH! FROM YOU, MY DEAR, ALWAYS!
WHAT WOULD YOU DO WITHOUT ME?
I CAN'T IMAGINE!
MISTRESS! MULTIPLE TARGETS ACQUIRED!
KEEP FIRING, K-9!
THAT'S A GOOD DOG!
DOESN'T IT SEEM STRANGE THAT THE AUTONS HAVE YET TO FIRE ON US?
I GOTTA SAY, THAT'S FINE BY ME!
INDEED. THIS SEEMS MORE LIKE A HOLDING MEASURE THAN AN EXECUTION, HMM?

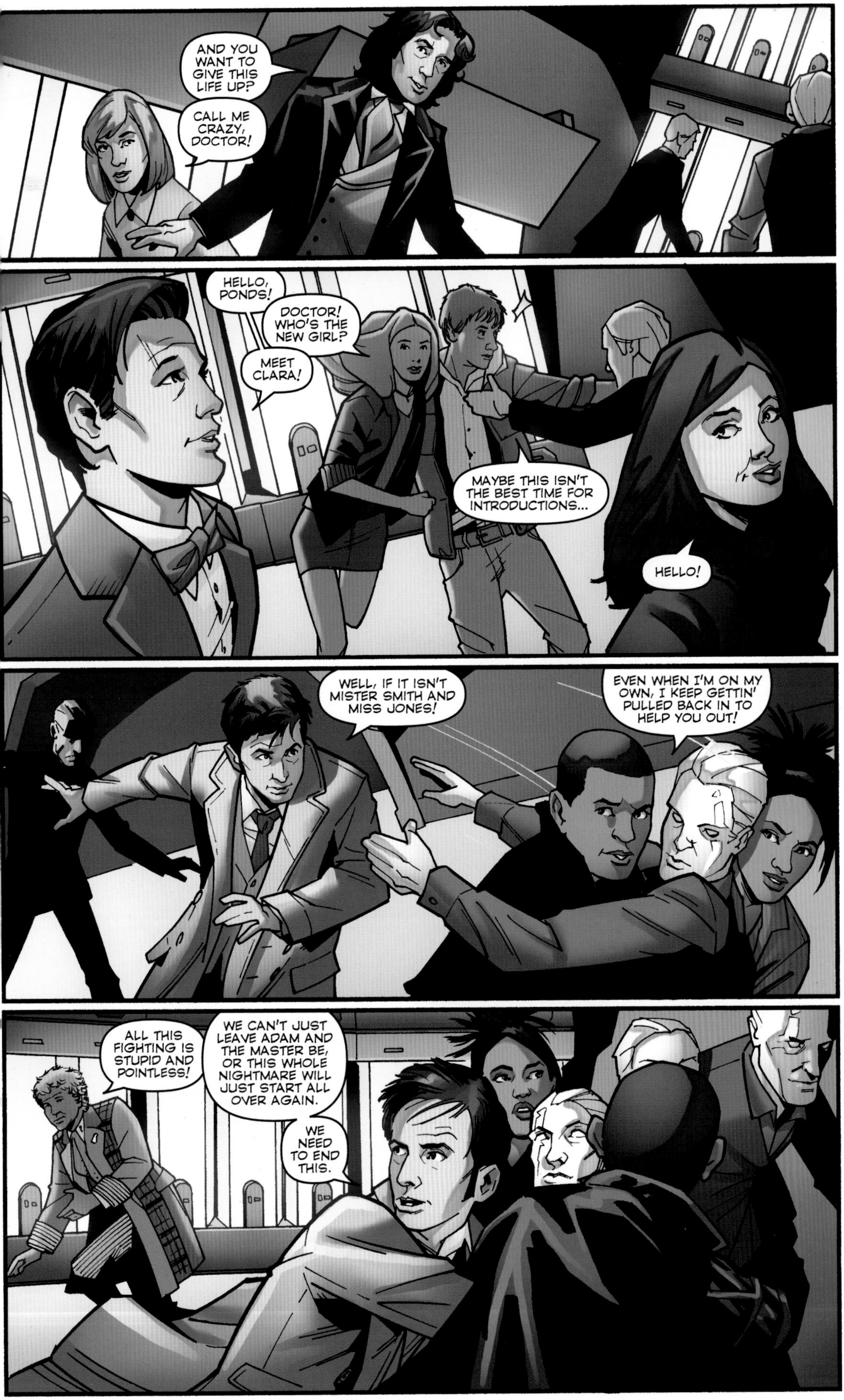
AND YOU WANT TO GIVE THIS LIFE UP?
CALL ME CRAZY, DOCTOR!
HELLO, PONDS!
DOCTOR! WHO'S THE NEW GIRL?
MEET CLARA!
MAYBE THIS ISN'T THE BEST TIME FOR INTRODUCTIONS...
HELLO!
WELL, IF IT ISN'T MISTER SMITH AND MISS JONES!
EVEN WHEN I'M ON MY OWN, I KEEP GETTIN' PULLED BACK IN TO HELP YOU OUT!
ALL THIS FIGHTING IS STUPID AND POINTLESS!
WE CAN'T JUST LEAVE ADAM AND THE MASTER BE, OR THIS WHOLE NIGHTMARE WILL JUST START ALL OVER AGAIN.
WE NEED TO END THIS.

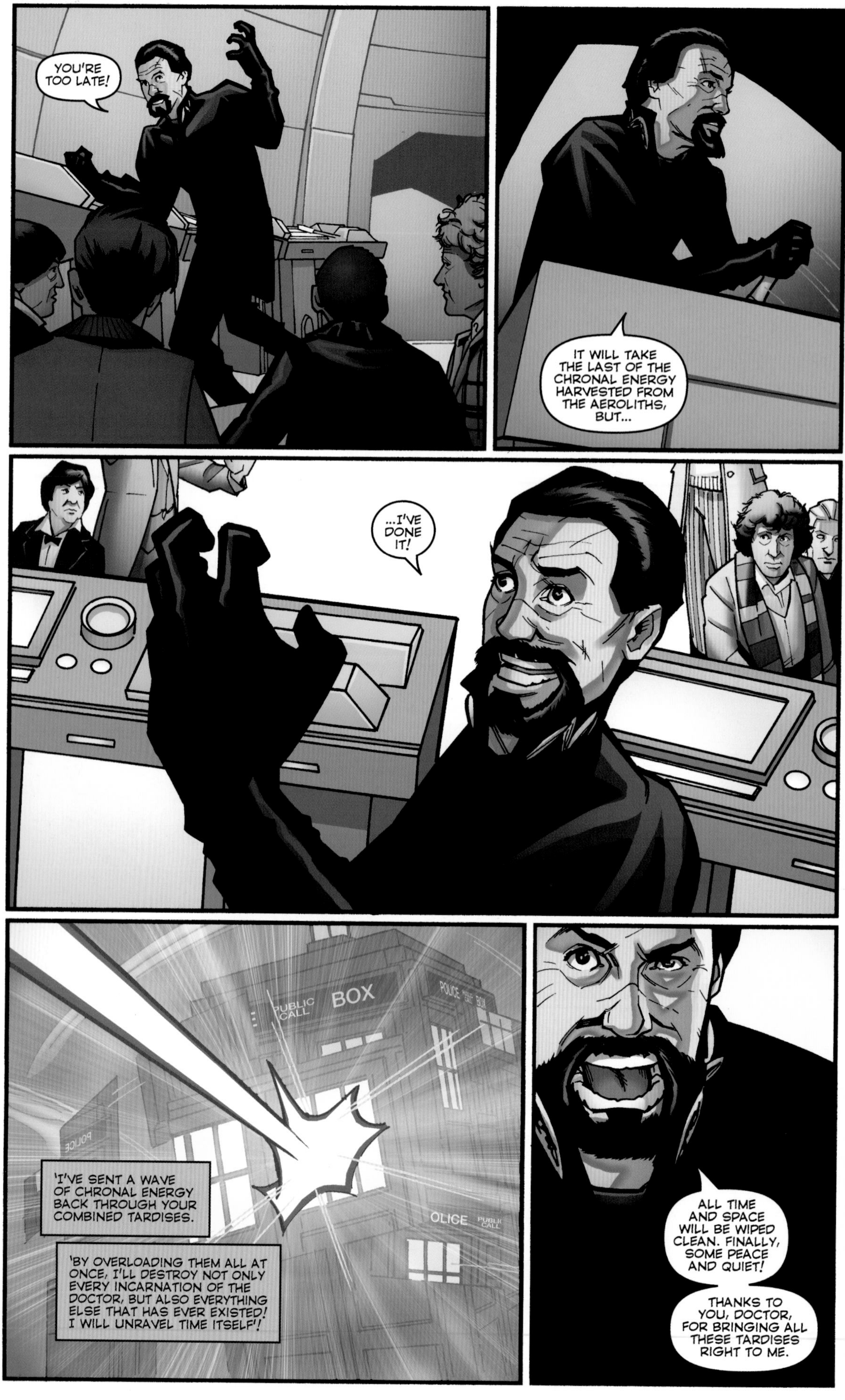
YOU'RE TOO LATE!
IT WILL TAKE THE LAST OF THE CHRONAL ENERGY HARVESTED FROM THE AEROLITHS, BUT...
...I'VE DONE IT!
PUBLIC CALL BOX
POLICE BOX
'I'VE SENT A WAVE OF CHRONAL ENERGY BACK THROUGH YOUR COMBINED TARDISES.
'BY OVERLOADING THEM ALL AT ONCE, I'LL DESTROY NOT ONLY EVERY INCARNATION OF THE DOCTOR, BUT ALSO EVERYTHING ELSE THAT HAS EVER EXISTED! I WILL UNRAVEL TIME ITSELF'!'
OLICE PUBLIC CALL
ALL TIME AND SPACE WILL BE WIPED CLEAN. FINALLY, SOME PEACE AND QUIET!
THANKS TO YOU, DOCTOR, FOR BRINGING ALL THESE TARDISES RIGHT TO ME.

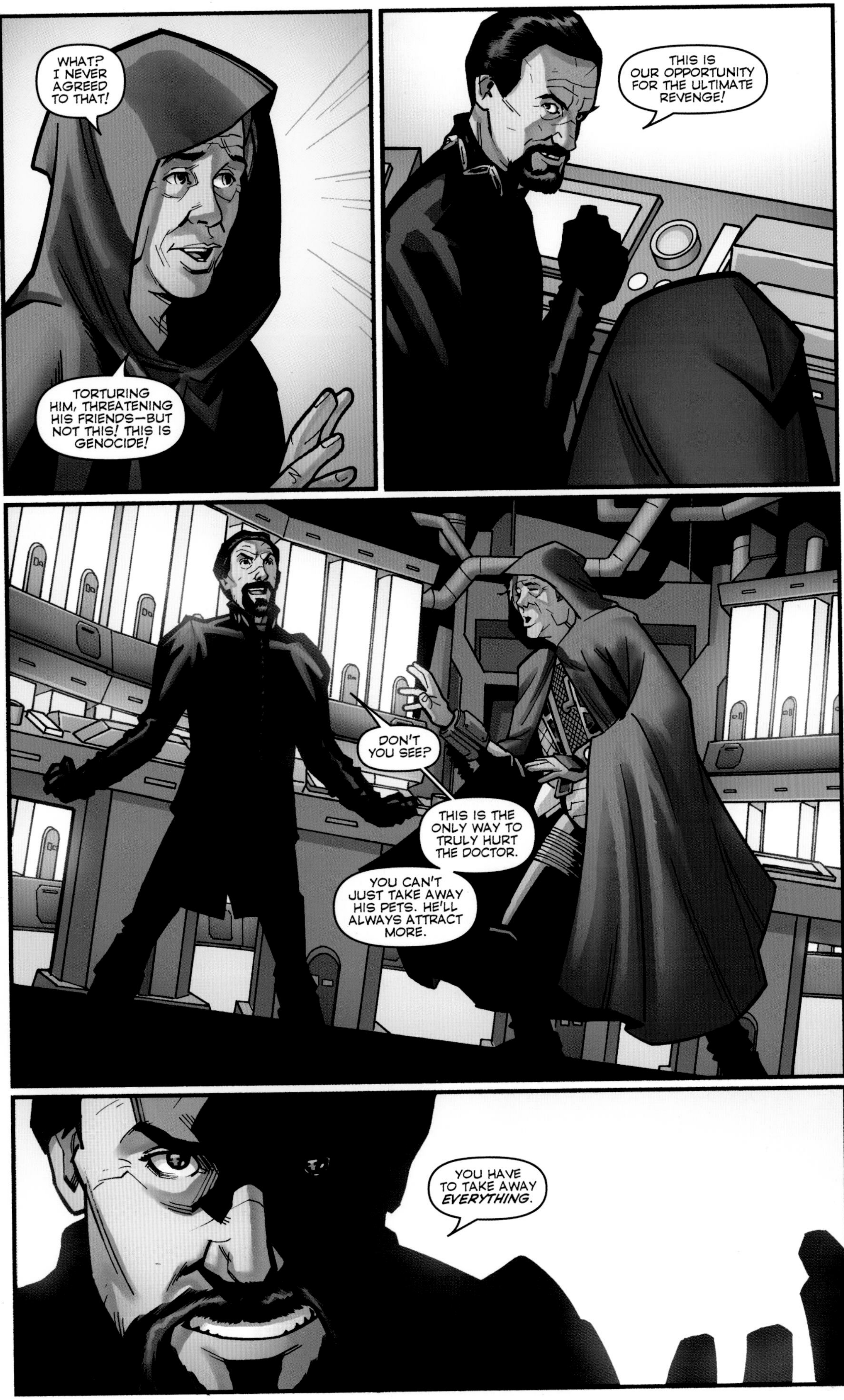
WHAT? I NEVER AGREED TO THAT!
TORTURING HIM, THREATENING HIS FRIENDS—BUT NOT THIS! THIS IS GENOCIDE!
THIS IS OUR OPPORTUNITY FOR THE ULTIMATE REVENGE!
DON'T YOU SEE?
THIS IS THE ONLY WAY TO TRULY HURT THE DOCTOR.
YOU CAN'T JUST TAKE AWAY HIS PETS. HE'LL ALWAYS ATTRACT MORE.
YOU HAVE TO TAKE AWAY *EVERYTHING*.

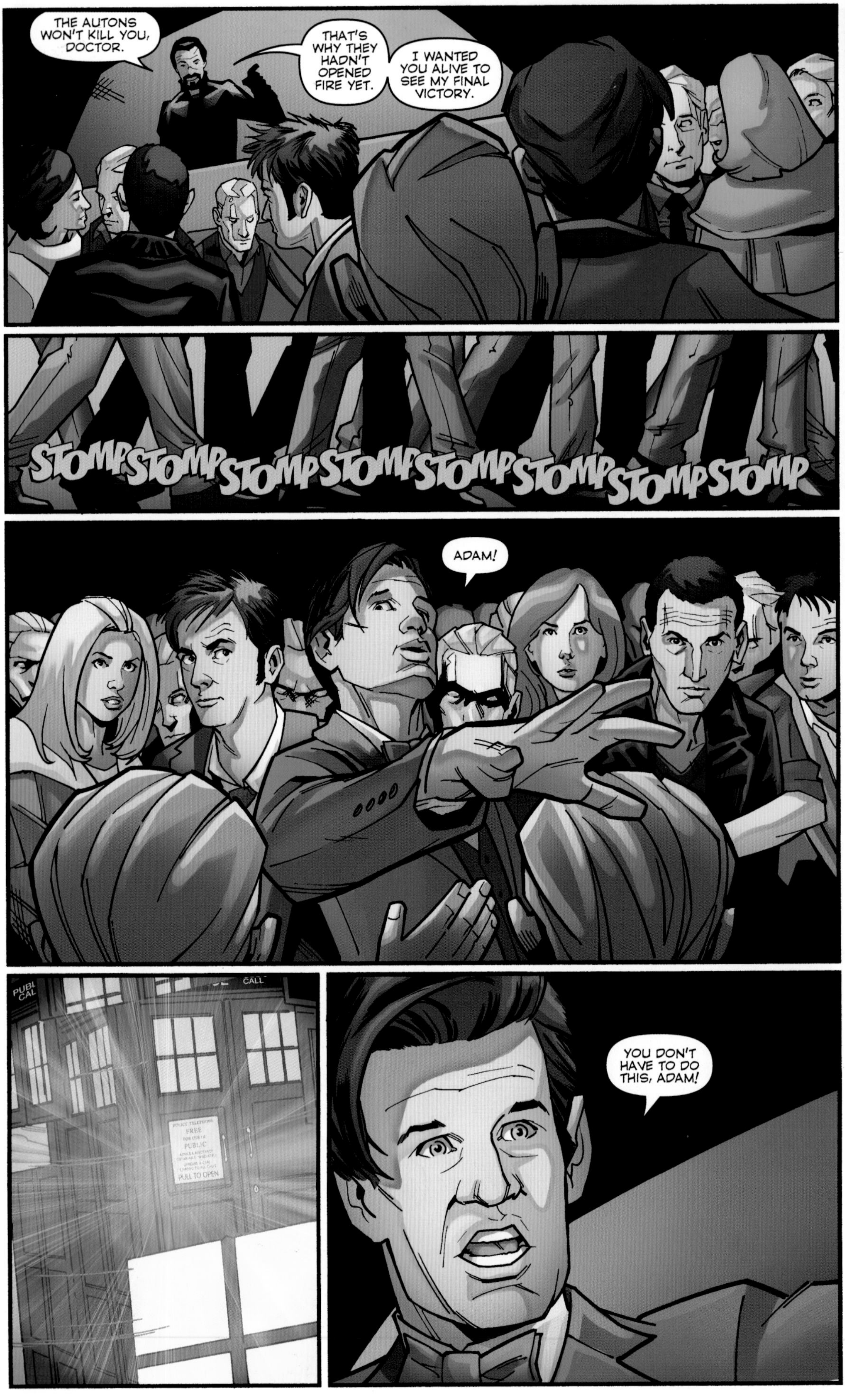
THE AUTONS WON'T KILL YOU, DOCTOR.
THAT'S WHY THEY HADN'T OPENED FIRE YET.
I WANTED YOU ALIVE TO SEE MY FINAL VICTORY.
STOMP STOMP STOMP STOMP STOMP STOMP STOMP STOMP
ADAM!
POLICE TELEPHONE FREE FOR USE OF PUBLIC
PULL TO OPEN
YOU DON'T HAVE TO DO THIS, ADAM!

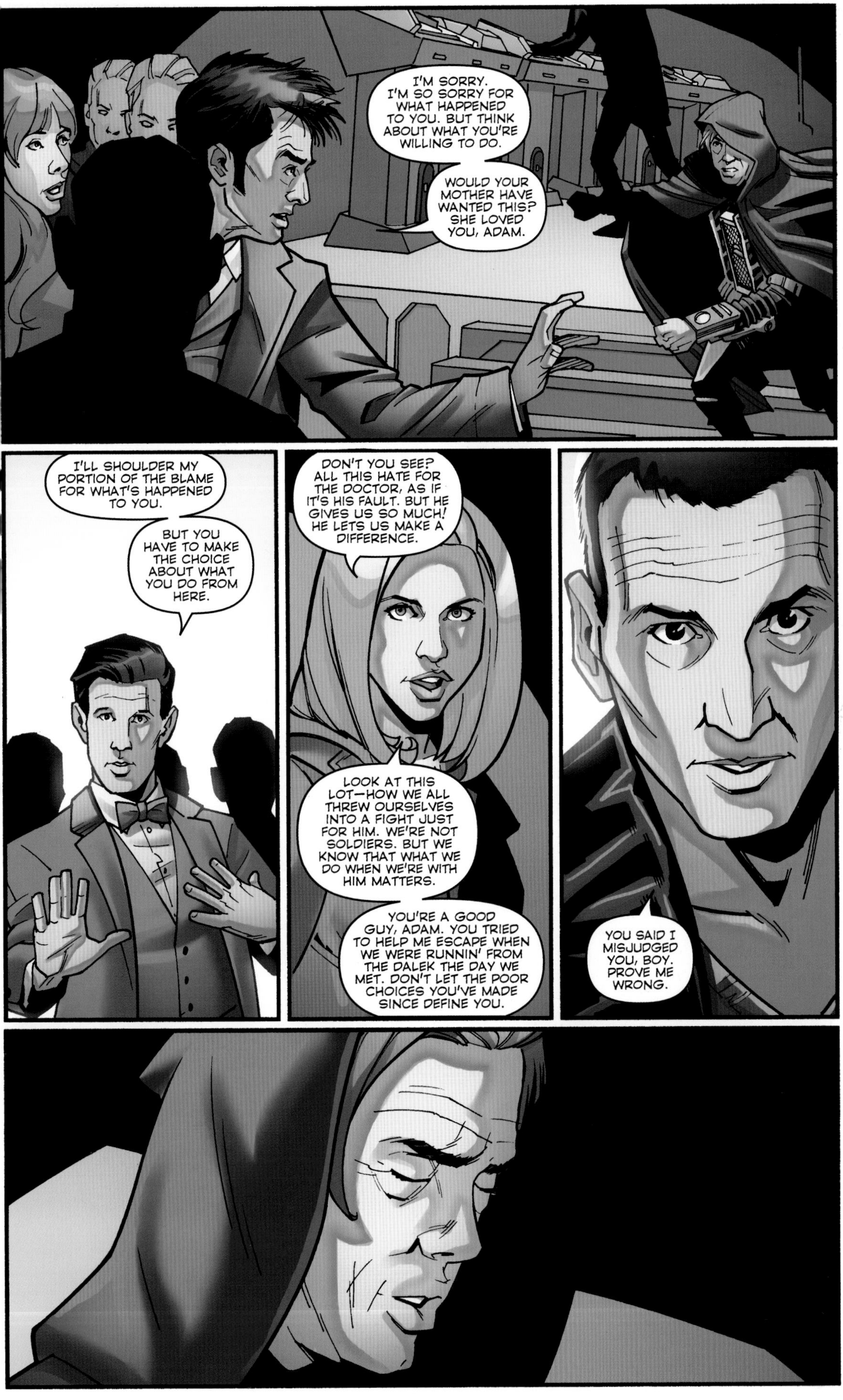

I'M SORRY. I'M SO SORRY FOR WHAT HAPPENED TO YOU. BUT THINK ABOUT WHAT YOU'RE WILLING TO DO.
WOULD YOUR MOTHER HAVE WANTED THIS? SHE LOVED YOU, ADAM.
I'LL SHOULDER MY PORTION OF THE BLAME FOR WHAT'S HAPPENED TO YOU.
BUT YOU HAVE TO MAKE THE CHOICE ABOUT WHAT YOU DO FROM HERE.
DON'T YOU SEE? ALL THIS HATE FOR THE DOCTOR, AS IF IT'S HIS FAULT. BUT HE GIVES US SO MUCH! HE LETS US MAKE A DIFFERENCE.
LOOK AT THIS LOT—HOW WE ALL THREW OURSELVES INTO A FIGHT JUST FOR HIM. WE'RE NOT SOLDIERS. BUT WE KNOW THAT WHAT WE DO WHEN WE'RE WITH HIM MATTERS.
YOU'RE A GOOD GUY, ADAM. YOU TRIED TO HELP ME ESCAPE WHEN WE WERE RUNNIN' FROM THE DALEK THE DAY WE MET. DON'T LET THE POOR CHOICES YOU'VE MADE SINCE DEFINE YOU.
YOU SAID I MISJUDGED YOU, BOY. PROVE ME WRONG.

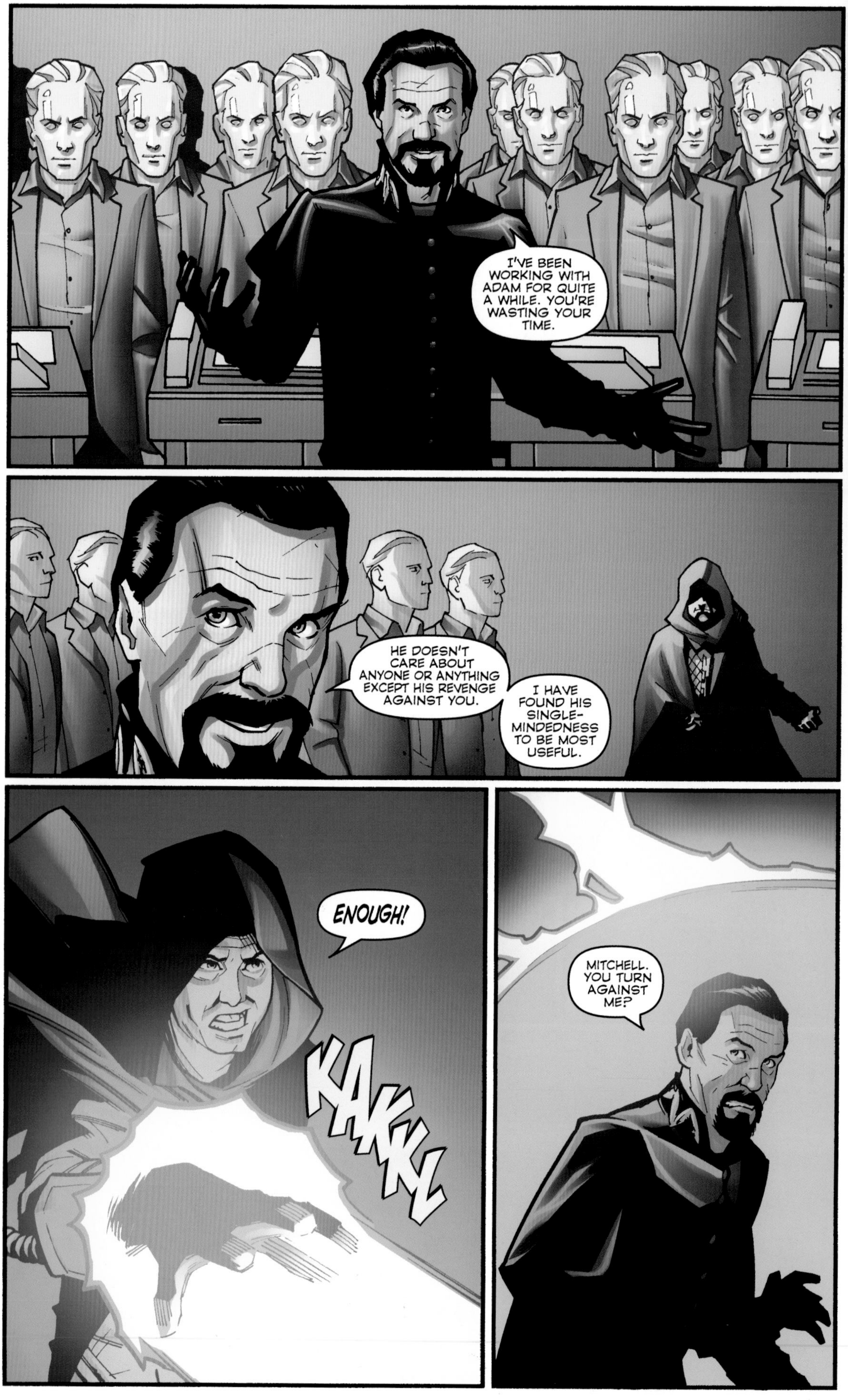
I'VE BEEN WORKING WITH ADAM FOR QUITE A WHILE. YOU'RE WASTING YOUR TIME.
HE DOESN'T CARE ABOUT ANYONE OR ANYTHING EXCEPT HIS REVENGE AGAINST YOU.
I HAVE FOUND HIS SINGLE-MINDEDNESS TO BE MOST USEFUL.
ENOUGH!
KAKKL
MITCHELL. YOU TURN AGAINST ME?

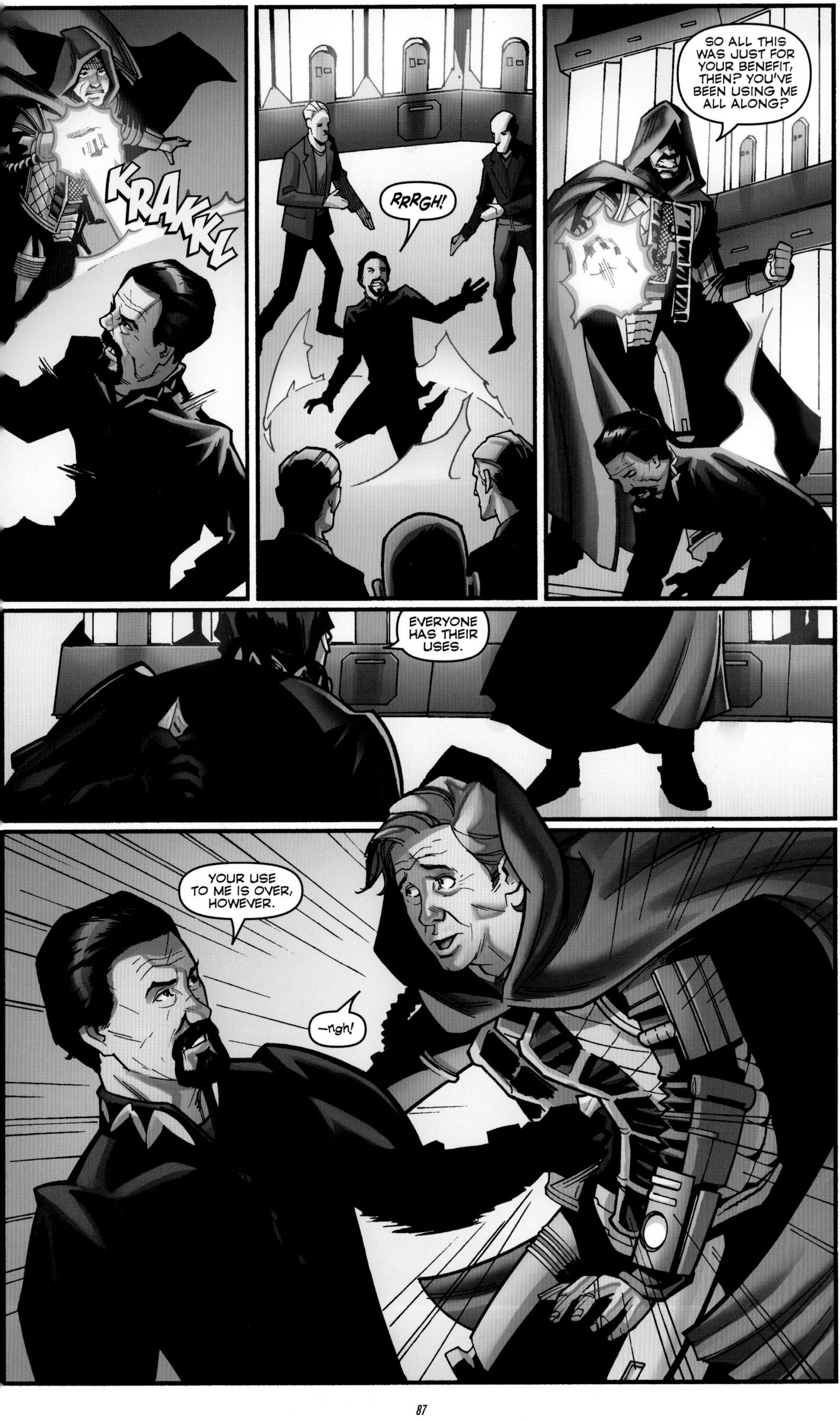
KRAKKL
RRRGH!
SO ALL THIS WAS JUST FOR YOUR BENEFIT, THEN? YOU'VE BEEN USING ME ALL ALONG?
EVERYONE HAS THEIR USES.
YOUR USE TO ME IS OVER, HOWEVER.
—ngh!

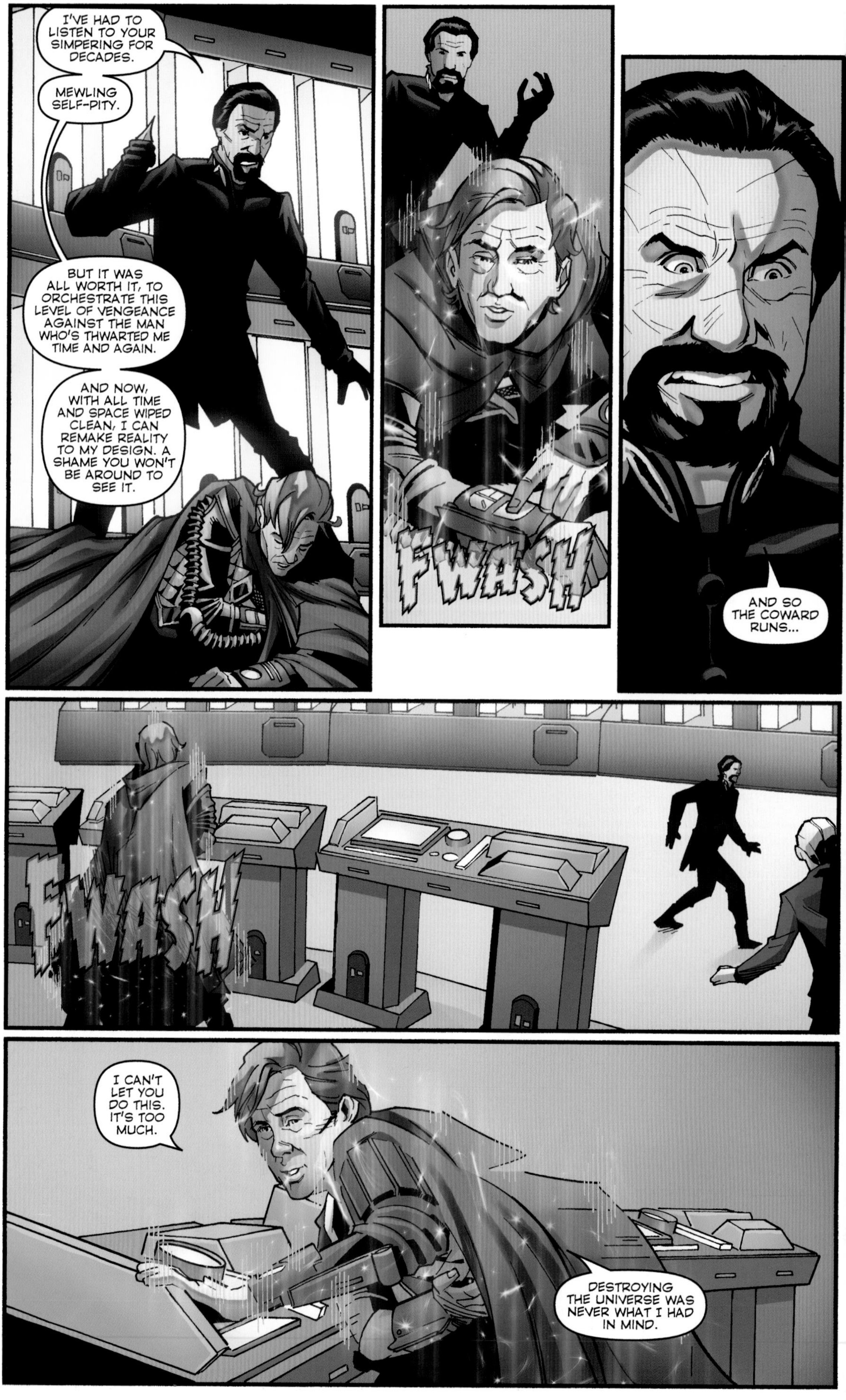
I'VE HAD TO LISTEN TO YOUR SIMPERING FOR DECADES.
MEWLING SELF-PITY.
BUT IT WAS ALL WORTH IT, TO ORCHESTRATE THIS LEVEL OF VENGEANCE AGAINST THE MAN WHO'S THWARTED ME TIME AND AGAIN.
AND NOW, WITH ALL TIME AND SPACE WIPED CLEAN, I CAN REMAKE REALITY TO MY DESIGN. A SHAME YOU WON'T BE AROUND TO SEE IT.
FWASH
AND SO THE COWARD RUNS...
FWASH
I CAN'T LET YOU DO THIS. IT'S TOO MUCH.
DESTROYING THE UNIVERSE WAS NEVER WHAT I HAD IN MIND.

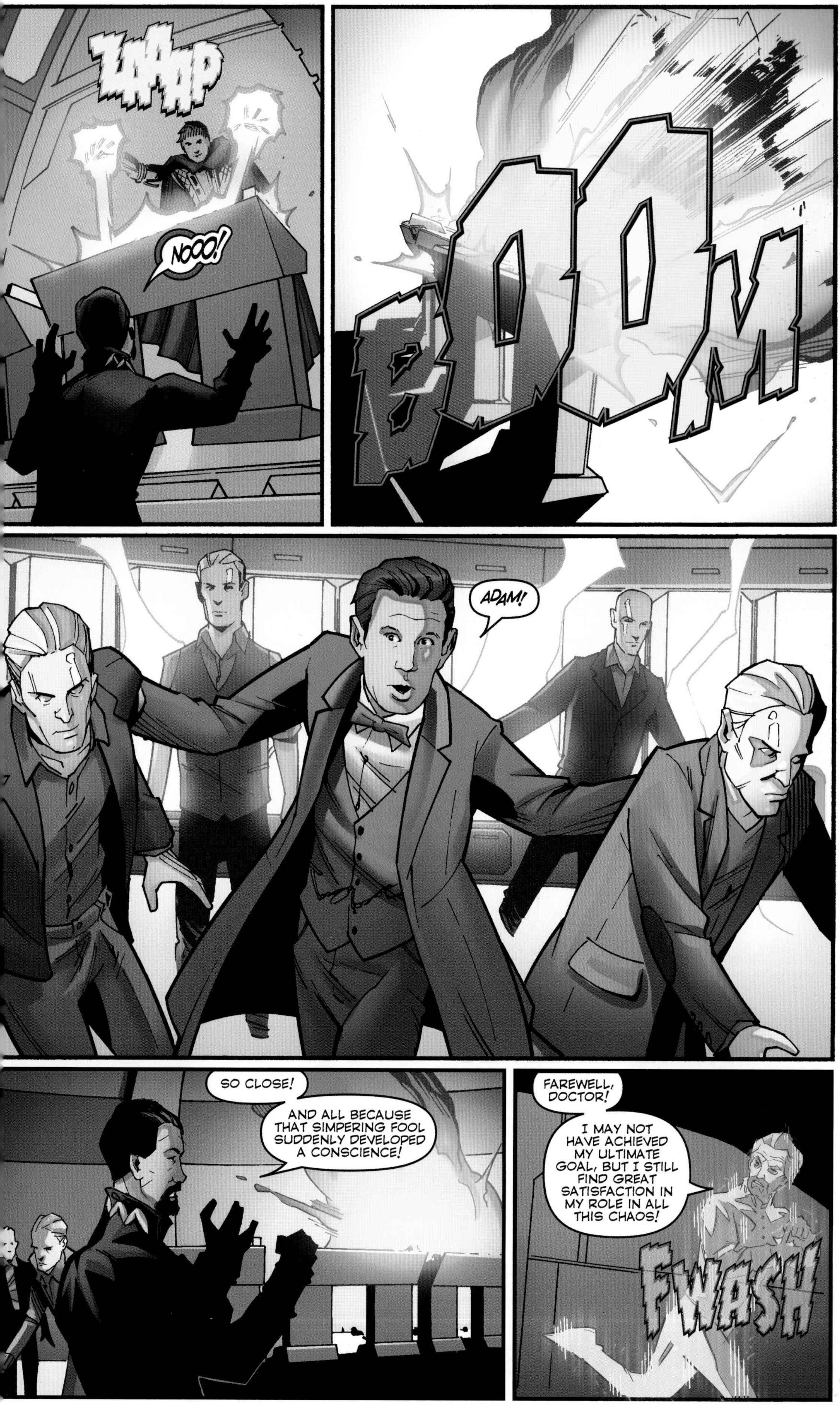
ZAAAP
NOOO!
BOOM
ADAM!
SO CLOSE!
AND ALL BECAUSE THAT SIMPERING FOOL SUDDENLY DEVELOPED A CONSCIENCE!
FAREWELL, DOCTOR!
I MAY NOT HAVE ACHIEVED MY ULTIMATE GOAL, BUT I STILL FIND GREAT SATISFACTION IN MY ROLE IN ALL THIS CHAOS!
FWASH

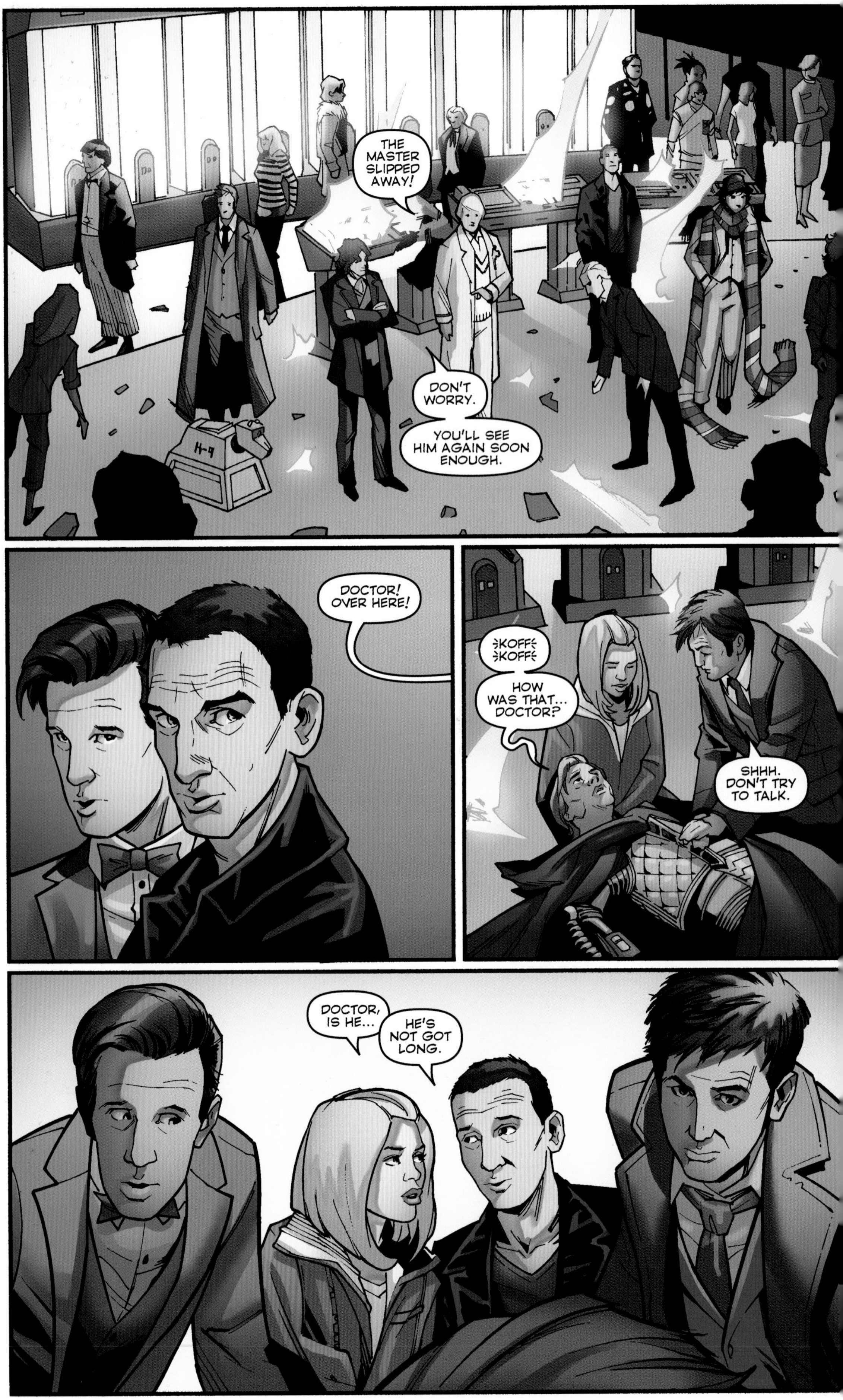
THE MASTER SLIPPED AWAY!
DON'T WORRY.
YOU'LL SEE HIM AGAIN SOON ENOUGH.
DOCTOR! OVER HERE!
KOFF *KOFF*
HOW WAS THAT... DOCTOR?
SHHH. DON'T TRY TO TALK.
DOCTOR, IS HE...
HE'S NOT GOT LONG.

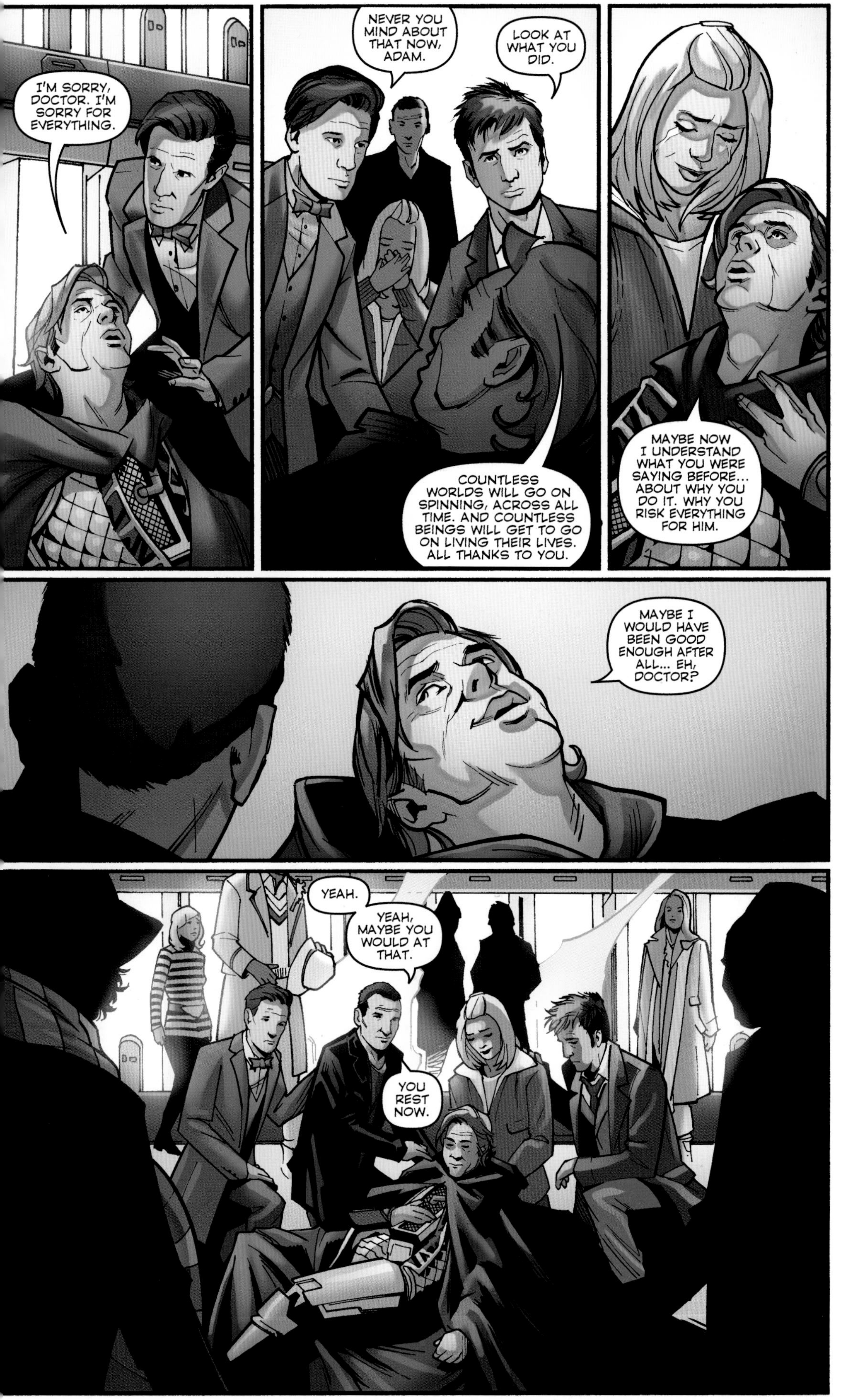
I'M SORRY, DOCTOR. I'M SORRY FOR EVERYTHING.
NEVER YOU MIND ABOUT THAT NOW, ADAM.
LOOK AT WHAT YOU DID.
COUNTLESS WORLDS WILL GO ON SPINNING, ACROSS ALL TIME. AND COUNTLESS BEINGS WILL GET TO GO ON LIVING THEIR LIVES. ALL THANKS TO YOU.
MAYBE NOW I UNDERSTAND WHAT YOU WERE SAYING BEFORE... ABOUT WHY YOU DO IT. WHY YOU RISK EVERYTHING FOR HIM.
MAYBE I WOULD HAVE BEEN GOOD ENOUGH AFTER ALL... EH, DOCTOR?
YEAH.
YEAH, MAYBE YOU WOULD AT THAT.
YOU REST NOW.

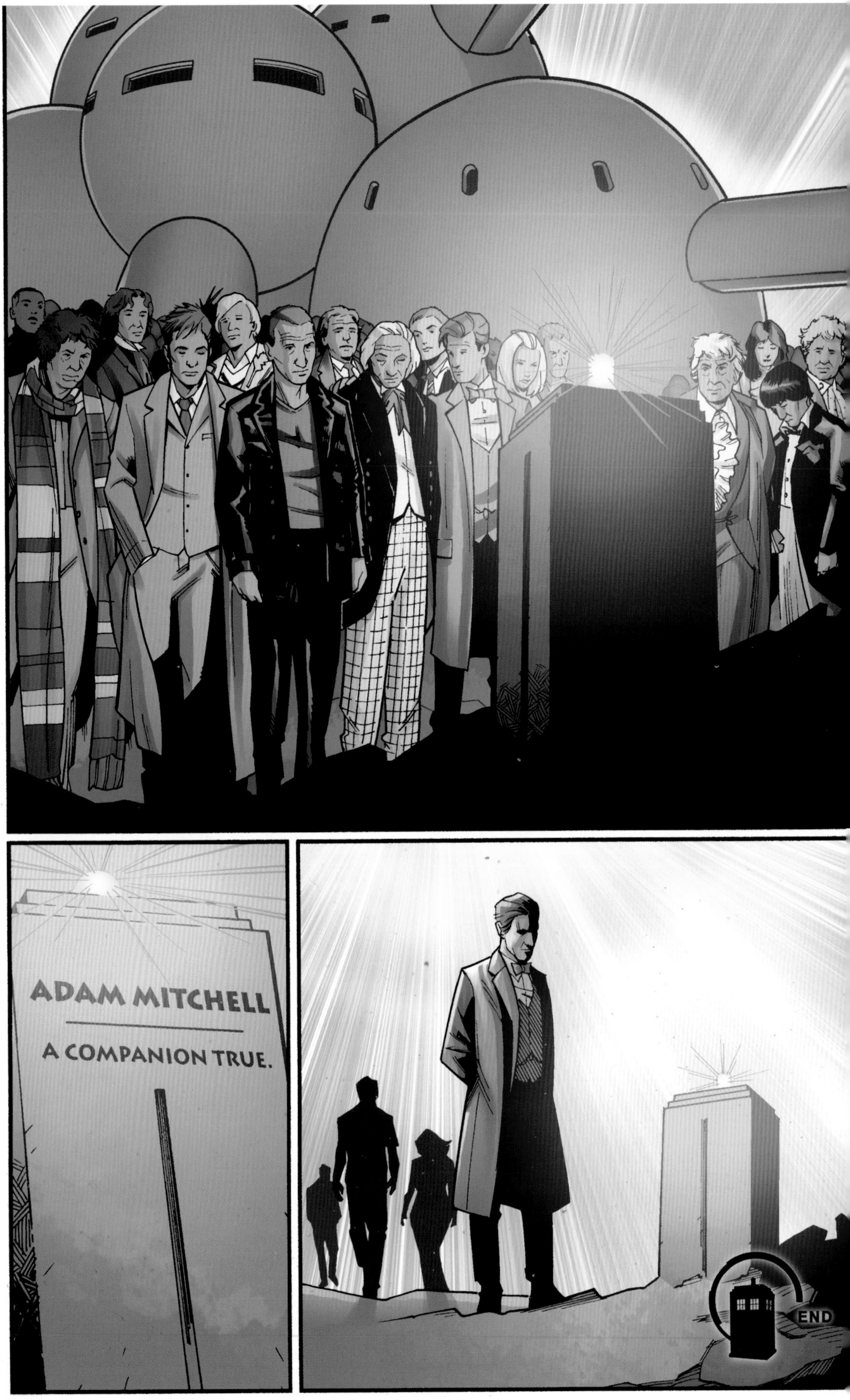
ADAM MITCHELL
A COMPANION TRUE.
END

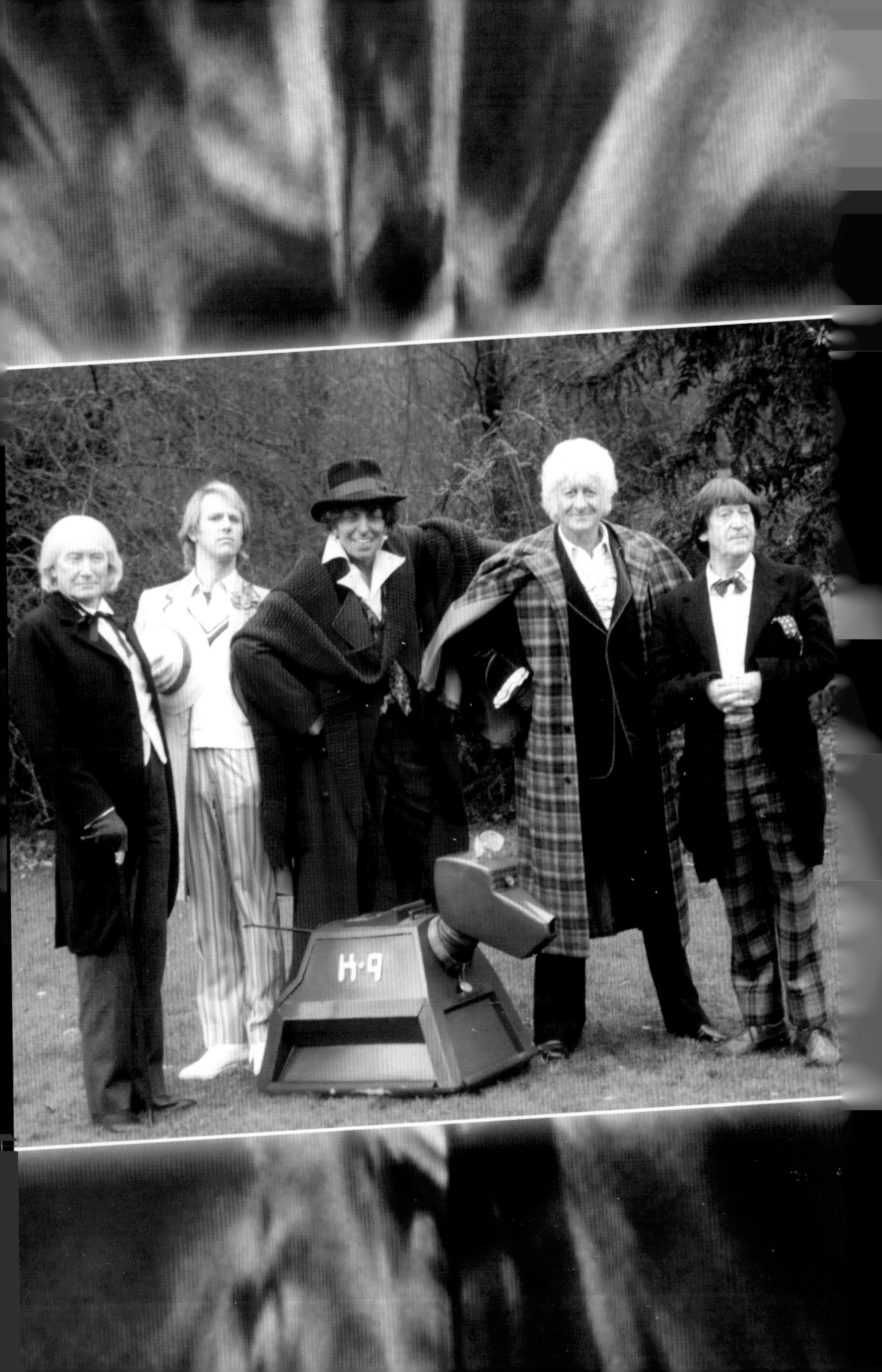
K·9

Art by Dave Sim
Colors by Charlie Kirchoff

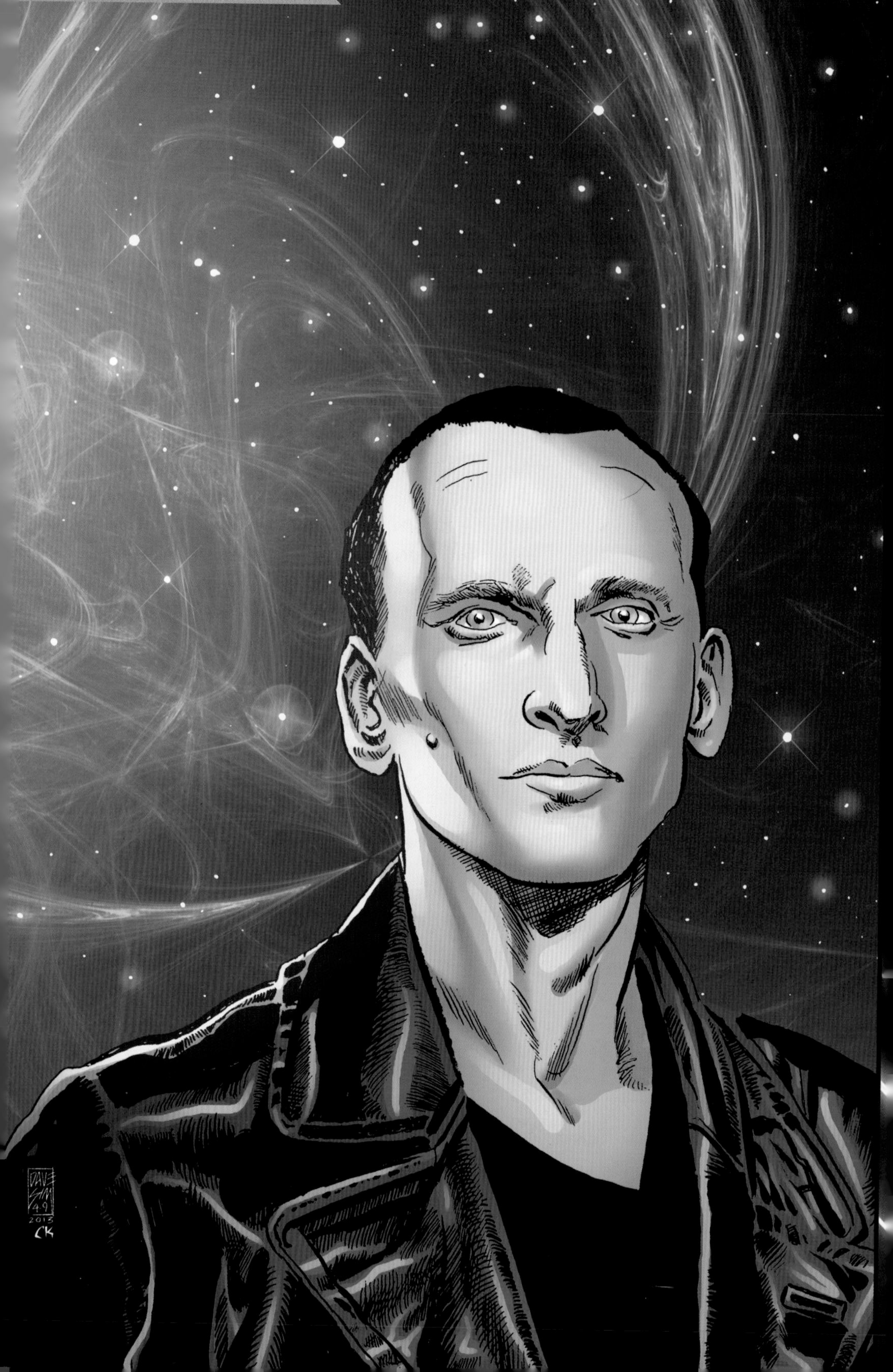
DAVE SIM 49 2013
CK

Art by Dave Sim
Colors by Charlie Kirchoff

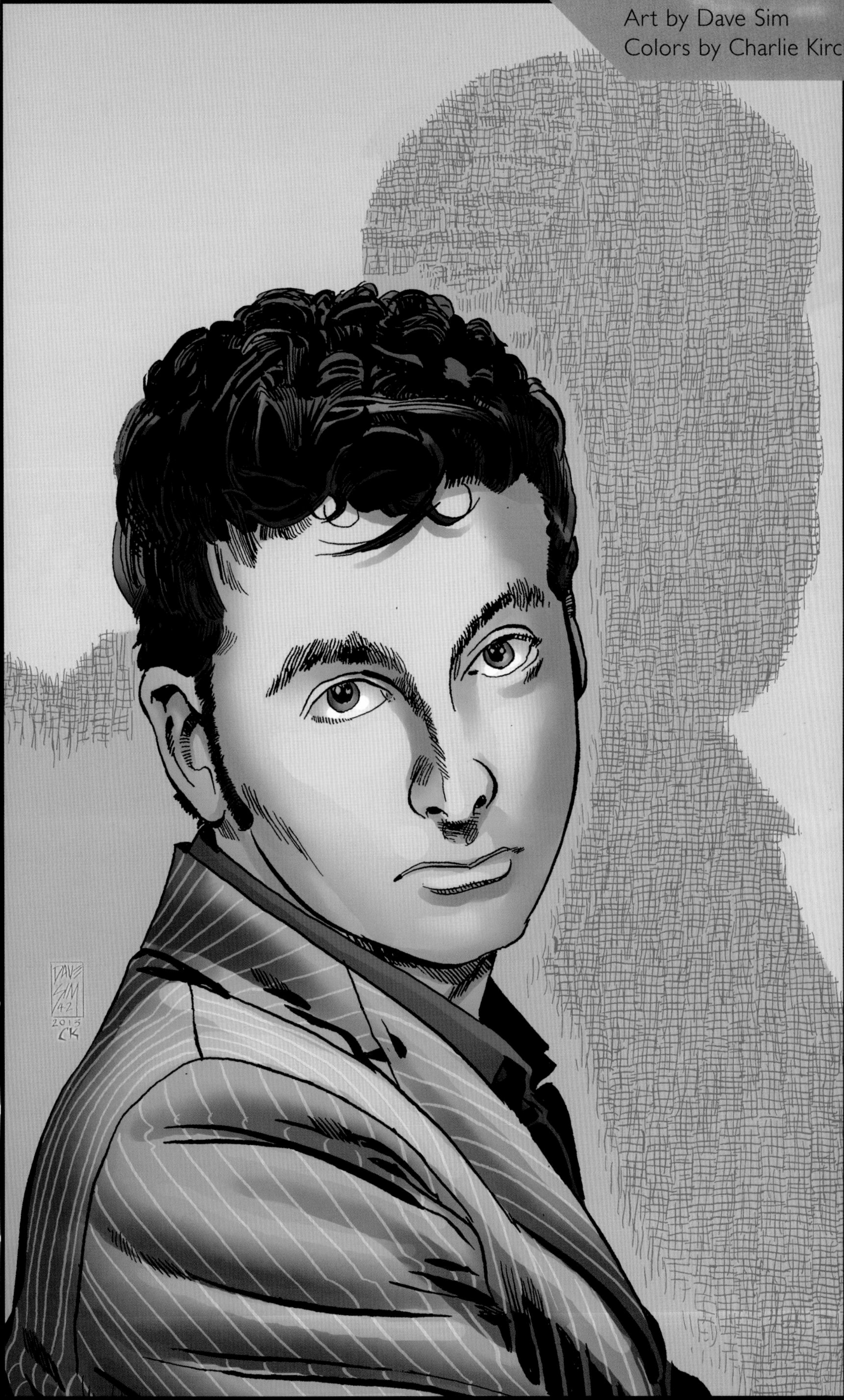

DAVE SIM
'42
2015
CK

Art by Dave Sim
Colors by Charlie Kirchoff

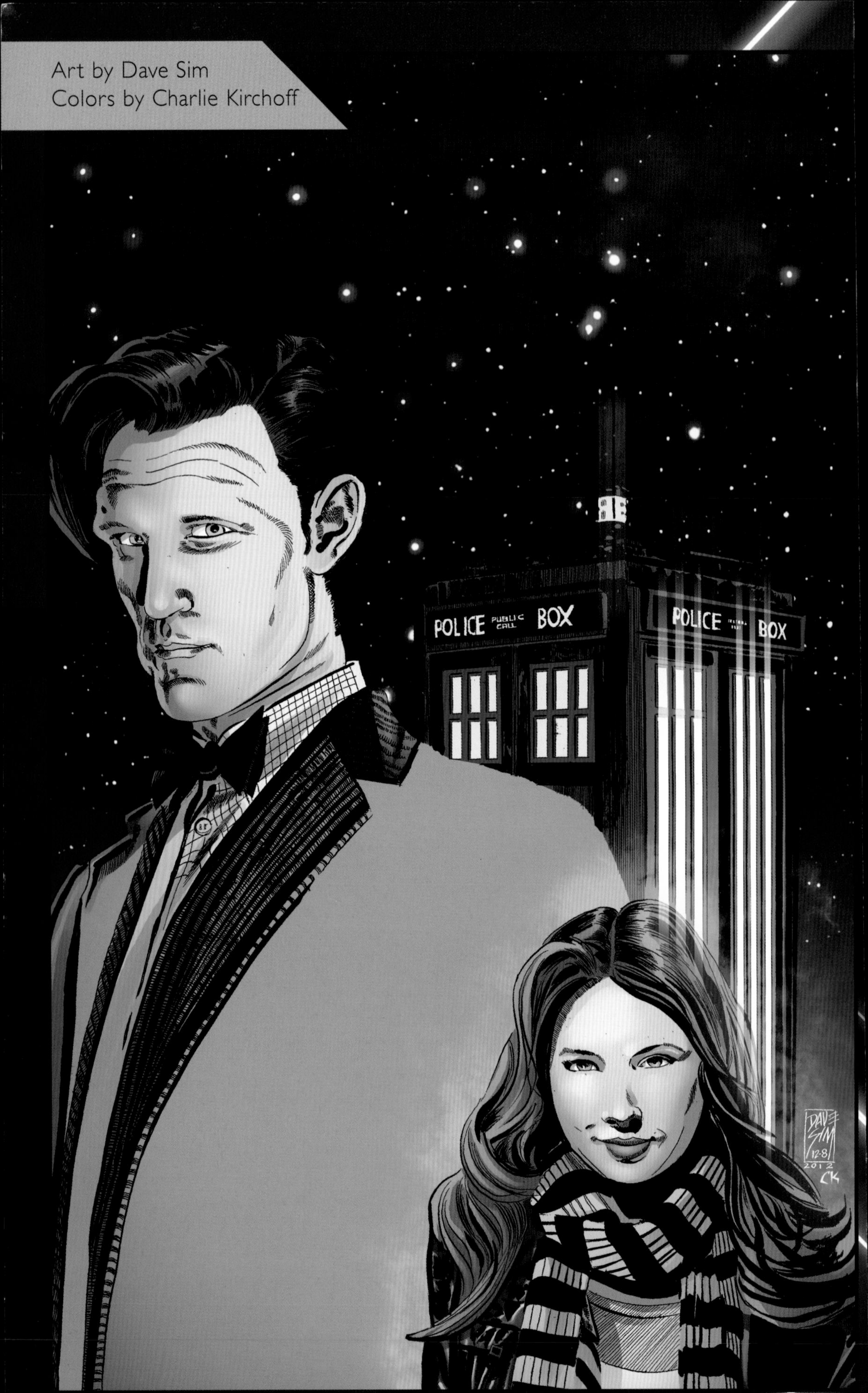
POLICE PUBLIC CALL BOX
POLICE BOX
DAVE SIM 12-8 2012
CK

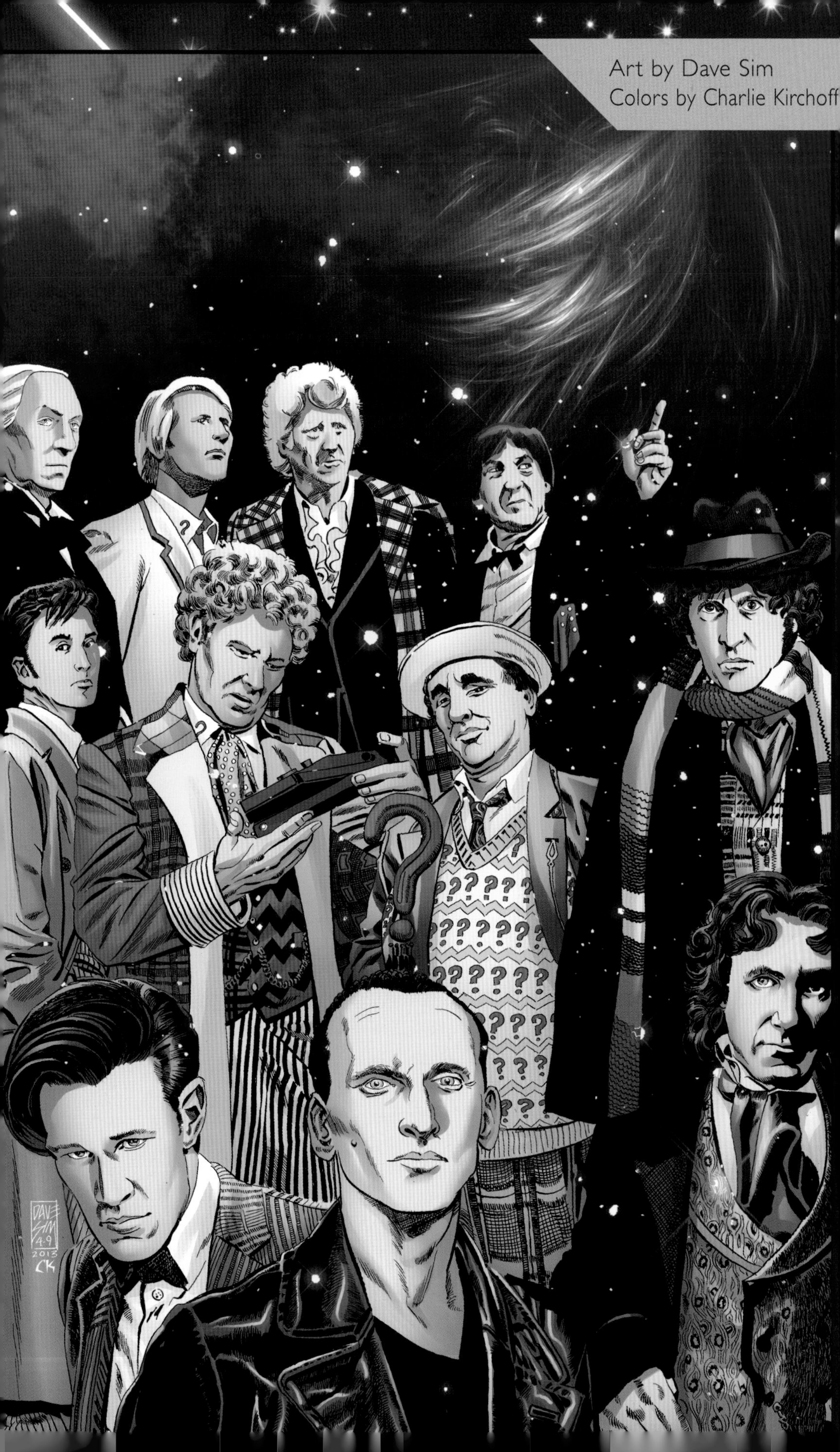
DAVE SIM
4·9
2013
CK

Art by Dave Sim
Colors by Charlie Kirchoff

Art by Robert Hack
Colors by Stephen Downer

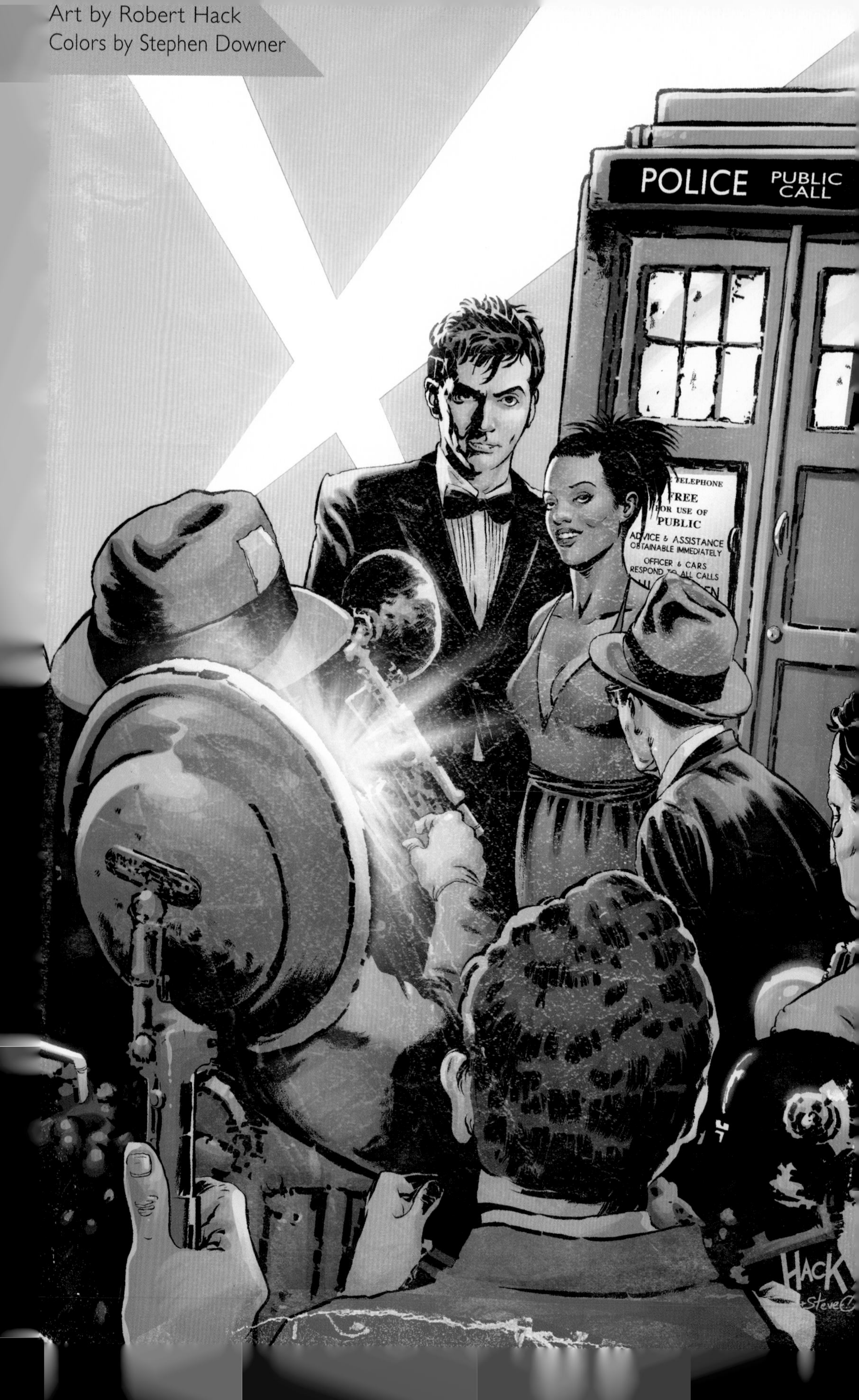
POLICE PUBLIC CALL
TELEPHONE
FREE
FOR USE OF
PUBLIC
ADVICE & ASSISTANCE
OBTAINABLE IMMEDIATELY
OFFICER & CARS
RESPOND TO ALL CALLS
HACK

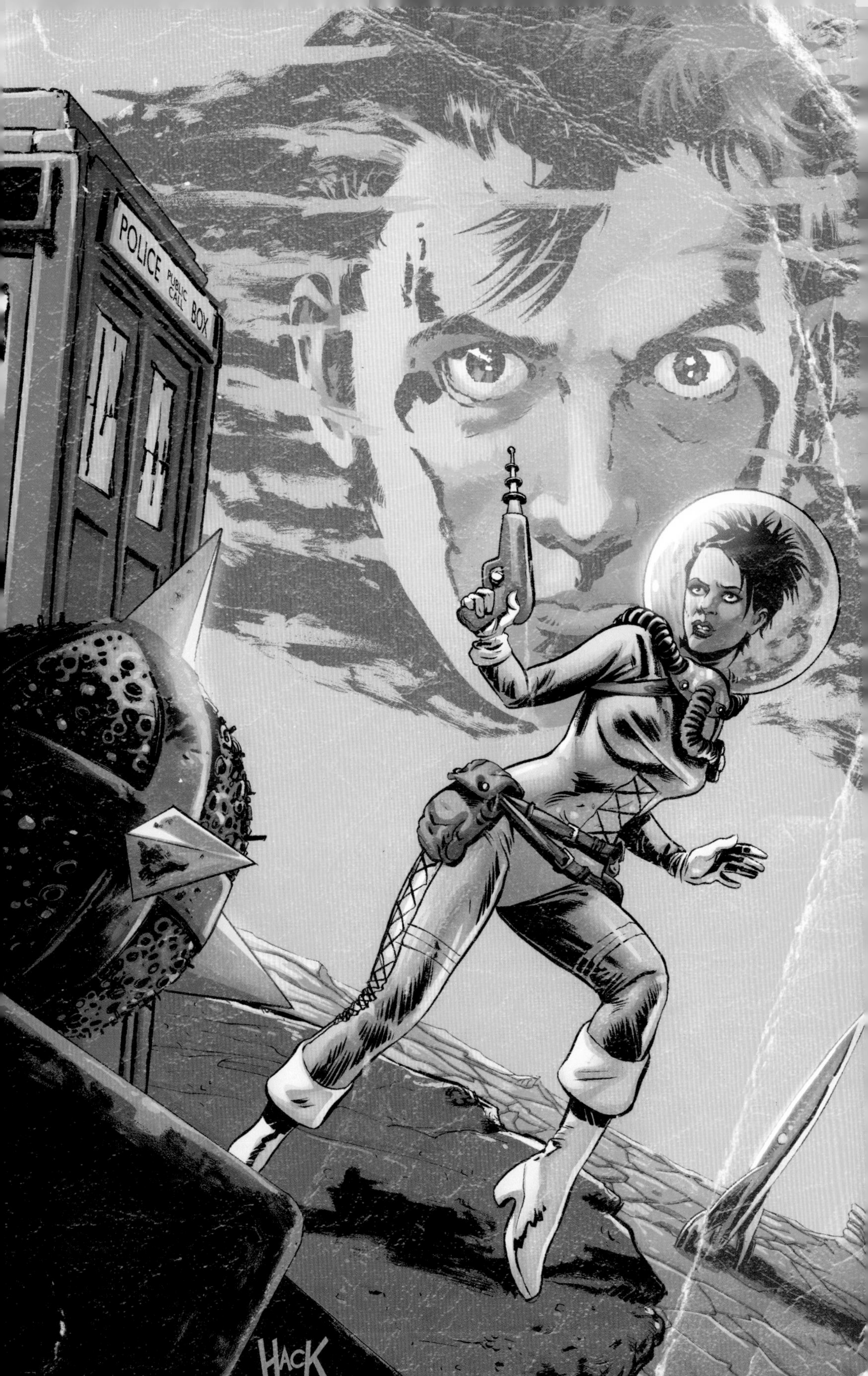
POLICE PUBLIC CALL BOX
HACK

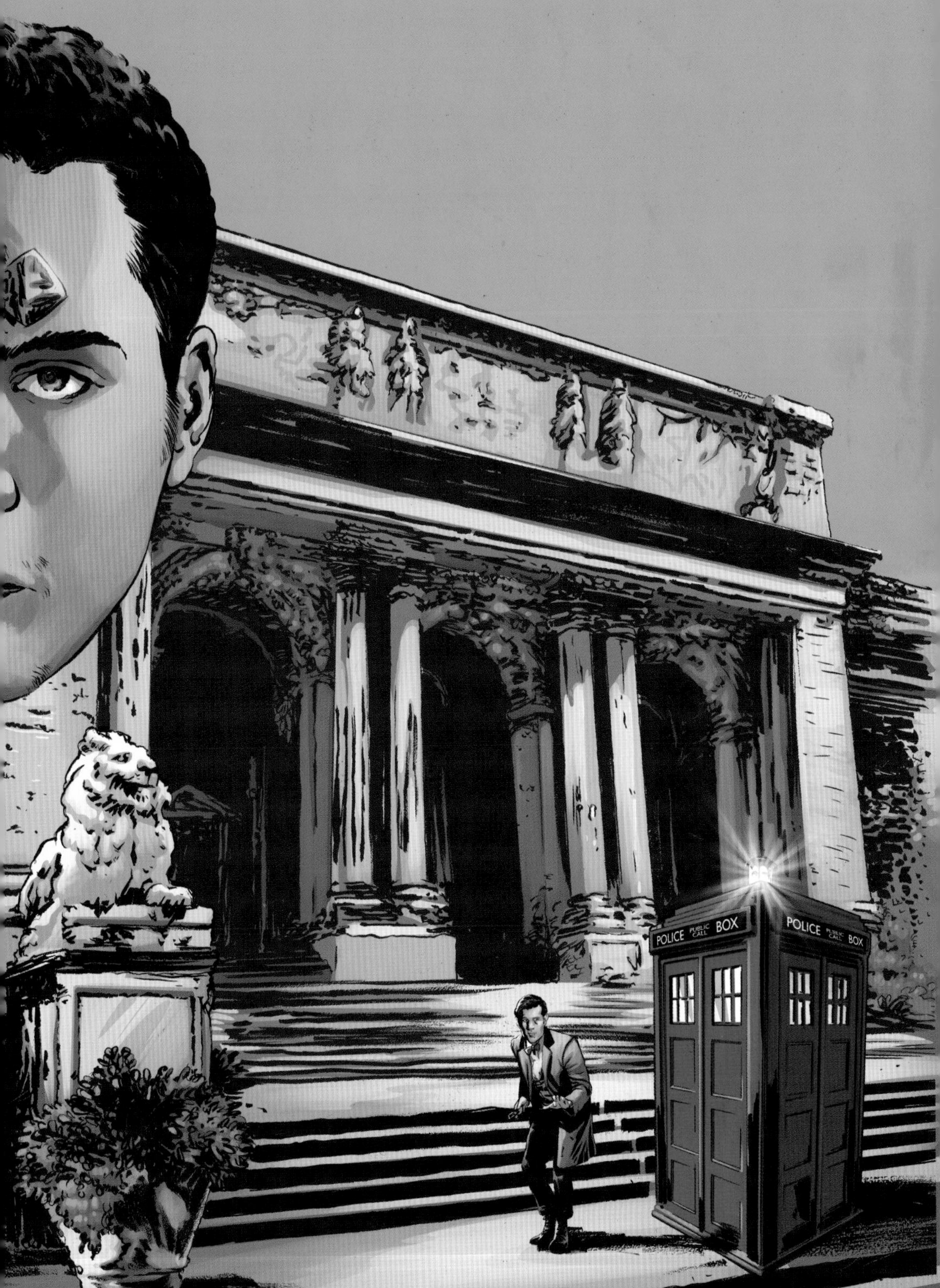
POLICE PUBLIC CALL BOX
POLICE PUBLIC CALL BOX

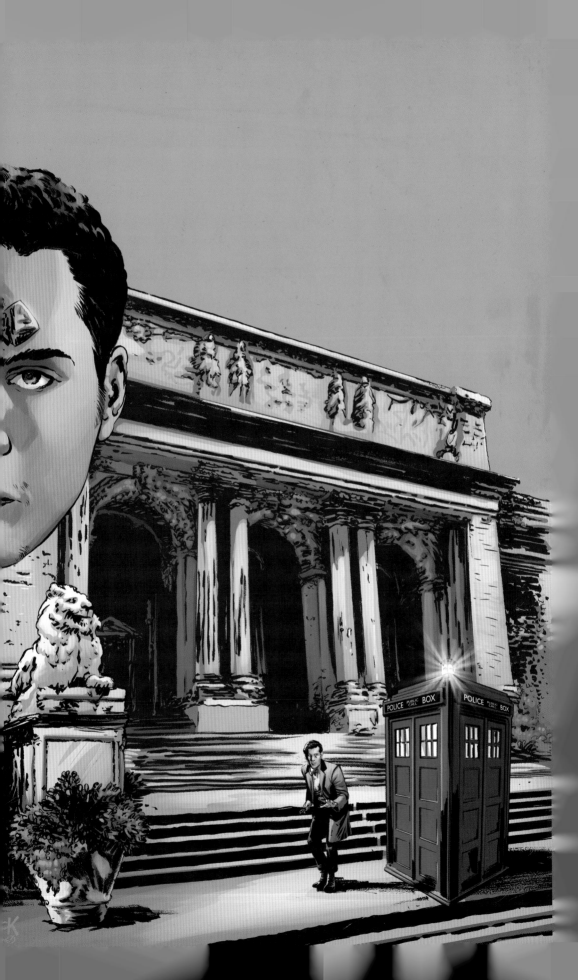

Art by Robert Hack
Colors by Stephen Downer

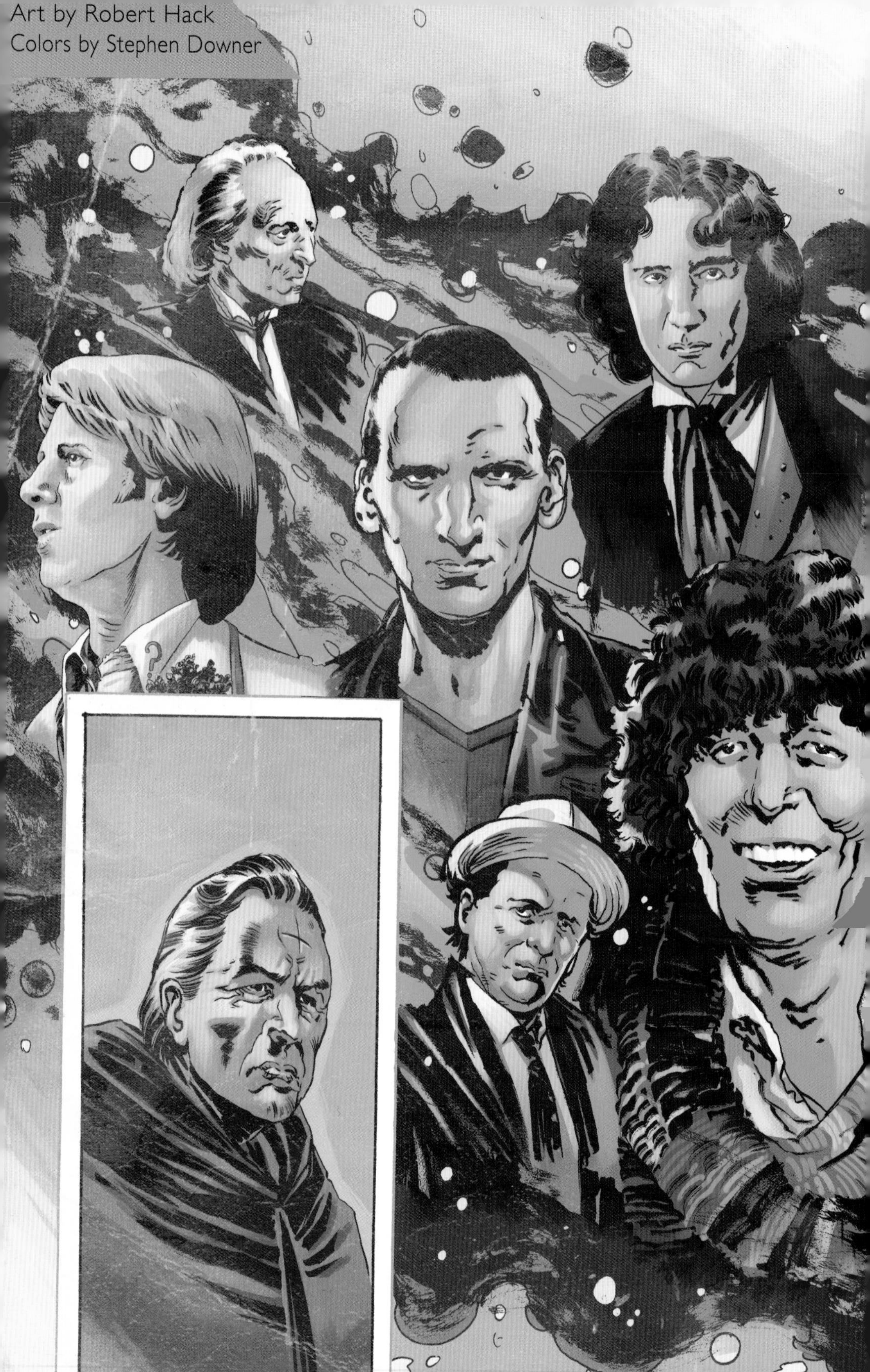

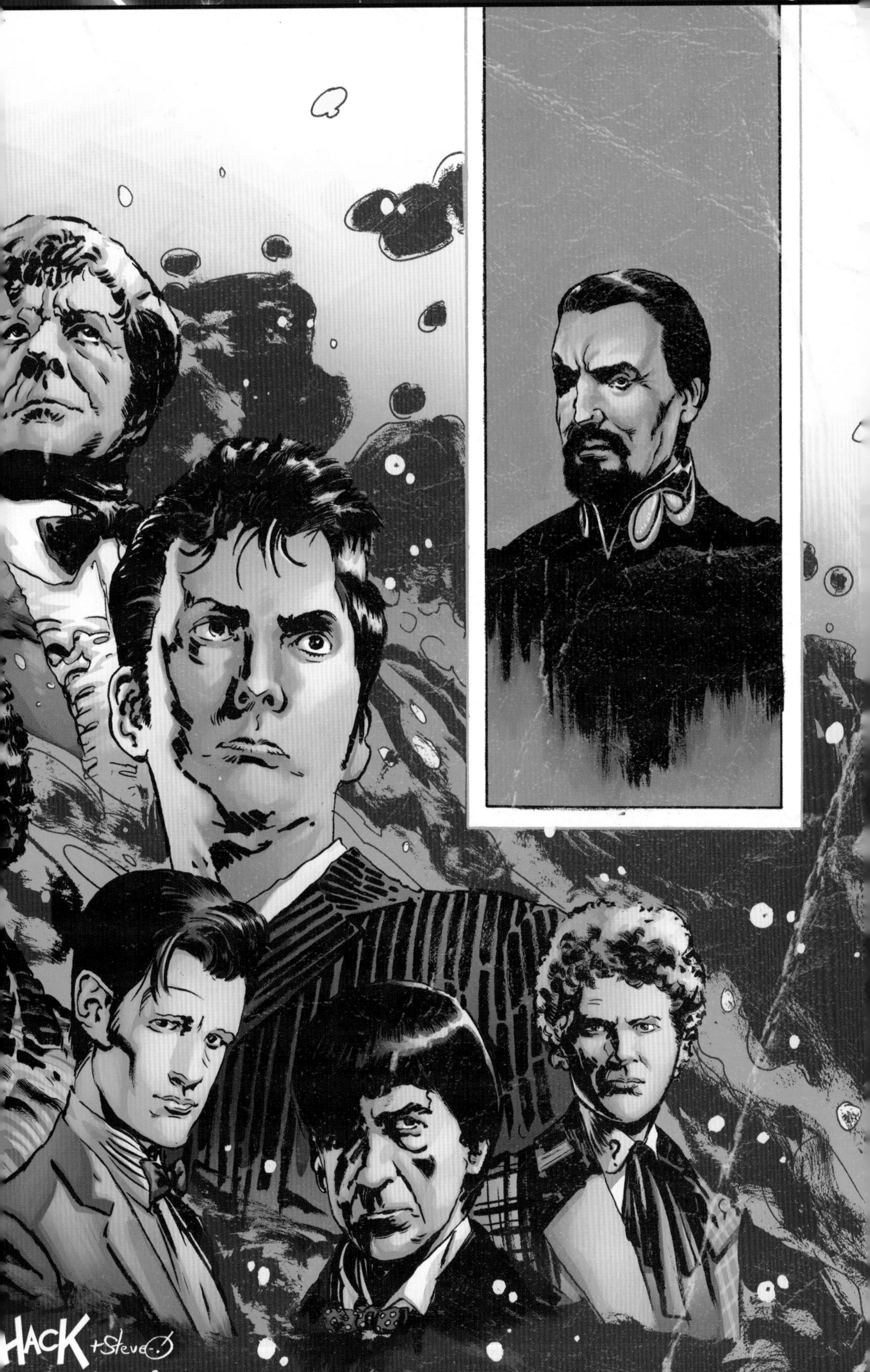
HACK +Steve

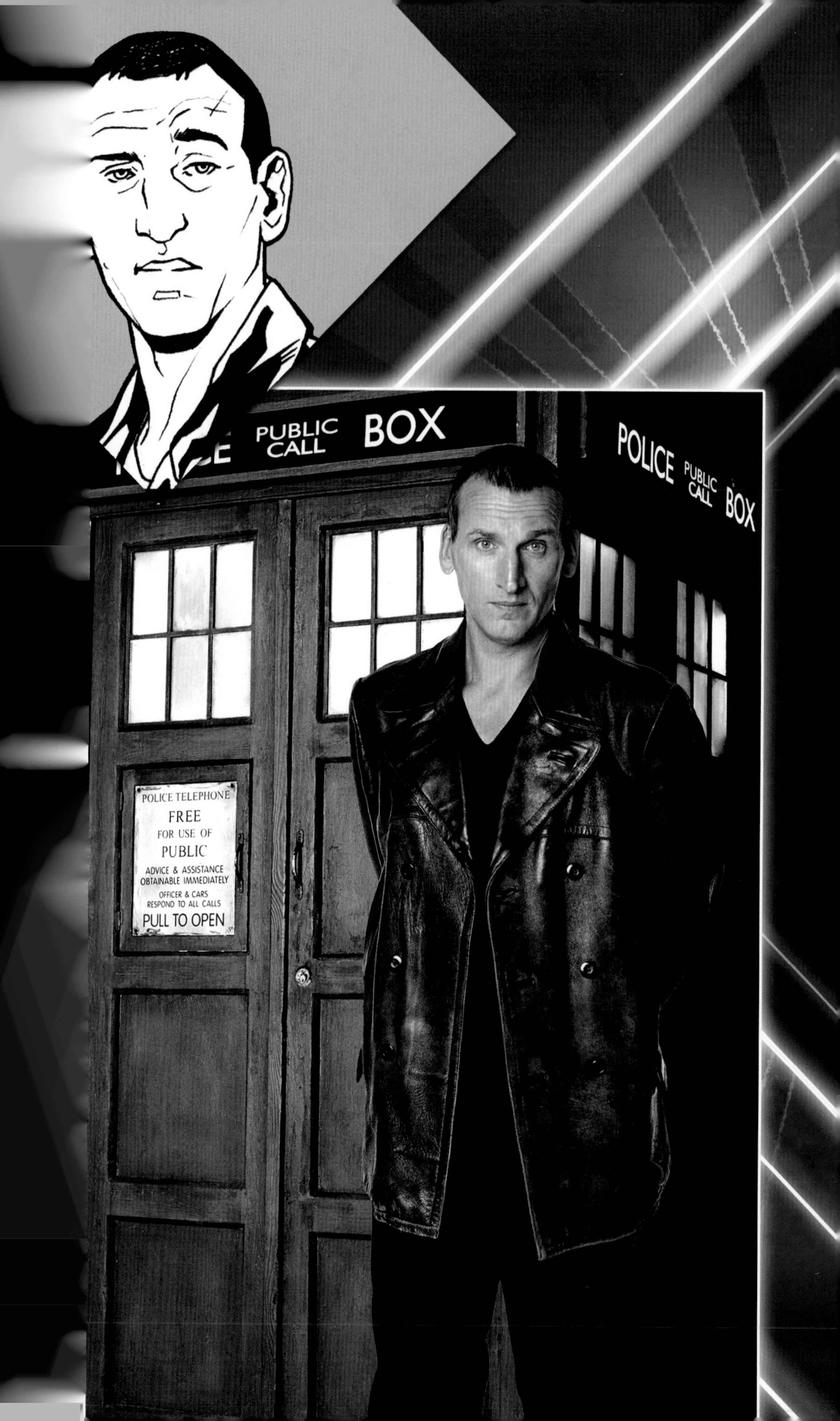
POLICE PUBLIC CALL BOX
POLICE PUBLIC CALL BOX
POLICE TELEPHONE
FREE
FOR USE OF
PUBLIC
ADVICE & ASSISTANCE
OBTAINABLE IMMEDIATELY
OFFICER & CARS
RESPOND TO ALL CALLS
PULL TO OPEN

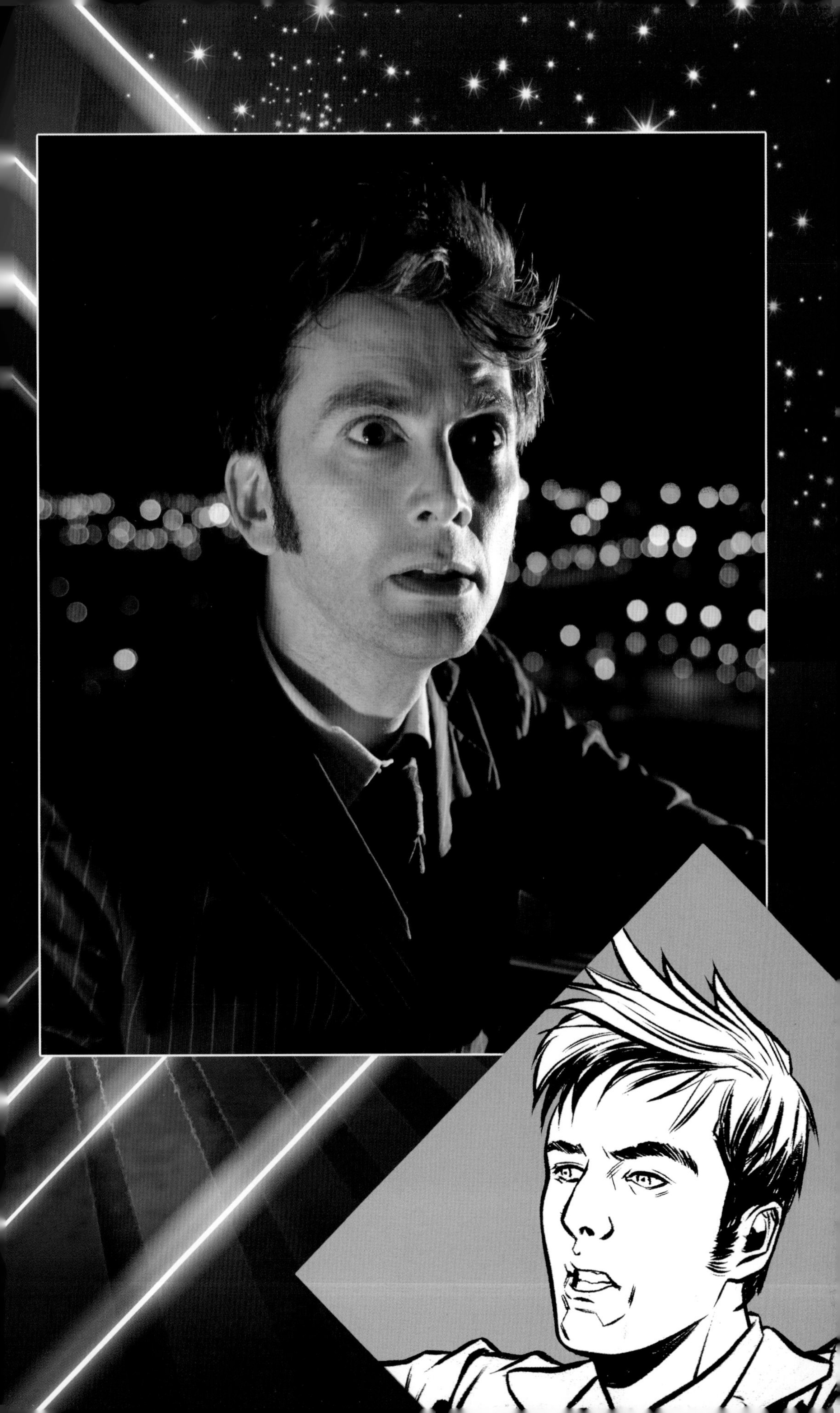

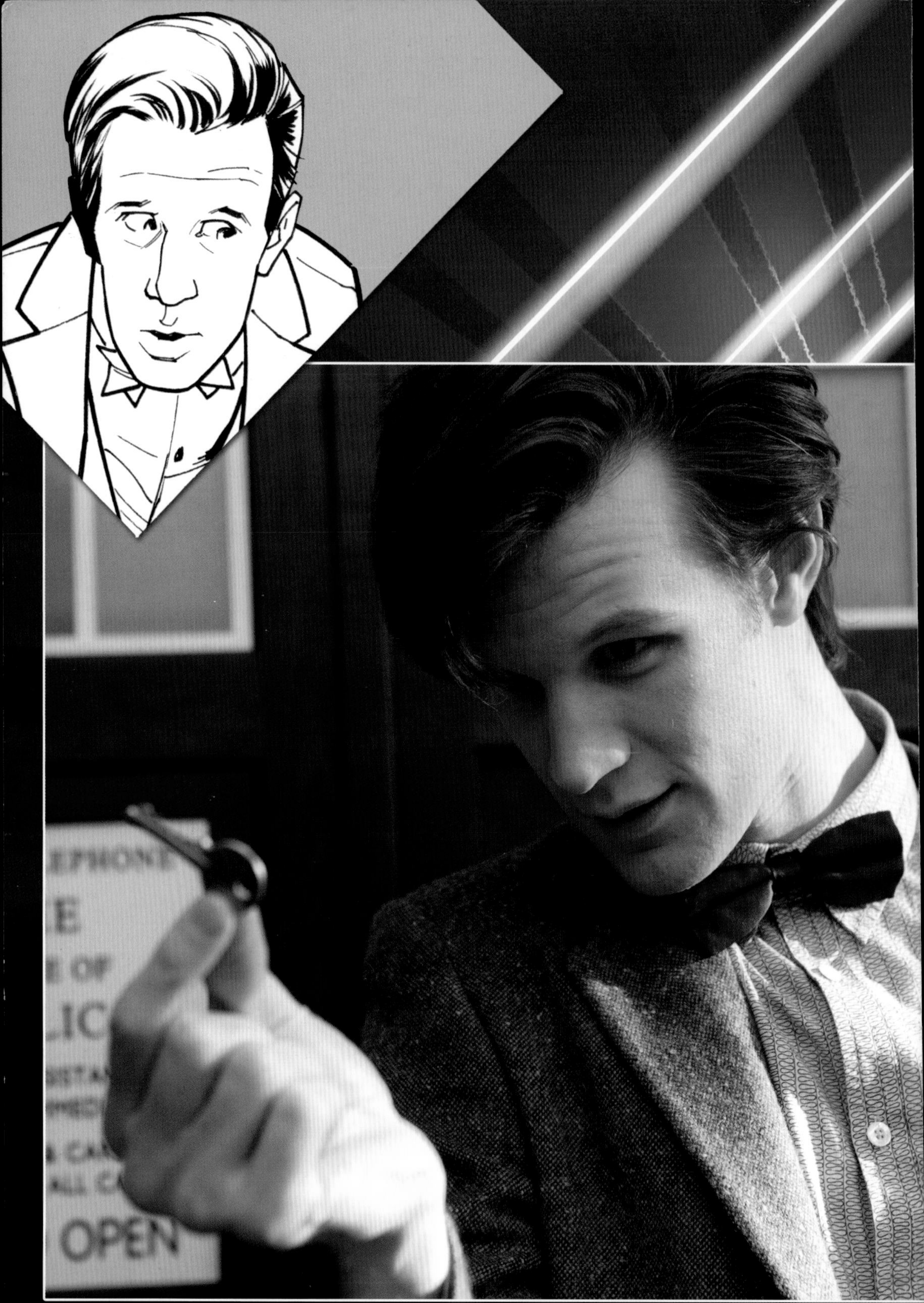
OPEN

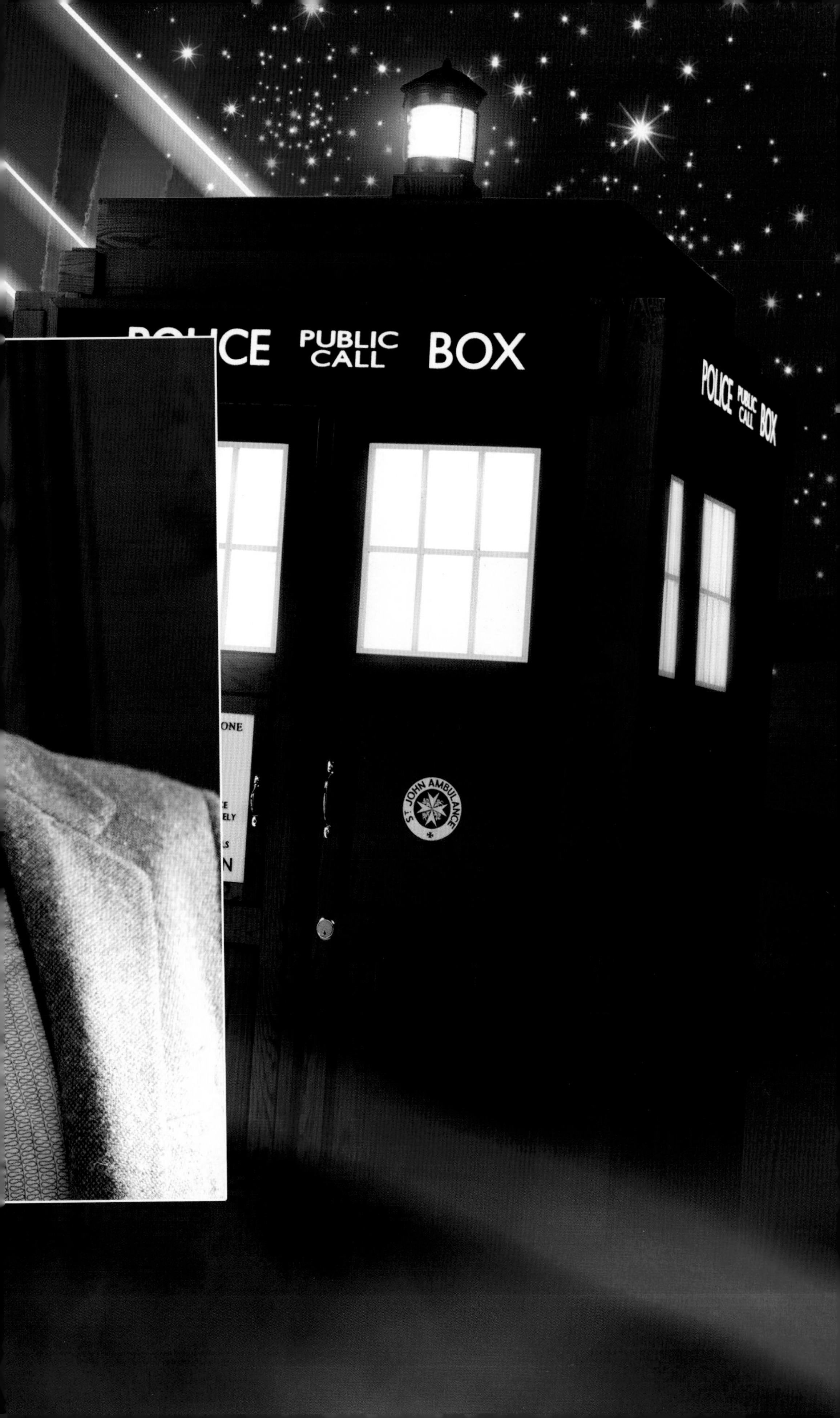
PUBLIC CALL BOX
POLICE PUBLIC CALL BOX
ST. JOHN AMBULANCE

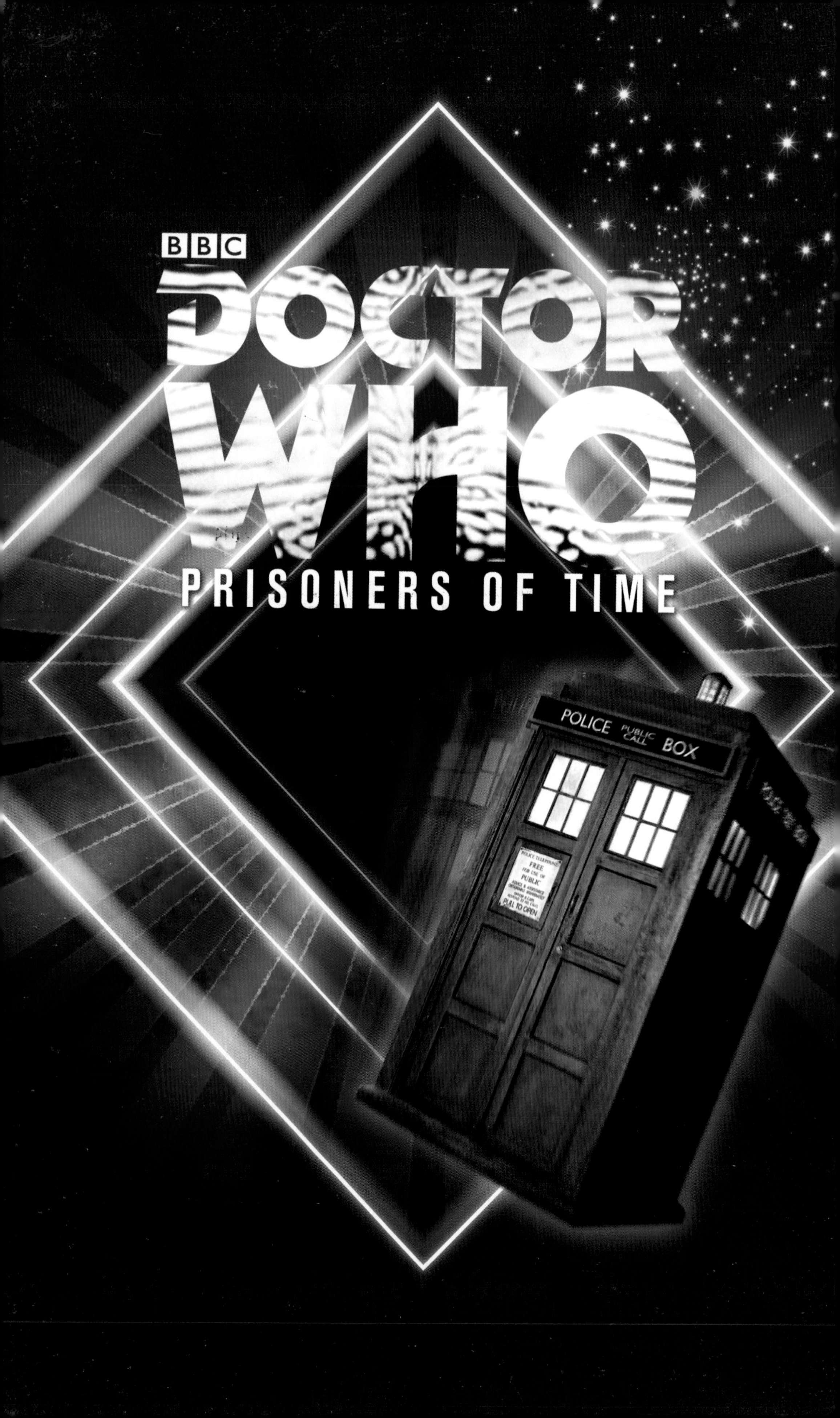
BBC
DOCTOR WHO
PRISONERS OF TIME
POLICE PUBLIC CALL BOX
POLICE TELEPHONE
FREE
FOR USE OF
PUBLIC
PULL TO OPEN